AQUINAS'S WAY TO GOD

AQUINAS'S WAY TO GOD

The Proof in *De Ente et Essentia*

GAVEN KERR, OP

OXFORD
UNIVERSITY PRESS

Oxford University Press is a department of the University of
Oxford. It furthers the University's objective of excellence in research,
scholarship, and education by publishing worldwide.

Oxford   New York
Auckland   Cape Town   Dar es Salaam   Hong Kong   Karachi
Kuala Lumpur   Madrid   Melbourne   Mexico City   Nairobi
New Delhi   Shanghai   Taipei   Toronto

With offices in
Argentina   Austria   Brazil   Chile   Czech Republic   France   Greece
Guatemala   Hungary   Italy   Japan   Poland   Portugal   Singapore
South Korea   Switzerland   Thailand   Turkey   Ukraine   Vietnam

Oxford is a registered trademark of Oxford University Press
in the UK and certain other countries.

Published in the United States of America by
Oxford University Press
198 Madison Avenue, New York, NY 10016

Library of Congress Cataloging-in-Publication Data
Kerr, Gaven.
Aquinas's way to God : the proof in De ente et essentia / Gaven Kerr, OP.
     pages cm
Includes bibliographical references and index.
ISBN 978–0–19–022480–6 (cloth : alk. paper)   1. Thomas, Aquinas, Saint, 1225?–1274. De
ente et essentia.   2. Ontology.   3. Substance (Philosophy)   4. God—Proof.   I. Title.
B765.T53D435 2015
212'.1—dc23
2014023867

9 8 7 6 5 4
Printed in the United States of America
on acid-free paper

CONTENTS

PREFACE

Western intellectual history bears witness to the fact that not a few thinkers have believed that the existence of a single principle from which all of reality is derived can be established in a satisfactory fashion. In other words, a number of people throughout history have thought that one can establish the existence of God on the basis of natural reason. Such demonstrations have taken many forms and are often categorised, many times out of context, within certain traditional categories of proofs for the existence of God, notably the cosmological, design, and ontological arguments. Whilst these three categories may be useful to students preparing for exams and may even indicate some of the salient features of such proofs of God, they rarely stand in place of detailed consideration of the argument in question.

The present study focuses on a proof of God offered by a thinker whose name is almost synonymous with attempts at proving God's existence: St Thomas Aquinas. It is true to assert that any textbook on the philosophy of religion which did not include the thought of Aquinas would be lacking in a significant respect, and often when dealing with proofs of God's existence, such textbooks will focus on the celebrated five ways of *Summa Theologiae*,

Ia, qu. 2, art. 3. It is right and just that non-specialists focus on the five ways, given that therein Aquinas offers some of his most sophisticated argumentation for God's existence, based on principles garnered over a lifetime of intense philosophical and theological research.

Whilst it is fitting that the five ways receive so much examination, I believe that the attention heaped upon the five ways occludes other proofs for God's existence offered by Aquinas—proofs which might not be so vulnerable to the traditional objections offered against the five ways. It is precisely because the five ways are so sophisticated and based upon a lifetime of speculation that, when read out of context, they may seem vulnerable to objection. Aquinas does not spell out in detail his philosophical presuppositions beforehand, and thus the five ways are taken to be dependent on a certain mode of thinking that non-Thomists find rather dubious. For the Thomist, however, the philosophical backdrop to the five ways is certainly defensible, but in order to defend it, entire monographs on Thomistic metaphysics are often required.

In this present study I have chosen to focus on a proof for God that Aquinas offers not towards the end of his career (the period in which the five ways are situated), but at the very beginning of his career, in the *De Ente et Essentia*. The *De Ente* is a small treatise on metaphysics written by Aquinas for his Dominican confrères in Paris. It does not have the grandeur of the two *Summae*, nor the detailed technicality of the disputed questions, but it does contain a simplicity and neatness of argumentation such that a non-specialist can read it and, if attentive, make some headway in the understanding of Thomist metaphysics.

In the *De Ente* Aquinas spells out certain metaphysical positions that he will more or less maintain for the remainder of his career. Moreover, he spells out this metaphysical framework *before* offering a proof for the existence of God. Thus, the proof for the existence of God in *De Ente*, unlike many other proofs in the Thomistic corpus, notably the five ways, does not presuppose the philosophical backdrop of the Thomistic system, but rather sets that backdrop up to begin with and then proceeds to the proof of God. This is most refreshing and offers to the non-specialist a nice entryway into the Thomistic system of thought.

In the present study, then, I seek to offer an interpretation and defence of the proof of God that Aquinas offers in *De Ente*, Cap. 4. The truth of a position ought to be the primary motivation for its defence, and it is because I find the proof of God offered in *De Ente*, Cap. 4 convincing that I choose to defend it. However, I could have defended any number of other proofs in Aquinas's corpus, all of which proceed along similar lines of reasoning, or are at least similarly defensible, for the same conclusion, such as *Summa Contra Gentiles*, Lib. 1, Cap. 15, 'Adhuc', *Summa Theologiae*, Ia, qu. 2, art. 3, 'Secunda Via'. However, I defend the *De Ente* proof because nowhere else have I found in the Thomistic corpus the philosophical backdrop to the proof spelt out in such detail immediately prior to the proof. Thus, the proof in the *De Ente* will at least go some way in convincing others, because it wears its philosophical presuppositions on its sleeve, as it were.

Up to this point, I have considered in general terms the proof of the *De Ente* in comparison to some of Aquinas's other, more popular proofs, and this immediately raises the issues of (i) how does the *De Ente* proof stand within the Thomistic system as a whole? and (ii) how does it stand within the general context of proofs for the existence of God?

Concerning (i), the *De Ente* proof does not explicitly reappear in any of the later proofs of God's existence that Aquinas offers; and in fact something similar to the *De Ente* proof emerges later in Aquinas's work only after he has established the existence of God, and where he intends to establish God's eternity (*SCG*, Lib. 1, Cap. 15, 'Adhuc'—mentioned above), or that essence and *esse* are identical in God (*Sth*, Ia, qu. 3, art. 4). This might lead one to infer that the *De Ente* proof is a youthful proof that Aquinas later abandoned for what he considered to be more profound proofs. My response to such a suggestion is twofold. Firstly, even if Aquinas did not consider the proof of the *De Ente* worthy of consideration in his later works, he still offered it in this early work on the basis of philosophical principles that he certainly makes use of in later works. That being the case, I as a contemporary Thomist can defend this proof as one of the Thomistic proofs of God based on Thomistic principles, even if Aquinas did not defend it in later works.

Secondly, I do not think it is entirely true that the *De Ente* proof does not re-emerge in later works, or at least something like the proof, because the proof structure of the *De Ente* is an inference from effects construed as being in potency in some respect, to a cause that is in potency in no respect. Now, as will become apparent, the potency in which effects are construed to be in *De Ente* is a potency to *esse*, and through a denial of an infinite regress of causes of *esse*, Aquinas infers a cause that is not in potency to *esse* but rather is pure *esse*. Later proofs typically consider the potency of effects as tied in with motion (*SCG*, Lib. 1, Cap. 13, *Sth*, Ia, qu. 2, art. 3, 'Prima Via', *Compendium Theologiae*, Cap. 3), causality (*Sth*, Ia, qu. 2, art. 3, 'Secunda Via'), or necessity (*Sth*, Ia, qu. 2, art. 3, 'Tertia Via'), but all these are particular applications of the act–potency distinction that Aquinas adopts and adapts to his purposes. Indeed, it is with regard to essence–*esse* distinction and composition that Aquinas's most personal metaphysical insights on act and potency come to the fore, so that the proof of God mounted on the back of that, as is the case in *De Ente*, can be said to be Aquinas's most personal application of his philosophical thought to the proof of God—so much so that the later proofs, such as those mentioned of the five ways, are derivative of the proof structure of the *De Ente*, and are constrained by Aquinas's context of writing, thereby signifying the particular application of the act–potency distinction and its use in proving the existence of God. Above all, what matters for Aquinas in proving the existence of God is the inference from participated being to un-participated being, from beings that stand in potency in some respect to a being who stands in potency in no respect, and this manner of procedure is most explicit in the *De Ente* proof. Thus, one could argue that whilst the *De Ente* proof does not reappear explicitly in later works, the mode of procedure of that proof can be said to govern the modes of procedure of most other proofs of God that Aquinas offers.

So much then for the standing of the *De Ente* proof in the Thomistic corpus; but how, then, does it stand with regard to other typical proofs of God? Above I mentioned general categories of proof: the cosmological, the design, and the ontological. Aquinas was explicit in rejecting something like the ontological argument (*SCG*, Lib. 1, Cap. 12, *Sth*, Ia, qu. 2, art. 1), and whilst some think that the fifth way displays properties that would render it a design argument, it is certainly not a design argument of the Paleyite variety, nor even of the more probabilistic kind offered by Richard Swinburne.[1] My own personal opinion on the fifth way is that it is not a design argument, but reflects something of Aquinas's more metaphysical tendencies concerning causal dependency, thereby bringing it more into line with the rest of the five ways, which are explicitly causal in scope, though this is not an interpretation I intend to push here.[2] Undoubtedly Aquinas offers something like a cosmological argument in many of his proofs of God, where a cosmological proof is one that focuses on some general feature of the universe and thence infers the existence of some cause thereof. This would seem to reflect Aquinas's arguments from motion and causality, but I do not think that it can cover Aquinas's proof in the *De Ente*, and here is why.

1. For those Thomists who consider the fifth way a kind of design argument, see Reginald Garrigou-Lagrange, *God, His Existence and His Nature* (London: Herder, 1934), I, p. 345; Walter Farrell, *A Companion to the Summa* (New York: Sheed and Ward, 1940), I, pp. 41–44; Frederick Copleston, *Aquinas* (Middlesex: Penguin, 1955), pp. 126–127.
2. Edward Feser shares a similar view of the fifth way; see his treatment thereof in *Aquinas* (Oxford: Oneworld, 2009), and 'Existential Inertia and the Five Ways', *American Catholic Philosophical Quarterly*, 85 (2011), 237–267.

The proof in the *De Ente* explicitly moves from a consideration of beings in which essence and *esse* are distinct to the existence of a being in which they are not so distinct, a being that is pure *esse*. Whilst Aquinas is undoubtedly concerned with a feature of the cosmos—or better, a feature of entities within the cosmos, viz. essence–*esse* distinction and composition—he is also concerned, as we shall see, with what is outside the cosmos as well, i.e. the angels of Christian theology. This is not to say that the proof in the *De Ente* requires a commitment to the existence of angels, rather that the proof of God offered therein seeks to account for the being of all things, whether within the cosmos or without. Cosmological arguments seek to account for some feature of the cosmos or of the beings therein and thence infer God, but that then leaves the existence of non-cosmological beings unexplained, and indeed it would invite the attack that such a mode of argumentation only leaves us with a supreme extra-cosmological being. The proof of God in the *De Ente* seeks to account for the existence of all beings, whether members of the cosmos or not, in which case it seeks to prove a creator God on which all things depend for their existence. By focussing on intra-cosmical beings, typical cosmological proofs neglect the possibility of extra-cosmical beings which may also require to have their existence caused, in which case the proof in the *De Ente* cannot be aligned with such cosmological proofs.

Given that Aquinas's proof of God in *De Ente*, Cap. 4, is one based on the metaphysics that he lays out beforehand, I think the best method of classification is to call it a metaphysical proof, such that it proceeds from an established metaphysical position and seeks on that basis to infer a primary principle for all that exists. Such a method of procedure, based as it is on certain fundamental metaphysical considerations, will surely appear in other proofs which, though not explicitly metaphysical, will draw upon such fundamental metaphysics; such a proof will always resist classification as a proof which moves from a consideration of intra-mundane features of the world to an extra-mundane creator.

The proof of the *De Ente* has thus been situated within Aquinas's more general system, and some indications have been given as to how it ought to be situated with regard to the standard proofs of the existence of God that are generally offered in philosophy. Let us now consider how to situate the proof of God in the more systematic context of Aquinas's vision of reality and man's engagement therewith.

Undoubtedly Aquinas was first and foremost a devout Catholic, a member of the Order of Preachers (the Dominicans) and thus an ardent preacher of the Gospel. The entire thrust of his life was the worship and love of God, and, coupled with the educational environment of the thirteenth century in which he worked, the entire focus of his mind was directed to religious matters. Thus, it is somewhat trivial to say that he was a religious thinker, i.e. a thinker of religious things; but it is not true to say that he was *solely* a religious thinker, i.e. somebody who devotes his thought only to things religious, and in order to understand why this is so, one must understand Aquinas's conception of the scientific hierarchy.

Aquinas envisaged the sciences as concerned with what can be known, and what can be known for Aquinas is the truth of being. It follows, then, that the divisions amongst the sciences will correlate with divisions of the kinds of knowledge of truth that one can have. Fundamentally, there are two general classes of science corresponding to whether our knowledge of truth is either (i) speculative or (ii) practical, thereby giving us the speculative and practical sciences.[3]

Concerning our speculative knowledge, there are three further classes of science the divisions of which track the divisions of the kinds of objects that can be known. There are things that can be known (i) that depend on matter and motion both for their being and for their being understood, (ii) that depend on matter

---

3. Aquinas, *Super Boethium De Trinitate et Expositio Librii De Ebdomadibus* (Rome: Commissio Leonina, 1992), *Super De Trinitate*, qu. 5, art. 1, p. 137:92–96.

and motion for their being but not for their being understood, and (iii) that depend on matter and motion neither for their being nor for their being understood.[4] The sciences corresponding to each class of speculative object are: (i) physics, (ii) mathematics, and (iii) divine science or theology. It is the science focussed on the third class of object which is of primary concern here.

Divine science or theology incorporates those objects that are immaterial. However, Aquinas makes a further division of the immaterial that goes on to subdivide this third science. There are objects open to scientific investigation that are immaterial in themselves but can be found in both material and immaterial things (e.g. being, one, act, potency, etc); such things are neutral with regard to being found in material things, that is, they could be without being in material things, and hence they are neutrally immaterial. There are things that are immaterial in themselves and can never be found to be in material things (e.g. God and angels), and they are such because they are immaterial substances, hence they are positively immaterial.[5]

Aquinas maintains that the theology of the philosophers (metaphysics) deals with the neutrally immaterial, that is, those categories of reality common to all things, both immaterial and material, whereas theology proper, that which is handed on in sacred scripture, deals with the positively immaterial, that is, God and the angels as they exist in themselves. Metaphysics can come to some sort of knowledge of the latter only insofar as it considers their effects, in which case it does not treat of divine things as part of its subject matter, but only as principles thereof.[6]

---

4. Ibid, p. 138:141–160.

5. Ibid, p. 138:154–160, see also John Wippel, *The Metaphysical Thought of Thomas Aquinas: From Finite Being to Uncreated Being* (Washington: Catholic University of America Press, 2000), pp. 4–8; the terminology of 'positively immaterial' and 'neutrally immaterial' is Wippel's.

6. *Super De Trinitate*, p. 154:175–182: 'Sic ergo theologia siue scientia diuina est duplex: una in qua considerantur res diuine non tamquam subiectum scientie, set tamquam principia subiecti, et talis est theologia quam philosophi prosequntur, que alio nomine metaphisica dicitur; alia uero que ipsas res

On the basis of these divisions, Aquinas holds that metaphysics can establish the existence of the objects of theology, but cannot establish anything proper to the objects of theology without their revealing themselves, since natural reason looks upon such objects as the eye of an owl looks upon the light of the sun.[7] Thus, for Aquinas, the scientific hierarchy is as follows: (i) theology, (ii) metaphysics, (iii) mathematics, (iv) physics, with the scale descending according to the degree to which the object of each science is involved with matter and motion. Given this hierarchy of the sciences, what are conclusions of a lower science will function as principles of a higher science, so that one cannot advance to a higher science without making sufficient progress in a lower science.

My point here is not to defend Aquinas's demarcation of the sciences, but rather to show why he ought not to be considered solely as a religious thinker, and in turn to give some indication as to the role of proofs for the existence of God in his thought. Aquinas does not think that one can engage in the thinking of the higher sciences unless there is attained a certain degree of proficiency in the lower sciences propaedeutic thereto. In that case, one's thinking about religious matters (presumably in the sphere of theology) will involve certain more fundamental thinking in metaphysics and the other speculative sciences, such that for Aquinas one can be a good philosopher without being a good theologian, but one cannot be a good theologian without being a good philosopher.

Aquinas was an excellent theologian and in turn an excellent philosopher; and so when it came to those studies immediately propaedeutic to theology, the highest of which is philosophy,

---

    diuinas considerat propter se ipsas ut subiectum scientie, et hec est theologia que in sacra Scriptura traditur'.

7. Ibid, p. 154:149–154: 'Quia autem huiusmodi prima principia quamuis sint in se maxime nota, tamen intellectus noster se habet ad ea ut oculus noctue ad lucem solis, ut dicitur in II Metaphisice, per lumen naturalis rationis peruenire non possumus in ea nisi secundum quod per effectus in ea ducimur'.

Aquinas took the task of understanding and clarifying the issues in philosophy to be just as important as the issues of theology proper.

The proper object of theology is God such that it is God that the theologian studies,[8] and it is obvious that Aquinas believes the existence of God to be demonstrable,[9] but the scientific context within which such a demonstration is to be located is not so obvious. Although there is no natural knowledge of God in Himself, Aquinas holds that God's existence is demonstrable prior to the theological study of Him, and this is because God's existence can be demonstrated on the basis of His effects that are known to us.[10] This means, then, that God's existence can be established as the cause of all that is, since a causal proof of His existence can be developed from which God can be inferred as the primary cause of anything that exists. However, this does not mean that the nature of God in Himself is philosophically established.[11] What philosophy can establish, and what Aquinas proceeds to establish about God in a number of places, are certain attributes concomitant upon His being the primary cause of all that is. Hence, Aquinas never concludes his proofs of God with 'therefore God exists'; rather, he always concludes with something like 'and this is what we understand God to be'.[12]

Aquinas's goal in his proofs for the existence of God is to establish the existence of some primary cause that God is typically

8. *Summa Theologiae* (Turin: Marietti, 1926), Ia, qu. 1, art. 7.
9. Ibid, Ia, qu. 2, art. 2.
10. Ibid.
11. Ibid, Ia, qu. 3, Proem.
12. Note the conclusion of each of the five ways: Prima via: 'Ergo necesse est devenire ad aliquod primum movens, quod a nullo movetur, et hoc omnes intelligunt Deum'; Secunda Via: 'Ergo est necesse ponere aliquam causam efficientem primam, quam omnes Deum nominant'; Tertia Via: 'Ergo necesse est ponere aliquid quod sit per se necessarium, non habens causam necessitatis aliunde, sed quod est causa necessitatis aliis, quod omnes dicunt Deum'; Quarta Via: 'Ergo est aliquid quod omnibus entibus est causa esse, et bonitatis, et cuiuslibet perfectionis, et hoc dicimus Deum'; Quinta Via: 'Ergo est aliquid intelligens, a quo omnes res naturales ordinantur ad finem, et hoc dicimus Deum'.

taken to be. Having done that and remaining within the confines of philosophy, certain of God's attributes concomitant upon His being the primary cause can be established; but it is only in theology that the nature of God as He has revealed Himself to us begins to be depicted; and the latter takes us outside of a philosophical context (though not outside of philosophical procedures) and into the very heart of theology.

Aquinas is not solely a religious thinker; this is because religion is not the sole topic of his thought, even though God is his sole concern. Aquinas utilises every means to ascend from knowledge of things dependent on matter and motion to things not so dependent. Thus, he has to think his way through all of those lower sciences in order to arrive at the highest science. In that respect, his thought is all encompassing and not limited solely to religious matters.

Within the Thomistic scientific hierarchy, proving the existence of God is not an interesting philosophical project that one undertakes in the same way as, for example, proving the existence of the external world. Rather, Aquinas is led to proofs for the existence of God out of a concern for a scientific understanding of reality. Having got to a certain point in metaphysics and the intelligible articulation of the nature of reality, Aquinas is led to consider whether or not there is a principle on which all of reality is based. The establishing of this principle will mark the high point of philosophy and the entryway of philosophy into theology.

The procedure in the *De Ente* bears testimony to Aquinas's scientific method insofar as having reached a certain stage in metaphysics, he proceeds to consider whether or not there is some principle from which all being is derived. This will mark the high point of his metaphysical vision, and the beginnings of his theology.

In this book I seek to interpret and defend the proof of God offered in the *De Ente* on the basis of the metaphysics established beforehand. Thus, in Chapters 1, 2, and 3 I shall explore Aquinas's metaphysics of *esse* which he articulates prior to the proof of God; then Chapters 4, 5, and 6 will focus on the proof of God proper; and finally Chapter 7 will consider the nature of God as creator of all that is, a theme not dealt with explicitly in the *De Ente*, but relevant to and consistent with the context. I shall conclude that Aquinas offers a philosophically satisfying proof for the existence of God, one that has been overlooked in the literature.

ACKNOWLEDGEMENTS

It is not a duty but a privilege to acknowledge and publicly thank those who have contributed to the completion of a work. To that end, I would like firstly to thank Cynthia Read, Marcela Maxfield, and the team at Oxford University Press for all their help in bringing this work to publication. I would also like to thank Rev. Prof. Brian Davies OP, who read the manuscript in its entirety and gave me some helpful advice.

An academic can never work in a vacuum, but requires an environment that will both stimulate him and offer him succor. To that end I have several people and groups of people I would like to thank. To the staff and students of Queen's University Belfast and St Malachy's seminary, I extend my sincerest thanks for providing me with a highly stimulating intellectual environment in which to work. In particular I would like to thank Dr Joseph Diekemper and Dr Jeremy Watkins, both for their ongoing encouragement and genuine interest in my work. A lot of the argumentation in this book, especially on causal infinities, was often class tested on the seminarians of St Malachy's; I would like to take this opportunity to thank them, not only for suffering me as a teacher, but for entering into the spirit of the argumentation and often posing deep and challenging questions. At this point I would also like to thank the Catholic chaplain at Queen's University Belfast, Fr Gary Toman, for his constant support (both intellectual and spiritual) over these past few years. Finally, I would like to thank several members of the Irish philosophical circuit whose collegiality and friendship, perhaps unknown to them, were of immense importance to me in writing this work: Mr Eamonn Gaines OP, Dr Catherine Kavanagh, Dr Declan Lawell, and Dr Frank Gourley.

A research environment is not just intellectual but also personal. In this respect I have two people I would like to thank: Dr Timothy Lynch and Rev. Prof. James McEvoy. I have the privilege of counting them not only as my teachers, but as my friends; sadly in the case of Prof. McEvoy, his untimely death severed that friendship much too early.

I have two families that I wish to thank. The first is my Dominican family, in particular the Dominicans of the Irish province, whose love and friendship helped me realise that God is not just the conclusion to a demonstration or the answer to a problem, but that God is a person with a heart, uniquely present in every aspect of my life. To them I extend my warmest thanks for teaching me this, not by their words, but by their love.

The second family I wish to thank is my wife Collette, and my children, Evelyn and Dominic. There are no other people with whom I would rather be, and their presence in my life daily reminds me of God's love and blessings. They have been with me when research has been going well, and not so well. This work is as much a fruit of their labours as it is mine.

The final person I wish to thank is someone Who is present throughout this book, without Whom this book would not have been written, without Whom none of us would be. I here give thanks to God, the unique and subsisting act of being from Whom all that is comes to be. It is to Him that I dedicate these meagre thoughts.

Some of this work has appeared in other formats. Portions of Chapter 5 and Chapter 6 appeared previously in 'Aquinas's

Argument for the Existence of God in *De Ente et Essentia* Cap. IV: An Interpretation and Defense', *Journal of Philosophical Research*, 37 (2012), 99–133, and in 'Essentially Ordered Series Reconsidered', *American Catholic Philosophical Quarterly*, 86 (2012), 541–555. Chapter 7 appeared in a slightly different format in 'A Thomistic Metaphysics of Creation', *Religious Studies*, 48 (2012), 337–356. I here thank the editors for permission to reproduce the material.

AQUINAS'S WAY TO GOD

ESSENCE–*ESSE* DISTINCTION

AND COMPOSITION

THE METAPHYSICAL BACKDROP to the proof of God in *De Ente*, Cap. 4 is stated quite succinctly in Aquinas's argument for the real distinction between essence and *esse*. Up until this point in *De Ente*, Aquinas has been considering being and essence as they are found in concrete substances, and in Chapter 4 he focuses upon an issue related to immaterial substances. Owing to certain Augustinian and Neoplatonic influences, it was thought by some that immaterial substances were composed of a kind of matter so as to distinguish them from the pure simplicity of God, and thereby account for their being in potency in some respect. Such matter possessed by immaterial substances was not thought to be the corporeal matter that bodily things possess, but rather an incorporeal matter possessed only by immaterial substances. What was central to such a view was that matter–form composition was the most all-encompassing form of composition, accounting for both the principle of act and the principle of potency in all things; such a view was known as universal hylemorphism.[1]

Aquinas rejects this view. He thinks that it is rightly rejected by the philosophers as well precisely because it is as separated from matter and all material conditions that such substances are immaterial substances, in proof whereof Aquinas argues that, insofar as forms are understandable on the basis of their separation from the material conditions in which they are found, so too that which understands such forms must be separated from material conditions. Consequently, an intelligent substance, such as an angel, must be wholly separated from matter.[2]

Having argued that immaterial substances cannot be material, Aquinas is still faced with the problem of how to account for the potency and thereby composition that such substances have in distinction from the pure simplicity of God, who is pure act. He proceeds to argue that immaterial substances are not wholly simple, not pure act, but do indeed have an element of potency. In order to support this position, he argues that there is a kind of composition, more fundamental than hylemorphic composition, involved in all substances, material and immaterial, other than God. This more encompassing composition is that of essence and *esse*, so that an immaterial substance, free from matter, is yet composed of essence and a distinct *esse*, thereby rendering it non-simple and in potency to God, Who grants it its *esse*.

In order to establish the latter, Aquinas must show (i) that in all things except one unique case there is distinction and composition

---

1. In *De Ente et Essentia* (Rome: Editori di San Tommaso, 1976), Cap. 4, p. 375:7–8, Aquinas cites Avicebron as the author of this position; for some historical details on the role of this doctrine in the intellectual climate contemporaneous with Aquinas see John Wippel, *The Metaphysical Thought of Godfrey of Fontaines* (Washington: Catholic University of America Press, 1981), pp. 275–77.
2. *De Ente*, Cap. 4, pp. 375:8–376:22.

of essence and *esse*, and (ii) that that unique case in which essence and *esse* are not so distinct actually exists, and all things derive their *esse* from it.

Part I of this book will explore Aquinas's thought with regard to (i), that is, essence/*esse* distinction and composition. Part II will focus on Aquinas's thought with regard to the existence of that being whose essence is its *esse*.

1

THE ARGUMENT FOR REAL DISTINCTION IN *DE ENTE*, CAP. 4

THOMAS AQUINAS'S ARGUMENTATION in the *De Ente* for the real distinction of essence and *esse* is quite compact and is as follows:

[Stage One] Whatever does not enter into the understanding of an essence or quiddity comes to it from without and enters into composition with the essence, because no essence can be understood without its parts. Now, every essence or quiddity can be understood without knowing anything about its *esse*. I can know, for instance, what a man or a phoenix is and still be ignorant whether it has *esse* in reality. From this it is clear that *esse* is other than essence or quiddity, unless perhaps there is something whose quiddity is its *esse*.[1]

[Stage Two] This thing [whose quiddity is its *esse*] must be unique and primary, because something can be multiplied only [i] by adding a difference, as the nature of the genus is multiplied in the species; [ii] by the form's being received in

---

1. *De Ente*, Cap. 4, p. 376: 94–104: 'Quicquid enim non est de intellectu essentie uel quiditatis, hoc est adveniens extra et faciens compositionem cum essentia, quia nulla essentia sine hiis que sunt partes essentie intelligi potest. Omnis autem essentia uel quiditas potest intelligi sine hoc quod aliquid intelligatur de esse suo: possum enim intelligere quid est homo uel fenix et tamen ignorare an esse habeat in rerum natura; ergo patet quod esse est aliud ab essentia vel quiditate. Nisi forte sit aliqua res, cuius quiditas sit ipsum suum esse'.

diverse matter, as the nature of the species is multiplied in diverse individuals; [iii] or insofar as something is one and absolute and received in something else, for example, if there were a separated heat, by the fact of its separation it would be distinct from the heat that is not separated. If there were something that is *esse tantum* so that it would be self-subsistent being, [i] this would not receive the addition of a difference, for then it would not be *esse* alone but *esse* with the addition of a form. Much less [ii] could it receive the addition of matter, because then it would not be subsistent *esse* but material *esse*. It follows that such a thing that is its own *esse* can be only one. In everything else, then, its *esse* must be other than its quiddity, nature, or form. Hence it must be that in intelligences their *esse* is over and beyond their form, so it is said that an intelligence is a form and *esse*.[2]

Whilst this argumentation is quite compact, it is by no means straightforward, and it will be the goal of this chapter to unpack what Aquinas is getting at; then, in Chapters 2 and 3 the underlying metaphysics of the position articulated herein will be explored. A few introductory remarks are merited before proceeding.

2. Ibid, p. 376: 'Et hec res non potest esse nisi una et prima: quia impossibile est ut fiat plurificatio alicuius nisi per additionem alicuius differentie, sicut multiplicatur natura generis in species; uel per hoc quod forma recipitur in diuersis materiis, sicut multiplicatur natura speciei in diuersis indiuiduis; vel per hoc quod unum est absolutum et aliud in aliquo receptum, sicut si esset quidam calor separatus esset alius a calore non separato ex ipsa sua separatione. Si autem ponatur aliqua res que sit esse tantum, ita ut ipsum esse sit subsistens, hoc esse non recipiet additionem differentie, quia iam non esset esse tantum, sed esse et praeter hoc forma aliqua; et multo minus reciperet additionem materiae, quia iam esset esse non subsistens sed materiale. Vnde relinquitur quod talis res, que sit suum esse non potest esse nisi una; unde oportet quod in qualibet alia re praeter eam aliud sit esse suum et aliud quiditas uel natura seu forma sua; unde oportet quod in intelligentiis sit esse praeter formam, et ideo dictum est quod intelligentia est forma et esse'.

Aquinas seems to set forth two discrete arguments for the distinction between essence and *esse*, so that it would appear that either would do the job of the other. I have labelled these arguments 'stage one' and 'stage two'. The greatest hermeneutical problem with this argumentation is whether or not Aquinas intends to establish, and in fact actually does establish, a real distinction between essence and *esse*. The bulk of this chapter will be devoted to the issue of when and where the real distinction is established, whether in stage one or stage two, so that a contemporary Thomist seeking to defend the real distinction may point to this argumentation as a success.

I have labelled these arguments 'stage one' and 'stage two' because I think that they are two stages of a single demonstration for the real distinction, rather than independent demonstrations in themselves. As will become apparent, I do not think that stage one establishes a real distinction unless supplemented by the argumentation in stage two. This is an important issue, because insofar as Aquinas's proof for God depends on the real distinction as a premise, it is vital that that is established beforehand, in which case it is necessary to determine when and how Aquinas establishes the real distinction.

Some (Joseph Owens in particular) have argued that neither stage one nor stage two establishes the real distinction, but rather that the latter is established at a third stage of argumentation with the proof of the existence of God. I shall not be considering that position in any great amount of detail here, because it is the goal of this study to defend the proof of God offered in *De Ente*. If, as Owens maintains, the existence of God is a necessary premise for the real distinction, then the real distinction cannot feature as a premise for the existence of God. But, as will be seen, the real distinction does feature as a premise for the existence of God, in which case the existence of God cannot be a premise for real distinction. I do not deny that elsewhere Aquinas, having previously established God's existence to his own satisfaction, makes use of God's existence in order to infer the real distinction; I simply maintain that that is not what he does here.

Throughout my translation above I have left the term '*esse*' untranslated; this is because Aquinas's use of that term betrays his peculiar understanding of *esse* as a metaphysical principle of beings. Indeed for Aquinas *esse* is the metaphysical principle of all reality par excellence and so does not admit of a straightforward translation. In Chapter 3 I shall consider Aquinas's thought on *esse* in some detail. For the non-specialist, one might for now read *esse* as existence, so that when Aquinas establishes the real distinction between essence and *esse*, it is a distinction between essence and existence. But, at the risk of anticipating material dealt with in Chapter 3, *esse*/existence for Aquinas is a real principle of act of a finite existent irreducible to anything more fundamental, such that the thing would not exist unless it has such a principle and without it there would be nothing *simpliciter*. *Esse*/existence is thus nothing like the usual construals given to it in contemporary analytical discussions. The non-specialist reader must bear the latter in mind when translating *esse* as existence.

Thus far I have referred to a 'real distinction' between essence and *esse*, and so as not to engender confusion, I shall tease out what is meant by a real distinction. There is a kind of real distinction that involves real separation of two things, in the way that the moon is really distinct from the earth or the heart is really distinct from the liver. If this is what Aquinas had in mind with the real distinction between essence and *esse*, then such a position is absurd; for if essence and *esse* were really distinct as two separate things, then one could separate them, and consider either in isolation from the other. But if essence could be separated from *esse*, then one wonders what *esse* might add to the essence so as to actualise it. If *esse* is a thing distinct from essence, then it would seem that essence enjoys enough actuality in itself, and has no need of another principle of actuality by which it can exist. Evidently, then, this cannot be what Aquinas meant (and indeed, it is not what he meant).

There is another kind of real distinction, wherein the items being considered are distinct but not separate from each other, such as the heart and its beating, or the liver and its functioning. In such a case there is a distinction between the two realities; such a distinction entails that neither reality is to be identified with the other, but also that the one cannot be separated from the other in the way that the heart is separate from the liver or the moon from the earth. In that case, what is distinct amongst our concepts of such realities is also found to be distinct in such realities (and this as contrasted with a merely conceptual distinction whereby what is distinct amongst our concepts is not so distinct amongst the realities that those concepts serve to pick out). Such a real distinction between essence and *esse* does not entail the prima facie absurdity that the distinction by separation entailed, because it does not entail that the essence pre-exists its *esse* in some way, only that the *esse* of the essence is not identical to the essence.

With these preliminary remarks in mind, let us enter into Thomistic metaphysics with Aquinas's argumentation for the distinction between essence and *esse*.

1.1 STAGE ONE: THE *INTELLECTUS ESSENTIAE* STAGE

Aquinas begins this stage with a consideration of how essences are understood; it is therefore often dubbed the *intellectus essentiae* argument. What follows is quite a succinct piece of argumentation, and it has raised considerable controversy amongst commentators as to what kind of distinction between essence and *esse* it establishes.[3] I have elsewhere examined some of the details of

---

3. For some of the details of this controversy see Wippel, *The Metaphysical Thought of Thomas Aquinas*, p. 136, n. 11. See also Steven Long, 'On the Natural Knowledge of the Real Distinction of Essence and Existence', *Nova et Vetera*, 1 (2003), 75–77.

this dispute, and so as not to repeat myself I shall not here go into those details in any significant amount of depth; rather, I shall focus on what I think the argument itself establishes.[4]

Aquinas begins by stating that if something does not enter into our understanding of an essence or quiddity, it is composed with it from without, since an understanding of an essence or quiddity will naturally involve an understanding of its parts. Now, an essence or quiddity can be understood without understanding anything about its *esse*; for instance, I can understand what it is to be a man or a phoenix, without thereby understanding that men or phoenixes exist. Consequently, *esse* is other than, or distinct from, essence—that is, unless there is something whose very essence is precisely its *esse*.[5]

4. See my article, 'Aquinas's Argument for the Existence of God in *De Ente et Essentia*, Cap. IV: An Interpretation and Defense', *Journal of Philosophical Research*, 37 (2012), §§. I.A and I.B.

5. Note the translation of the opening sentence: 'Quicquid enim non est de intellectu essentie uel quiditatis, hoc est adueniens extra et faciens compositionem cum essentia . . .' as 'Whatever does not enter into the understanding of an essence or quiddity comes to it from without and enters into composition with the essence'. Scott MacDonald translates this as: 'Whatever is not of the concept of an essence or quiddity comes from without and effects a composition with the essence'. See 'The *Esse/Essentia* Argument in Aquinas's *De Ente et Essentia*', *Journal of the History of Philosophy*, 22 (1984), 171. Strictly speaking, as MacDonald translates it, this opening gambit is false (MacDonald points this out on p. 160), given that there are many things that are not of the concept of an essence, yet do not enter into composition with it. In order to obviate the falsity of this opening sentence, MacDonald reformulates what he sees as implicit therein. Thus, he construes Thomas as meaning: 'Whatever belongs to a thing and is not part of its essence', and this MacDonald readily recognises as interpolation on his part (pp. 160–61). However, I consider MacDonald's translation a poor translation, since Aquinas does not use the genitive in speaking of the understanding or concept of essence (as MacDonald's translation suggests); rather, he uses the ablative with the preposition '*de*', and this entails that the opening line takes into consideration whatever is concerned or not concerned with (does or does not enter into) the understanding of an essence or quiddity. On this better translation, the problems and thereby the corrections that MacDonald envisages for Aquinas need not arise. This would also explain why MacDonald does not think the *intellectus essentiae* argument is actually to be found in this stage of the *De Ente* (p. 162), since he interprets

This argumentation raises several significant questions. First (i), how exhaustive is the act of understanding envisaged to be when Aquinas states: 'Whatever does not enter into the understanding of an essence or quiddity comes to it from without and enters into composition with the essence'? Must one understand every intelligible note of a thing, observe that none of those notes involves a thing's *esse* and thereby conclude to the otherness of essence and *esse*? Surely this course of action is undermined by Aquinas himself, who claims in the very next chapter of the *De Ente*, that not every intelligible feature of a thing can be understood.[6] Secondly (ii), what role do the examples of man and phoenix play in the argument? Clearly men exist and one can talk about their essences, but can one really talk about the essence of non-existing things such as phoenixes? Is Aquinas suggesting that there is something like a Meinongian slum of non-existing essences that can be understood with regard to their essential natures but not with regard to their *esse*? Surely one can cut through the latter and say that with regard to non-existing essences, such as a phoenix, there is precisely nothing to understand—the phoenix example is at best irrelevant and at worst an embarrassment. Finally (iii), and most importantly, what sort of otherness of essence and *esse* is envisaged at this stage?

To deal with (i), that is, the exhaustiveness of the understanding of essence, Steven Long has suggested that what Aquinas has in mind when he refers to the 'parts of essence' are its generic elements, that is to say, matter and form for a material essence and

Aquinas as primarily focussed on what belongs to things that have essences and not on our understanding of essences; and this can only be upheld on the basis of what I believe to be an inadequate translation of the opening line of argumentation.

6. Aquinas, *De Ente*, Cap.5, p. 379:76–78: 'In rebus enim sensibilibus etiam ipse differentie essentiales ignote sunt'. For a list of occasions wherein Thomas retains this intellectual modesty about our knowledge of the intelligible notes of a thing, see M.-D. Roland-Gosselin, *Le 'De Ente et Essentia' de s. Thomas d'Aquin* (Paris: Librairie Philosophique J. Vrin, 1948), p. 40, n. 2.

form for an immaterial essence.[7] A full discussion (and defence) of the Thomistic notion of essence will have to wait until the next chapter, but suffice to say, the essence of a (material) thing for Aquinas is the unity of its matter and form, in which case a knowledge of essence is attained through a knowledge of the thing's form as individuated by its matter. Essence then is not identified with and not understood through a series of essential notes. The understanding of essence, then, cannot be the understanding of all of the (essential) intelligible notes of a thing (*vide* Aquinas's denial that we can even know all the essential differences of sensible things above in n. 6). What this entails is the recognition of a determinate object before us, in distinction from other such objects, and the grasp of this object, in distinction from others, as of a determinate kind. And *esse* is not understood in our understanding of the latter.

Accordingly, Aquinas presents two examples of matter/form composites, one existing (a man) the other non-existing (a phoenix). His suggestion is that the understanding of essence is neutral with regard to *esse*, since one can equally well understand the essence of something existent (a man) and something nonexistent (a phoenix), insofar as they are both understood to be kinds of matter/form composites, one of which exists and the other of which does not. This entails, then, that understanding the matter and form and thereby the essence of a thing does not entail the understanding of a thing's *esse*—otherwise the essence of a phoenix could not be understood. Consequently, a thing's *esse* does not enter into the understanding of essence and is thereby not identified with the essence. But this argumentation turns on the intelligibility of being able to understand nonexisting essences, and so, in relation to (ii) above, is it intelligible to speak of the essence of nonexisting things?

---

7. Steven Long, 'On the Natural Knowledge of the Real Distinction', 81–82. Owens offers the same interpretation in 'Quiddity and the Real Distinction in St Thomas Aquinas', *Mediaeval Studies*, 27 (1965), 6.

The focus of this argument is the *understanding* of essence (*de intellectu essentiae*), that is, of essence as absolutely considered in the mind, in abstraction from *esse*.[8] In other words, the argument is about the conceptual content that is employed in understanding the essence of material objects and not about the objects themselves. The concern then with this argument is closer to that of second intentions rather than first intentions.[9] Given that Aquinas is concerned with concepts, the phoenix example can be seen to make some sense, since one can conceive of things that do not exist, such as phoenixes, and thence employ some intricate semantical machinery to guarantee the meaningfulness of propositions about such nonexisting things.[10] Otherwise some unwieldy metaphysical framework is employed that situates the possibility of nonexisting possibles in the mind of God and holds that such possibles have essences insofar as they express a

8. This point is emphasised by Owens, 'Quiddity and the Real Distinction', 1–7.
9. Long, on the other hand, argues in the aforementioned article as well as in 'Aquinas on Being and Logicism', *New Blackfriars*, 86 (2005), §. C, that the whole concern of the *intellectus essentiae* argument is with first intentions. For my reaction to Long, see my article referred to in n. 4. See also what Aquinas says earlier in the *De Ente*, Cap. 3, p. 374:68–70: 'Ergo patet quod natura hominis absolute considerata abstrahit a quolibet esse, ita tamen quod non fiat precisio alicuius eorum'. This passage indicates that the nature of a thing, when considered absolutely in the mind, abstracts from *esse*, in which case *esse* does not enter into our understanding of things, which is the context of the *intellectus essentiae* argument in the immediately succeeding chapter of the *De Ente*. Owens makes a similar point (though he too believes that the argument is concerned with first intentions) in 'Quiddity and the Real Distinction', p. 6, whereas I believe this goes to show that, in the *intellectus essentiae* argument, Aquinas is thinking of essence as it is absolutely considered in the mind, and not as it is present in the objects to which the mind is directed in knowing the world, i.e., the objects of first intentions.
10. For a discussion of Aquinas's view that we can think of nonexistents, see Gyula Klima, 'The Semantic Principles underlying St Thomas Aquinas's Metaphysics of Being', *Medieval Philosophy and Theology*, 5 (1996), §. II, and for a list of instances wherein Aquinas distinguished between real beings and beings of reason see p. 92, n. 9. This of course raises thorny issues over possibility and actuality and our referring across possible worlds. I will deal with these issues in Chapters 2 and 3; see also Klima's article, §. III, for a discussion of the same.

non-contradictory finite quiddity that is available to God's power to create; and whilst in accord with an overall Thomistic metaphysics, this seems to go beyond the actual *intellectus essentiae* argument as laid out in the *De Ente*.[11] Thus, the phoenix example, when taken hand in hand with the example of the man, goes to show that the possession of conceptual content, such as what would signify a man or a phoenix, is no guarantee of the actual existence of the essence that such conceptual content serves to signify.[12] This then entails that conceptually speaking, essence and *esse* are distinct. Thus, in connection with point (iii) above, the *intellectus essentiae* argument establishes primarily a conceptual distinction between essence and *esse*, since it begins with the understanding, and thus the conceptual content involved in that understanding, of essence. There are accordingly distinguished two concepts: the essence of a thing and its *esse*; but is this the only distinction that the argument exhibits, that is to say, does it go beyond, or is it capable of going beyond, a conceptual distinction?

It is tempting to presume that unless the distinction is already thought to obtain in things, talk of essence as neutral with respect to *esse* is simply an embarrassment, given that one can only talk of essences that have *esse* and thereby exist, in which case any distinction between essence and *esse* which is made on the back of an inspection of the understanding of essence will be a distinction applicable to real beings. This contention shares something

---

11. This is Long's strategy in 'On the Natural Knowledge of the Real Distinction', 78–80 and 'Aquinas on Being and Logicism', 339.

12. Klima points out that for Aquinas, it was not necessarily the case that the phoenix was a mythical bird, and that it could be that Aquinas believed that he was referring to a species of actually existing bird. Be that as it may, Klima points out that the force of the argument at this point is that knowing the essence of a thing, either by quidditative definition (as with a man) or confusedly (as with a phoenix), is not the same as knowing the existence of such; and, in my opinion, this entails that in our understanding of them, essence and existence are distinct. See 'On Kenny on Aquinas on Being: A Critical Review of *Aquinas on Being* by Anthony Kenny', *International Philosophical Quarterly*, 44 (2004), Issue 176, 579.

of the flavour of the view that talk of the essence of a phoenix is an embarrassment, since phoenixes do not exist, and thereby have no essence to be understood. On this account then, the distinction between essence and *esse* must be envisaged as a distinction between two real metaphysical principles, and the distinction of associated concepts is derived from such a real distinction. However, as I have indicated, if the *intellectus essentiae* argument is read primarily about the *understanding* of essence, as Aquinas's actual terminology (*de intellectu essentiae*) would suggest, the concern is with the conceptual content involved in that understanding, in which case the phoenix example will not be so mystifying, since we can certainly conceive of such nonexistents. Not only that, if the *intellectus essentiae* argument is taken as being concerned with the understanding of essence and thereby the conceptual content involved therein, the distinction is primarily one amongst concepts. But if this is the case, then, unless bolstered by further philosophical considerations, any attempt to transfer the distinction between the concepts of essence and *esse* to the real order will be an illegitimate move from thought to reality; in effect, such a move would amount to a projection of the objects of two distinct mental operations—understanding, correlated with essence, and judgement correlated with *esse*—onto extra-mental reality.[13] In the absence of any bolstering considerations at this

13. Such bolstering considerations have indeed been offered. Lawrence Dewan believes that the real distinction *must* be established in the *intellectus essentiae* argument in order that it may enter as a premise in the proof of God later on: see 'St Thomas, Joseph Owens and the Real Distinction between Being and Essence', *The Modern Schoolman*, 61 (1984), 151. Long, on the other hand, holds that the inference at stage two, the topic of the next section, from the impossibility of multiplication of subsistent *esse* to the distinction between essence and *esse* in multiple entities, will result only in a conceptual distinction if essence and *esse* are not already—that is, at the *intellectus essentiae* stage—taken to be real principles of the finite entity and thereby really distinct. See Long, 'On the Natural Knowledge of the Real Distinction of Essence and Existence', 82; 'Aquinas on Being and Logicism', 341. However, I maintain that these contentions can only be vindicated if Thomas does *not* offer independent argumentation at stage two for real distinction, and thus they will stand or fall

stage, I see no reason to apply the distinction between the concepts of essence and *esse* to the real order.[14]

Still, if the distinction is only conceptual, one may wonder about Aquinas's conclusion: 'From this it is clear that *esse* is other than essence or quiddity, unless perhaps there is something whose quiddity is its *esse*'. Aquinas does not here say that conceptually speaking, essence is other than *esse*, but simply that essence and *esse* are distinct; and since it is not stipulated that what is here being dealt with is the understanding of essence, unless the argument is interpreted as delivering a real distinction, it would appear that Aquinas has in fact moved illegitimately from the conceptual plane to the metaphysical plane. And indeed, the *intellectus essentiae* argument has been criticised for moving from a distinction

on the strength of the argumentation offered at stage two. Furthermore, David Twetten has shown that if the *intellectus essentiae* argument is to conclude to real distinction of essence and *esse*, not only will further considerations need to be taken into account, but further premises must be added to the actual argument. See David Twetten, 'Really Distinguishing Essence from *Esse*', in *Proceedings of the Society for Medieval Logic and Metaphysics*, 6 (2006), 64–65; this article also appears in *Wisdom's Apprentice: Thomistic Essays in Honour of Lawrence Dewan* (Washington: The Catholic University of America Press, 2007).

14. A number of commentators agree that *at this stage* there is established only a conceptual distinction, foremost among them: Cornelio Fabro, *La Nozione Metafisica di Partecipazione secondo S. Tommaso D'Aquino* (Turin: Società Editrice Internazionale, 1950), pp. 218–19 (Fabro calls it a logical distinction); Leo Sweeney, 'Essence/Existence in Thomas Aquinas's Early Writings', *Proceedings of the American Catholic Philosophical Association*, 37 (1963), 105–109; Owens, 'Quiddity and the Real Distinction', 8–14, 'Stages and Distinction in *De Ente*: A Rejoinder', *The Thomist*, 45 (1981), 103–08, and 'Aquinas's Distinction at *De Ente et Essentia* 4.119–123', *Mediaeval Studies*, 48 (1986), §. IV; Wippel, 'Aquinas's Route to the Real Distinction', *The Thomist*, 43 (1979), 282–87, and *The Metaphysical Thought of Thomas Aquinas*, pp. 137–142; Armand Maurer, *Thomas Aquinas: On Being and Essence* (Toronto: Pontifical Institute of Medieval Studies, 1968), pp. 21–24 (Maurer states that Thomas established *at least* a conceptual distinction, he does not say that he established *only* a conceptual distinction). For a list of authors who hold that at this stage there is only a conceptual distinction, see Long, 'On the Natural Knowledge of the Real Distinction', 76, nn. 2–3.

in the order of concepts to a distinction of real metaphysical components of a thing.[15]

However, one way of reading this conclusion that can obviate such criticism is to see it as transitional to a further stage of argumentation (stage two), wherein essence and *esse* will be shown to be really distinct principles of a thing through a consideration of the unity of subsistent *esse*, as opposed to the multiplicity of finite beings. Such a reading would preserve the conceptual nature of the *intellectus essentiae* argument, as indicated by its opening gambit ('whatever does not enter into the *understanding* of an essence or quiddity'), whilst obviating the charge that it moves illegitimately from a concern about the concepts of essence and *esse* to a consideration of them as real principles of things in the conclusion ('*esse* is other than essence'), since, viewed as only a stage within a larger argumentative framework and not a complete argument in itself, the *intellectus essentiae* argument has not culminated in a final conclusion, but rather has entered into a new stage of argumentation.[16] On this reading, the argument concludes with a distinction of essence and *esse* in everything, unless there were a being whose essence is its *esse*; and if there were such a being, it would be one and first. Aquinas argues for the unicity of this being in the second stage of argumentation; he argues for its primacy in a further third stage wherein a proof of the existence of God is offered. Let us now turn to the argumentation in favour of its unicity.

---

15. See Wippel, *The Metaphysical Thought of Thomas Aquinas*, p. 142, n. 29, for details.

16. The view that the conclusion of the *intellectus essentiae* argument is simply one step in a larger argumentative framework is supported by several commentators: Owens, 'Quiddity and the Real Distinction', 17 *et seq*, 'Stages and Distinction in *De Ente*', 103, 'Aquinas's Distinction', 281; Wippel, 'Aquinas's Route to the Real Distinction'. MacDonald's analysis supports the judgement of one continuous argumentative framework ('The *Esse/Essentia* Argument', 158–59), but he does not recognise anything like the *intellectus essentiae* argument, because he misconstrues the opening argumentation as being about what belongs to things, rather than about what enters into the understanding of essence.

1.2 STAGE TWO: THE IMPOSSIBILITY OF MULTIPLICATION

Having ended the *intellectus essentiae* stage with the statement that essence and *esse* are distinct in all things, except for that whose essence is its *esse*, Aquinas goes on, in what I take to be a second stage of argumentation, to tease out the significance of the *hypothesis* of that whose essence is its *esse*. Accordingly, Aquinas here begins with a consideration of the different types of multiplication that may apply to things. He then considers whether such forms of multiplication could apply to a being whose essence is its *esse*, and he concludes that they could not. However—and this is crucial—he does not here assume the existence of that whose essence is its *esse*, rather, the existence of such is considered only as a hypothetical possibility. *If* there were something whose essence is its *esse, then*, assuming that the argumentation is correct, the denial of its multiplicity would obtain in reality; but as yet only the hypothesis of such a being is presented at this stage of argumentation. Why, then, the emphasis on the hypothetical nature of this argumentation?

If stage one only considers the concepts of essence and *esse* as distinct, then one would expect the argumentation in stage two to be hypothetical in nature and bound up with a discussion of concepts, as opposed to real things. So given that in my interpretation stage one is bound up with concepts, then the argumentation in stage two must be hypothetical, and thereby bound up with concepts as well. I emphasise this because it is Long's contention that if stage one is conceptual, then stage two must be also; this is surely correct, given that the hypothetical nature of stage two demands that its concern be with concepts. However, the hypothetical, and thereby conceptual, nature of stage two does not preclude the possibility of drawing real conclusions about essence and *esse*, as will be shown later.

Accordingly, Aquinas begins with a statement that if there were a being whose essence is its *esse*, it would be one and primary.

In order to show that this being could only be one, Aquinas begins with a consideration of the modes of multiplication. In his eyes, there are three:

(i) Multiplication can occur through the addition of some difference; as the nature of a genus is multiplied into its species.

(ii) Multiplication can occur through a form's being diversified in matter; as the nature of a species is diversified in its individuals.

(iii) Multiplication can occur when something separate is received in something concrete; say if there were a separated heat from which all hot things were hot.

Let us pause for a moment to consider these forms of multiplication.

Types (i) and (ii) clearly presuppose the Aristotelian classificatory system of genus and species and the ontological principles of matter and form, whereas type (iii) is more Platonic in nature. The first type of multiplication considers some generic nature and holds that such a nature is specified through the addition of a differentiating feature (or features): for example, a generic notion, such as 'animal', signifies a wider domain of entities than some specific type of animal, such as the species 'human'. On the Aristotelian account that Aquinas is here adopting, the domain of signification of the species 'human' is narrower than that of 'animal', because there is some specific feature(s) of 'human' that sets it apart as a species of animal; and if the species 'human' did not have the specific feature(s) it has, then it could not be specified as a particular type of animal.

The second type of multiplication considers how individuals of a particular species are multiplied. In some species, such as 'human', the species in itself is not self-individuating—that is to say, individual humans are not the individuals that they are through their being the types of things that they are, but rather through their being individual members of the species. Reference to the type, that is, the species, that the individuals are will not refer to the individuals of that type, in which case some further element is required for individuation; and this, as Aquinas notes, will involve the matter out of which such individuals are made. Thus, the species is realised in material instances, that is, in diverse clumps of designated matter occupying space and time, so that when reference is made to an individual of a type, there is referential success when one not only refers to the type of which the individual is an individual, but also to the type as instantiated in the individual occupying 'this place' at 'this time'. Thus, the realisation or reception in matter of a type brings about individuals of that type.

Finally, the third form of multiplication considers how some separated universal property can be received and thereby multiplied in particular instances. On this account, particular things receive from the exemplar the universal property in question. So in the example that Aquinas uses, if there were a separate heat, particular instances of heat would receive from that separated heat the heat that they possess, so that the heat of the separated heat is thereby multiplied in the particulars. Notice that this third type of multiplication, insofar as it focuses on the reception of something universal into something intrinsically particular, bears resemblance to the second type of multiplication: the reception of form in matter.[17] Though one difference between the two types of multiplication might be that in (ii), prior to the reception of form in matter, no material individuals are presupposed, whereas in (iii), prior to the reception of the universal in the particular, certain individuals capable of receiving the universal property in question are presupposed. However, this may be a trivial difference because the receiving principle (matter/concrete particulars) and what is received (form/separate

---

17. Wippel notes that in later years Aquinas conflated the second type of multiplication with the third type. See *The Metaphysical Thought of Thomas Aquinas*, p. 145, 156–57.

universal) are indeed presupposed for multiplication types (ii) and (iii).

Aside from these hermeneutical issues, the more important issue is whether or not these modes of multiplication are exhaustive. The importance of this issue cannot be overstated, for immediately after listing these types of multiplication Aquinas attempts to show that a being whose essence is its *esse* cannot be multiplied in any way, in which case the exhaustiveness of the forms of multiplication becomes an issue, because if he has left out any form of multiplication, his overall conclusion—namely, that there could only be one being whose essence is its *esse*—will be considerably weakened.

One can read Aquinas's listing of the types of multiplicity as either (i) inductive or (ii) deductive. If the listing is read as inductive, then Aquinas is simply observing multiple things and listing the types of multiplicity that are seen to be involved therein; from this perspective, Aquinas is generalising from particular instances of multiplicity to universal norms that apply to those instances. In the latter view, as with most inductive generalisations, there is always the possibility of some further type of multiplicity arising, because there is always the possibility that there is some instance that was either unobserved or not adequately considered, which could render a new type of multiplicity apparent.

If, however, the listing of types of multiplicity is read as deductive, then there must be some principle at work from which the deduction is made and which determines the types of multiplicity that Aquinas believes there are. The principle at work would seem to be that possibility is a necessary condition for multiplicity, such that things can only be multiple if it is possible for there to be more than one of those things. Thus, in all the cases listed, we begin with something more general whose range of possibility is capable of being determined in some respect.

I think that the deductive reading sits better with the overall reading of stage two that I have been emphasising. Recall that given my view that stage one results only in a conceptual distinction, stage two must begin by considering the concepts of essence and *esse*, in which case stage two must be conducted on the conceptual plane. Confirmation that the latter is in fact the case was found in the fact that at this stage the focus is on the hypothesis of a being whose essence is its *esse*. Thus, the argument of stage two is being carried out on the hypothetical and thereby conceptual plane, in which case one would expect the type of reasoning involved to be a deductive argument based on principles determined by a priori reasoning, as opposed to a generalisation made on the back of a posteriori recordings. I thus submit that Aquinas's elucidation of the types of multiplicity is deductive insofar as he is considering the types of multiplicity that can obtain on the basis of the principle of the necessity of possibility for multiplicity.

Now, one can of course argue that multiplicity of types (i), (ii), and (iii) are by no means exhaustive of the implementation of the principle of the necessity of possibility for multiplicity. But that would be to disagree with the details of the argument whilst missing its point. The whole point of the argument in stage two is to show that a being whose essence is its *esse* could not be multiplied in any fashion. If the principle of the necessity of possibility for multiplicity is assumed, then *whatever* we take the types of multiplicity to be, every type of multiplicity will involve possibility in what is to be multiplied, in which case the more fundamental question is whether or not possibility is itself applicable to that whose essence is its *esse*.[18] And clearly Aquinas does not think that possibility is applicable to that whose essence is its *esse*.

Accordingly, Aquinas goes on to ask whether or not that whose essence is its *esse* could be multiplied in any fashion. Before going on to deny any form of multiplicity to such a being, Aquinas first states that if there were such a being, it would be *esse tantum*, that is, pure *esse*, and if it is such, it would be subsistent *esse*. The

---

18. Long, 'On the Natural Knowledge of the Real Distinction', 82.

importance of these clarifications insists upon some reflection. According to Aquinas, that whose essence is its *esse* would be pure *esse*, that is to say, what it is would not in any way differ from its *esse*; rather, it would be *esse* itself (*ipsum esse*), and would signify in itself the very fullness of *esse*, insofar as it simply is precisely what it is 'to be'. Given the latter, such a reality would be subsistent *esse* (*esse subsistens*), since it would be not in virtue of some principle distinct from it, but simply in virtue of what it is, since what it is, its essence, is *esse*. Thus, such a being, if it exists, would be subsisting *esse* itself, i.e. *ipsum esse subsistens*. And on the basis of these clarifications, Aquinas denies that there could be any more than one such being.

He begins by stating that such a being could not be subject to the first mode of multiplication, as a generic nature is determined through the addition of specifying characteristics, for then, according to Aquinas, it would not be pure *esse*, but *esse* plus some form. Such a being could not be subject to the second mode of multiplication, for then it would not be subsistent *esse*, but material *esse*. Aquinas then concludes that such a being cannot be multiplied in any way, that is to say, there is at most one being whose essence is its *esse*. But immediately three questions present themselves: first, has Aquinas adequately eliminated multiplication types (i) and (ii) from the picture? Second, what about multiplication type (iii), given that Aquinas has not explicitly rejected this? Third, could there be any other type of multiplication applicable to that whose essence is its *esse*? Let us consider each of these questions in turn.

Aquinas denies multiplication of type (i) for pure *esse*, because to admit it would entail that such a being would not be pure *esse*, but *esse* plus some form. Recall that multiplication of type (i) involves multiplying the nature of a genus into its various species, and that this is achieved through the addition of specifying features that serve to pick out some form of that genus. Accordingly, through the addition of various features, the species 'human' is determined as a form of animal. The same cannot be said for pure *esse*, for if pure *esse* were multipliable as a genus into its species, then the multiple instances of *esse* realised in its species would not be pure *esse* itself, but rather each would be a specific form of *esse*, just as the species 'human' is a form of animal, but does not convey animality to its full extent. Accordingly, Aquinas denies multiplication of type (i) for pure *esse* insofar as its multiplication would not preserve its purity as *esse*, but instead would result in some form of *esse* and not pure *esse* itself.

When considering Aquinas's denial of multiplication type (ii) for pure *esse*, it must be recalled that pure *esse* is subsistent *esse*, because if it exists, it exists not in virtue of something distinct from itself, but in virtue of itself. Now, recall that multiplication type (ii) occurs through the reception and thereby individuation of some form in matter, in which case if applied to pure *esse*, what would result would be the reception of pure *esse* in matter and thereby the production of material instances of *esse*. Aquinas denies the possibility of the latter, stating that such would be incompatible with the subsistence of pure *esse*.

Whatever is material is subject to generation and corruption. But pure *esse*, as subsistent through existing in virtue of what it is, cannot be subject to generation and corruption. That this is so is clear from the fact that whatever is generated and corrupted is such on the basis of certain principles through which it exists (matter and form in this instance). If one either adds or removes the principles through which the generable and corruptible thing exists, then the thing is thereby either generated or corrupted; but all the while such a thing as generable and corruptible is dependent on another for its existence as a generable and corruptible thing. Pure *esse* exists in virtue of what it is and is therefore not dependent on another for its existence, in which case it cannot depend on matter for its being and is therefore not subject to multiplication through material instantiation.

The denial of multiplication of types (i) and (ii) leads to the conclusion that there is nothing outside of pure *esse* that could serve to differentiate it into particular instances of itself, *à la* type (i); moreover, pure *esse* could not be multiplied into material individuals, for then it would cease to be subsistent and would be subject to the generation and corruption that besets all material creatures, *à la* type (ii). Assuming that these are the only forms of multiplication, Aquinas has succeeded in showing that if there indeed exists pure *esse*, not only is it unitary, signifying in itself the fullness of what it is to be, but as pure and thereby subsistent *esse* it is essentially immaterial, and not subject to material conditions. Yet it is the assumption that these *are* the only types of multiplication that is worrying. As yet Aquinas has not considered his own third form of multiplication, nor has he considered any other possible forms of multiplication. It is to these issues that I now turn.

Once the nature of type (iii) multiplication is understood, it will be clear why Aquinas has not considered it. On this account, he asks us to imagine some separate property on which depend all instances of the property in question. But notice something peculiar about this type of multiplication: whereas in types (i) and (ii), the more general feature (the genus and the form) was itself multiplied *in* that which multiplies it (species and matter), in this third form of multiplication, the general feature is not multiplied in the things that multiply it; it remains one and separate, whereas the multiple individuals depend on it for the property in question. Aquinas's example is that of a separated heat on which individual heats depend for their hotness; an instance of this type of relationship is not difficult to find. Consider the heat or energy from the sun. There are many ways in which this heat is realised here on earth from its reception in lakes, rivers, or stones, through to the technologically advanced canvassing and distribution of the sun's energy by means of solar panels. However, so many realisations of the sun's energy do not signify so many suns; rather, all realisations of the sun's energy are but participations in the energy of the sun and not actual multiplications of the sun itself. On the other hand, in type (i) multiplication, specific animals are actual instances and thereby multiplications of the type 'animal', and in type (ii) material individuals of some type are actual instances and thereby multiplications of that type. Consequently, in type (iii) multiplication, there is not the actual multiplication of the general property *in* the individuals, but the participation of the individuals *in* the general property, in which case the separate property remains one and single. And this is precisely the type of relationship that Aquinas wishes to spell out between pure *esse* and creatures: pure *esse* is not properly multiplied *in* creatures, rather, multiple creatures depend on pure *esse* in order to be.[19] So much then for the third form of multiplication; what of the issue of further forms of multiplication?

It was noted that in the deductive reading of this whole section, Aquinas is applying a principle of plurification and deducing its various types. The underlying principle appears to be the necessity of possibility for multiplicity, given that, except for type (iii), the forms of multiplicity adduced presuppose that for what is to be multiplied (the generic or specific nature), it must be possible of multiplication. So, as has been seen, the reference frame of a generic nature admits of further specification through the addition of various differentiating features, and a specific nature can be multiplied through being received in distinct clumps of matter.

---

19. This of course anticipates the participation relationship of the finite creature in its act of being, a theme that predominates Aquinas's metaphysics of *esse* and is crucial in understanding his solution to the problem of the one and the many. I shall touch on this theme in Chapter 3 when I discuss the composition of essence and *esse* in creatures, though I shall not dwell on it in any great amount of depth. The most important discussions of it are as follows: Louis-Bertrand Geiger, *La Participation dans la philosophie de s. Thomas d'Aquin* (Paris: Librairie Philosophique J. Vrin, 1942); Cornelio Fabro, *La Nozione Metafisica di Partecipazione secondo S. Tommaso d'Aquino; Participation et causalité selon s. Thomas d'Aquin* (Louvain: Publications Universitaires de Louvain & Paris, Béatrice-Nauwelaerts, 1961); William Norris Clarke, 'The Meaning of Participation in St Thomas', in *Explorations in Metaphysics: Being—God—Person* (Notre Dame-London: University of Notre Dame Press, 1994), pp. 89–102; Rudi te Velde, *Participation and Substantiality in Thomas Aquinas* (Leiden: E. J. Brill, 1995); John Wippel, *The Metaphysical Thought of Thomas Aquinas*, Chapter 4.

Now it must be asked whether or not pure *esse* is such that it is intrinsically multipliable.

This whole discussion turns on the following question: is there something about pure *esse* as there is about a general or specific nature that would permit its multiplication even if, hypothetically speaking, there in fact is only a single pure *esse*? Let us consider what it is about the things multiplied in types (i) and (ii) that permits their multiplication. In both cases, they signify some reality indeterminately, and they accordingly are determined by some principle distinct from themselves. Thus, the generic nature 'animal' signifies all animals, but only indeterminately, and thereby stands to be further determined through the addition of specifying features—features that are formally distinct from the generic notion itself. The same goes for the multiplication of some species into its individuals through reception in matter; the species signifies its individuals as individuals of such and such a kind, but not their individuality. In order to signify the individuals in their individuality, recourse to some principle other than the species in question is required, and this principle is matter. When it comes to pure *esse*, it is not the case that *esse* indeterminately signifies all of the things that could possibly be, and therefore stands to be determined by something distinct from itself. Pure *esse* is precisely what it is to be. Accordingly, anything not envisaged by pure *esse* is precisely an impossibility of being and beyond the scope of being. Given the latter, there can be nothing distinct from pure *esse* which stands to determine it in some fashion, whereas in types (i) and (ii) multiplication, their scope of application is determined through some principles distinct from themselves. Therefore, pure *esse* considered precisely as pure *esse* does not stand to be determined in any way by anything distinct from itself, in which case, unless it is self-determining, pure *esse* is intrinsically indeterminable and thereby non-multipliable.

Given these considerations, I think Aquinas is right to conclude in favour of the unicity of pure *esse*, not only because multiplication of types (i) and (ii) do not apply and type (iii) does not count against his overall conclusion, but also because pure *esse* does not stand to be determined by anything distinct from itself, in which case, unless it is self-determining, pure *esse* will not admit of the possibility of multiplication.

If pure *esse* exists, then it can be only one. But if there can only be one pure *esse*, that is, if there can be at most one reality whose essence is its *esse*, then in all else essence and *esse* are distinct. And so it must be asked: what kind of distinction has the argument delivered us?

Steven Long contends that unless essence and *esse* are already taken to be real metaphysical principles of things at the beginning of this stage of argumentation, then the distinction at this stage can only be conceptual; for, unless one wants illegitimately to move from thought to reality, if one enters this stage with nothing but a conceptual distinction, one must leave with a conceptual distinction.[20] The point tracks a similar one made by Owens, to the effect that any conclusion at this stage to a real distinction is an illegitimate jump from thought to reality and would show tendencies of the ontological argument.[21] And whilst Owens and Long disagree over how to characterise the first stage of argumentation (Owens envisaging therein a conceptual distinction, whereas Long interprets a real distinction) they are agreed that one cannot move from a conceptual distinction at stage one to a real distinction at stage two. According to them, stage two only serves to universalise the distinction established at stage one—that is to say, whereas stage one applied the distinction (real or conceptual) to material beings only, stage two applies the distinction to all beings other than pure *esse*, and thereby extends the applicability of the distinction to immaterial creatures.[22]

20. Long, 'On the Natural Knowledge of the Real Distinction', 82–83; 'Aquinas on Being and Logicism', 341.
21. Owens, 'Stages and Distinction in *De Ente*: A Rejoinder', 100, 117–21.
22. Owens, 'Aquinas's Distinction', 282, 286; Long, 'On the Natural Knowledge of the Real Distinction', 93. As noted at the beginning, this was one of Thomas's intended outcomes: to show that essence and *esse* can be distinguished in immaterial creatures.

Wippel, on the other hand, has consistently defended his view that this stage of argumentation delivers a real distinction between essence and *esse*. He contends that once it has been established (conceptually no doubt) that at most there can be one being whose essence is its *esse*, then irrespective of the actual existence of that being, there is a distinction between essence and *esse* in all else. In other words, if it is granted that there are multiple entities, then such entities, whatever they may be, will be subject to essence/*esse* distinction; for whatever such entities may be, *qua* multiple they are *not* that being whose essence is its *esse*, because that being can only be one. If the fact of real multiplicity is recognised, then it must also be recognised that this stage delivers us a distinction between essence and *esse* in such things that are really multiple. But given that in a realist construal of things there do exist multiple entities, these entities cannot be pure *esse*. Consequently, such really existing multiple entities, as not pure *esse*, must be composites of essence and *esse*, in which case there is distinguished in those things themselves essence and *esse*. And at this stage, according to Wippel, there is established a real distinction of essence and *esse*.

The force of Wippel's interpretation rests on the following modal argument. What is intrinsically impossible cannot be actual and is therefore precisely nothing, because possibility is a necessary, though not sufficient, condition for actuality. As shown above, it is impossible for there to be more than one pure *esse*, in which case, if there is any at all, there is never actually more than one pure *esse*. Consequently, multiplicity is a sign of non-identity of essence and *esse*, and if one grants that there exist multiple things, then one must grant the non-identity, or distinction, of essence and *esse* in such things.

This reasoning does not move from the positive concepts of essence and *esse* in the mind to the projection of them on reality, as Owens and Long would suggest. It is a modal argument that seeks to move from the impossibility of a given state of affairs to the denial of its possibility and thereby the affirmation of the obtaining of the inverse of that state of affairs. As such the argument is philosophically sound and does not contain shades of the ontological argument which would seek to project some positive conceptual content onto reality from some mere possibility. Furthermore, insofar as this stage (stage two) directly precedes the argumentation for the existence of God, Dewan's concern—namely, that the real distinction must figure in the argument for God and must therefore be established *prior* to such argumentation—is accounted for, because it is not until a stage of argumentation subsequent to the one here considered that proof for God's existence is offered. I thus conclude that at this stage of argumentation, Aquinas has established that essence and *esse* are really distinct, given that he has transformed the modal claim that it is impossible for there to be more than one being whose essence is its *esse* (a highly conceptual claim) into the claim that in multiple things essence and *esse* are non-identical.

Before concluding this chapter, there is an objection to the argumentation for real distinction that must be addressed.

1.3 DAVID TWETTEN'S ARISTOTELIAN QUESTION-BEGGING OBJECTION

Whilst supportive of the doctrine of the real distinction, David Twetten has urged a hypothetical question-begging objection to all of Aquinas's arguments for the real distinction.[23] I do not here propose to go over the application of this objection to all of Aquinas's arguments in this respect, only the arguments that feature in *De Ente*, Cap. 4.

The question-begging objection goes as follows. An Aristotelian can countenance equating material essence with

23. David Twetten, 'Really Distinguishing Essence from *Esse*'.

matter–form composition.[24] But unless it is antecedently assumed that beyond matter and form Thomist *esse* is a metaphysical principle of a thing, the Aristotelian does not see the attraction of appealing to anything beyond matter and form in order to account for the being of the essence in question. So, argues Twetten, Aquinas's arguments for the real distinction turn on the presupposition that *esse* is a real metaphysical principle over and beyond matter and form; and all the arguments show is that *esse* is neither matter nor form. The arguments *do not* tell us why Thomist *esse* should be included in our ontology in the first place.

As applied to the argumentation in the *De Ente*, the objection goes as follows. The *intellectus essentiae* argument makes the tacit assumption that ignorance of the existence of some nonexistent essence is in fact ignorance of some ontological principle distinct from that essence, i.e., *esse*. Granted this latter assumption, if one does not understand that some essence, such as a phoenix, exists, then what renders the phoenix existent, its *esse*, is distinct from its essence. But the Aristotelian will likely counter: ignorance of the existence of some essence is not ignorance of an ontological principle, such as *esse*; rather, it is an ignorance of there being any material instances of that essence. So, ignorance of the existence of a phoenix is not ignorance of the *esse* of the phoenix; rather, it is ignorance of (that is never having come across) any instance of a phoenix. Thus, understanding the essence of something without understanding its existence does not establish that essence and *esse* are distinct, so that *esse* should be countenanced as a metaphysical principle of things over and above matter and form. So much then for the application of Twetten's objection to stage one. What about stage two?

The inference from the unicity of pure *esse* to the distinction between essence and *esse* in all multiple things rests on the tacit assumption that if essence and *esse* are indistinct, then the being

---

24. Ibid, 60, n. 8.

in which they are indistinct is pure *esse*; and this in turn rests on the assumption that *esse* is a metaphysical principle already included in our ontology, so that lack of distinction of essence and *esse* entails that the reality not so distinct is pure *esse*. The Aristotelian counters: why can't that which lacks distinction of essence and *esse* simply be pure essence, why must it be pure *esse*?[25]

So Twetten is clear, one can perhaps follow Aquinas in his Aristotelianism only so far, but if one wants to go beyond the Aristotelian principles of Aquinas's metaphysics and affirm that essence and *esse* are distinct, then either Aquinas or his commentators will have to offer positive reasons not only for the real distinction, but also for the assumption that *esse* is a principle that presently existing things must have, and this over and beyond the Aristotelian principles of matter and form. The Aristotelian insists: what does *esse* add to the metaphysical analysis of a thing not already explained by matter and form? After all, form for Aristotle is the principle of the being of a thing; things have their existence through their form, that is to say, material things exist insofar as they are formed chunks of matter. What more is needed?

It would be merely dodging the bullet to claim that Aquinas is not being a good Aristotelian, but rather introducing his own metaphysical principles. The pure-blooded Aristotelian will ask precisely why Aquinas, or anyone else for that matter, is not being a good Aristotelian in this respect; it is precisely the introduction of Thomist *esse* into the metaphysical analysis of finite beings that cries out for substantiation. The Aristotelian (amongst others) will ask, does Aquinas's overall framework make good philosophical sense, that is to say, are there any good reasons for admitting *esse* as a principle of our ontology? Thus, a solid refutation of Twetten's hypothetical objection is called for.

---

25. See Ibid, 64–68 for reformulation of the argumentation from *De Ente*, Cap. 4 and criticism.

To my mind, the case for Thomist *esse* rests on the lack of an affirmative answer to the following question: can form account for the existence of the thing, that is to say, does the form of a matter–form composite have the wherewithal to account for the existence of a thing?[26] And the Thomist will reply that it does not, because form *qua* form, that is, *qua* structuring principle of matter, does not entail actual existence. Let us return to Aquinas's phoenix example: the form of a phoenix is, presumably, what structures a clump of matter into a bird that explodes into flames when it expires and rises from its own ashes. There is nothing about this form that signifies the actual existence of a phoenix; what signifies the actual existence of a phoenix is there actually existing a thing that is such. But, the Thomist continues, the actual existence of a phoenix is not necessitated by the form that it has—if it were, then all forms would exist. In other words, if form is so construed as to be not only a structuring principle of a thing but also a principle of the existence of a thing, then all forms would self-exist, since if form and existence are identical, then that form (of whatever kind) must exist. But the Thomist objects that one can only posit that some form exists *if* in fact that form does indeed exist; just as with the ontological argument, Aquinas objects that whilst a 'that than which nothing greater can be conceived' can be conceived to exist in reality, it doesn't actually exist in reality through our conceiving it as such. Similarly, whilst form can be conceived to exist in reality, it doesn't actually exist as such through our conceiving it to be so. Consequently, there is room here for an actualising principle of form, the possession of which signifies the existence of forms such as cat, dog, human, and horse, and the lack of which renders forms such as phoenix, phlogiston, and hippogryph,

---

26. I here gloss over inquiring into matter as a principle of the existence of a thing, given that matter for Aristotle is a principle of potency and therefore does not actualise a thing in existence, but only serves to delimit the scope of form to some individual instance.

nonexistent, yet conceptually possible. And this actualising principle is Thomist *esse*.

There is scope then for including *esse*, over and above matter and form, in one's ontology, because *esse* is the principle that accounts for the present existence of something, if that something actually exists, and this existence cannot be accounted for by form, for then all forms (of whatever kind) would exist. Having established then the need for *esse* in our ontology, the Thomist must determine *esse*'s relation to essence; and as Aquinas's argumentation in the *De Ente* shows, essence and *esse* are really distinct.

1.4 CONCLUSION

Whilst scholarly opinion is divided over the stage at which Aquinas established the real distinction, I hold firmly to Wippel's interpretation that it is with stage two, the impossibility of multiplying pure *esse* and the implications that follow therefrom, that Aquinas has established there to be a real distinction between essence and *esse*. However, this is to say nothing of their composition in the finite entity. How in fact are they so composed?

Subsequent to establishing the actual existence of a being whose essence is its *esse* (that is, subsequent to the proof of God), Aquinas infers that God is the principle from which all *esse* flows. If that is the case, then that which stands to *esse* as a receiver to something received stands in potency to *esse*, and *esse* stands to it as actualising principle. But it is the essence of the finite being that *esse* actuates, in which case essence stands to *esse* as potency to act. All finite beings are thus composites of potency and act, and essence and *esse* are composed in finite creatures as potency and act. A unified substantial entity is produced out of the composition of essence and *esse*.

To return to the original point of the discussion, the potency of immaterial substances, Aquinas has established that in them there is a principle of potency, their essences, which is not material, but which is yet not actual—they are not pure *esse*. As such, immaterial finite entities are distinguishable from God, who is pure act and not a composite of potency and act. Aquinas has thus succeeded in his original aim of establishing the finititude of immaterial non-divine entities without thereby postulating a spiritual matter therein.

The more pressing issue now is the metaphysical background of Aquinas's notions of essence and *esse*. So far all that has been established is something that nearly all commentators, except Owens, agree upon: that Aquinas held there to be a real distinction between essence and *esse* in the argumentation considered in this chapter. The bulk of this chapter has been focussed on clarifying exactly where and how Aquinas concluded to real distinction, but it is taken by most that it is a fact that he did. It is however not clear at this point what Aquinas actually thought about essence and *esse*, other than that they are distinct. And so now these fundamental principles of Thomist metaphysics must be considered before moving on to the proof of God's existence proper.

2

ESSENCE

IN THE PREVIOUS chapter, two terms central to Aquinas's metaphysical thought were introduced: 'essence' and *'esse'*. These terms are crucial to Aquinas's proof of God in *De Ente*, Cap. 4. As has been noted, for Aquinas these two terms signify central metaphysical principles of a finite entity, and are found to be really distinct therein. The previous chapter was focussed primarily on establishing that essence and *esse* are really distinct for Aquinas, and when exactly he establishes them as such in the *De Ente*. Here the focus shifts somewhat, such that in the present chapter and the next the concern will be with the nature of essence and *esse* considered in themselves.

Insofar as this chapter and the next are propaedeutic to Aquinas's proof of God in *De Ente*, I shall explore what Aquinas thought of essence and *esse* in the *De Ente* itself and in works consistent with the *De Ente*. Thankfully, aside from developments signifying the maturing of a philosophical mind with age, Aquinas's thought on essence and *esse* in the *De Ente* remained with him throughout the rest of his career. Aquinas was a systematic thinker of a profound intelligence in whose early thought can be found the excitement and crispness of youth, and whilst with age comes the development of key themes, those key themes themselves remain, essence and *esse* being in fact essential to his own characteristic metaphysical thought.

This chapter is concerned with essence, and as such it will be divided into three sections: (i) a historical account of Aquinas's thought on essence; (ii) a contrast of the Thomist account with more contemporary accounts of essence; and (iii) a conclusion and transition to the next chapter.

2.1 THOMISTIC ESSENCE

As noted in Chapter 1, Aquinas distinguishes between essence and *esse* such that essences exist each through an act of existence (*esse*) which is distinct from them. Essence, then, is a principle of a finite being such that it is a necessary though not sufficient condition for the existence of such a being; essence, then, is that through which and in which a thing has *esse*.[1] Aquinas accordingly holds that beings are things that have essences such that beings are the type of things they are on account of the essences that they have. In coming to characterise essence, Aquinas distinguishes between two types of per se being (*ens* per se) and holds that the term 'essence' is derived from one type but not from the other.

For Aquinas, *ens* per se is divided into: (i) what is divided through the ten categories and (ii) what signifies the truth of propositions. According to (ii) anything about which an affirmative proposition can be formed can be called a being, even if it posits nothing in reality; for example, according to this mode of being, blindness could be called a being insofar as it is one of the truth conditions for the proposition that 'x is blind'. According to (i), only that which posits something in reality, i.e. a substance, can be called a being, in which case not all beings in the (ii) sense can be considered beings in the (i) sense.

Aquinas claims that the term 'essence' is derived from being taken in the first sense and not the second, since in the second sense something could be called a being that does not have an

---

1. Aquinas, *De Ente*, Cap. 1, p. 370:51–52: 'Essentia dicitur secundum quod per eam et in ea ens habet esse'; *Scriptum Super Libros Sententiarum* (Paris: Lethielleux, 1929), Lib. 1, d. 23, qu. 1, art. 1: 'Essentia dicitur cujus actus est esse'.

essence. For example, if essence were derived from the (ii) sense of being, privations signifying a lack of something and nothing positive would be thereby said to have essences, but this cannot be since a privation signifies a lack of something, whereas essence is that in which and through which a thing has *esse*, in which case essence cannot signify a lack of something, a privation, but something positive. Thus, essence is derived from the (i) sense of being.[2]

Now insofar as essence is signified by the first definition of being (i.e., as what is divided through the ten categories), and thus signifies something in reality, essence must be a principle of things by which they are locatable within a classificatory system signifying what they are in both general (genus) and specific (species) terms. Thus, essence for Aquinas is the principle by means of which a concrete thing is the type of thing that it is and no other. It follows, then, that the essence of a thing is signified by its definition indicating what (*quid*) the thing in question is. And thus essence has commonly been taken to be synonymous with *quiddity*.[3]

According to the (i) sense of being, being is signified as divided by the ten categories. On this account, the primary

---

2. *De Ente*, Cap. 1, p. 369:14–18: 'Nomen igitur essentie non sumitur ab ente secundo modo dicto: aliqua enim hoc modo dicuntur entia que essentiam non habent, ut patet in priuationibus; sed sumitur essentia ab ente primo modo dicto'. See also: *In I Sent.*, d. 19, qu. 5, art. 1, ad. 1, d. 33, qu. 1, art. 1, ad. 1; *In II Sent.*, d. 34, qu. 1, art. 1, d. 37, qu. 1, art. 2, ad. 3; *Quaestiones Disputatae De Potentia Dei* (Turin: Marietti, 1927), qu. 7, art. 2, ad. 1; *Summa Contra Gentiles* (Turin: Marietti, 1927), Lib. 3, Cap. 8; *Summa Theologiae* Ia, qu. 48, a. 2, ad. 2; *In Metaphysicam Aristotelis Commentaria* (Turin: Marietti, 1935), Lib. 5, n. 889. I have followed closely Gyula Klima's listing of the relevant passages wherein Aquinas makes the twofold distinction with regard to being. See Klima, 'The Changing Role of "Entia Rationis" in Medieval Semantics and Ontology: A Comparative Study with a Reconstruction', *Synthese*, 96 (1993), 51, n. 4. Klima traces this twofold distinction to Aristotle's *Metaphysics*, Bk. 5, Chapter 7, 1017a23–35, and he holds (pp. 27–31) that the distinction is in place in order to safeguard the inherence theory of predication adopted by Aquinas.

3. *De Ente*, Cap. 1, p. 369:27–31; *In V Met*, n. 902, *Summa Theologiae*, Ia, q. 29, art. 2, *Summa Contra Gentiles*, Lib. 4, Cap. 81: *De Humanitate*.

referents of being are substances about which or in which various accidents are predicated. Thus, substances are primarily *beings*, things that *be*, whereas accidents, which are only said to be of or in substances, are secondarily beings, i.e., they derive their 'being-ness' from the being of substance. Given that essence is signified by the (i) sense of being and that such signification admits of a primary sense (substance) and a secondary sense (accident), essence will too have both primary and secondary senses. Essence is thus properly said of substance, to the effect that it is a substance which properly has an essence, whereas essence is said only secondarily of accidents, to the effect that the essence of accidents is said only in relation to the essence of the substance of or in which they are predicated.[4]

The primary signification of the term 'essence' for Aquinas is thus the definitional content of the concrete substance signifying that the substance is one particular kind of thing rather than another. This, then, raises an issue for Aquinas, because for him, many concrete substances are composed of parts, and the question thus arises as to how essence is related to the parts of a thing whose essence it is. The most common concrete substances are material substances, and according to the Aristotelian ontology that Aquinas consciously adopts, such substances are composites of matter and form. The question is thus how essence relates to the components (matter and form) of such a substance.

Aquinas considers three possible ways by which essence may relate to matter and form, all of which he ultimately rejects: (i) that essence is synonymous with the matter of a thing; (ii) that essence is synonymous with the form of a thing; and (iii) that essence signifies a relation between matter and form.

---

4. *De Ente*, Cap. 1, p. 370:53–57: 'Sed quia ens absolute et primo dicitur de substantiis, et per posterius et quasi secundum quid de accidentibus, inde est quod etiam essentia proprie et uere est in substantiis, sed in accidentibus est quodammodo et secundum quid'.

First, Aquinas denies that matter is the essence of a material substance because, as has been noted, essence signifies the definitional content of a thing by which it is classifiable as one type of thing rather than another. Essence is thus the principle of knowability of a thing insofar as it permits us to recognise the thing as one type of thing rather than another. But matter is neither (i) capable of signifying the full definitional content of a thing nor (ii) capable of rendering a thing knowable, because (i) many things can be made of the same materials but be different things (e.g., cats, dogs, horses are all made of flesh and bone, but they are different types of things), and (ii) matter does not situate a thing within a classificatory system whereby the thing is known as this or that type of thing, in which case matter does not make a thing knowable.

Given the foregoing considerations, one might wish to propose that form is the essence of a thing, because form does seem to be a principle by which a thing is recognised to be of a particular type and through which a thing is known.[5] Nevertheless, Aquinas refuses to identify essence with form, because the essence of a thing signifies its definitional content, but the definitional content of a material substance must include some reference to the matter of which it is made, otherwise it will not be the definitional content *of* a material thing.[6]

Finally, essence cannot be anything signified by the relation between matter and form or, to put it another way, anything added over and above matter and form; for then essence would be outside of the thing and accidental to it, and the thing would be thus unknowable in terms of its essence thus construed, which runs contrary to the very nature of essence.

---

5. Aquinas takes this to be the position of Averroës; see Armand Maurer, 'Form and Essence in the Philosophy of St Aquinas', *Mediaeval Studies*, 13 (1951), §. 1.

6. *De Ente*, Cap. 2, p. 370:13–16: 'Essentia est illud quod per diffinitionem rei significatur; diffinitio autem substantiarum naturalium non tantum formam continent sed etiam materiam'. See also, *In V Met*, n. 902; *In VI Met*, nn. 1155–1161; *In VII Met*, nn. 1467–1469, and for commentary Maurer, 'Form and Essence', 166–67.

Having denied that essence can be equated with either (i) matter, (ii) form, or (iii) something over and above the composition of (i) and (ii), Aquinas concludes that the essence of the material thing is just the matter–form composite itself, and taken as such the essence of a thing is signified by its definitional content, which includes reference to both the thing's matter and its form.

The foregoing reasoning characterised essence in terms of the elimination of various possibilities; thus it was denied that essence is (i) matter, (ii) form, or (iii) a relation between the two, in which case essence is the composite of matter and form. Aside from such an eliminationist argument, one can offer a more positive reason, taking in the entire breadth of Aquinas's metaphysical thought, for the same.

Above it was noted that for Aquinas essence is that through which and in which a being has *esse*. Essence then for Aquinas is subject to *esse*, such that no material essence would exist unless it possessed a distinct act of existence. But if it is the case that essence is subject to *esse* and that no essence exists unless composed with *esse*, then essence must encompass all that is subject to *esse* in the material substance, which includes both its matter and its form; because, if essence did not cover both, and only encompassed the form, as Averroës thought, then only the form, and not the matter, would be subject to *esse*, in which case only the form of a material individual would exist. But this is absurd. Thus, the essence of a thing must include its matter, in which case the essence of a thing as signified by its definitional content is the composite of matter and form.

Now, Maurer raises an interesting point with respect to Aquinas's reasoning here.[7] Within Aquinas's metaphysical framework, wherein the distinction between essence and *esse* is fundamental, form is no longer the supreme principle of actuality and intelligibility of a thing, as it was for Aristotle. Rather, *esse* is of

---

7. Maurer, 'Form and Essence', 173 *et seq.*

such fundamental importance that things would be neither in act nor intelligible without it.[8] Consequently, when essence is viewed from the existential standpoint—that is, when viewed as subject to *esse*—it is the entire composite of matter and form that is brought into view; this then entails a greater role for matter than Aristotle (and Averroës following him) had envisaged. Consequently, from the perspective of the real distinction between essence and *esse*, Aquinas is motivated to envisage the essence of the thing as including both its matter and its form.

Given that matter plays a role in the signification of the essence of a thing, matter has to be capable of being included in the definitional content of a thing. But traditional Aristotelianism, represented in this case by Averroës if not by Aristotle himself, tends to view matter as unintelligible and thereby refrains from including it in a thing's definition. Nevertheless, insofar as for Aquinas matter plays a key role in the essence and thereby the definition of a thing, he is committed to thinking of it as in some way intelligible, and this leads him to make a key distinction, found principally in Avicenna, between (i) the matter that an individual matter–form composite possesses and which functions as the principle of individuation, and (ii) the matter that goes to play a role in the definition of a thing's essence. This is the distinction between designated matter (*materia signata*) and non-designated matter respectively.[9]

Designated matter is matter considered under determined dimensions, such that it serves to locate a thing in a defined space. This matter functions as the principle of individuation insofar as it goes to locate individual members of a species in space and thereby distinguish the one from the other. Thus Peter

---

8. *De Potentia*, qu. 7, art. 2, ad. 9: 'Hoc quod dico esse est actualitas omnium actuum, et propter hoc est perfectio omnium perfectionum', *Summa Contra Gentiles*, Lib. 1, Cap. 71: 'Unumquodque, quantum habet de esse, tantum habet de cognoscibilitate'.

9. See Roland-Gosselin, *Le 'De Ente et Essentia' de s.Thomas d'Aquin*, pp. 59–69, for details of this distinction in Avicenna.

and Paul are individual humans insofar as their humanity is located in designated matter. However, it is not designated matter that is included in the essence of a thing, for designated matter is that which serves to locate a thing in three-dimensional space and is thus only capable of ostensible recognition, in which case if matter so construed were to be included in the essence of a thing, that essence would be indefinable. Rather, it is non-designated matter which is included in a thing's essence, where non-designated matter is not the individual matter that a thing has, but the matter considered as a property of things of that particular type.

Consider Peter and Paul. They are individual humans insofar as their humanity is located in designated matter; their humanity consists in a certain way that their matter is structured, i.e. their form, but it also consists of being made of flesh and bones. Peter is made of this flesh and these bones, which are not Paul's flesh or bones. Nevertheless one can abstract from the individual flesh and bones of Peter or Paul and simply consider flesh and bones as such. When one thinks of flesh and bones not in terms of a determinate this, but in generic terms as such, one thinks of non-designated matter, i.e. the type of matter out of which the individuals of the species are made. And it is such matter that is included in the definitional content of the essence of a thing.[10]

It follows, then, that the difference between the essence of man considered as such and the essence of the individual man, Peter or Paul, is that between the non-designated and the designated; and this is not a real distinction but a distinction of reason. The essence of man considered as such is the overall definitional

---

10. See *De Ente*, Cap. 2, p. 371:67–84. It must be emphasised that the distinction between designated and non-designated matter is not a distinction between two types of matter, but a distinction applicable to how one and the same matter is considered. All matter that exists is designated, but such matter can be considered qua designated, i.e. qua a determinate this, or qua a type of matter that the members of a species have.

content that the individual man manifests. Elsewhere Aquinas calls this essence the *forma totius*, and this is because it is, speaking loosely, the overall form that the essence of the thing displays—that is, the form of the whole; when individuated, this *forma totius* signifies an individual of that type. The *forma totius* is to be distinguished from the *forma partis* which is the form that, in Aristotelian ontology, informs and thereby actualises prime matter—it is the form of the part, or a form that is part of the overall substance. The *forma partis* is really distinct from the matter that it actualises and perfects. The individual man, then, is a real composite of form (*forma partis*) and prime matter, and as such counts as an instance of the essence (the *forma totius*) of the species of which he is a member.

Thomistic essentialism can be characterised by a commitment to the view that things can be defined and located within a classificatory system on the basis of their definitional content, and this is because of a certain metaphysical view as to the constitution of such things. As has been shown, that metaphysical view is in principle Aristotelian insofar as it views material things as composites of matter and form, but it goes beyond Aristotle insofar as it grants a certain intelligibility to matter (non-designated matter) which plays a role in the definitional content of a thing. As distinguished from this intelligible matter is designated matter, which serves to guarantee the individuality of members of the same species. Both matter and form have a role to play in the definitional content and thereby the essence of a thing, and this is what Aquinas calls the *forma totius*, which is the overall nature that a thing takes. This *forma totius* is to be distinguished from the *forma partis* which is what is more traditionally understood by form in the Aristotelian tradition, i.e., what actualises and perfects prime matter.

Aquinas's essentialism amounts to the rather uncontroversial view that an object has a certain definitional content, the lack of which would entail that the object in question would not be that very object but some other. This definitional content is rooted in, and indeed synonymous with, the ontological principle termed 'essence', and is what serves to place a thing within its proper genus and species. If a thing has essential properties, then, it is because it has an essence off which such properties can be read.

2.2 CONTEMPORARY ESSENTIALISM

Contrast Thomistic essentialism with more contemporary versions. Contemporary essentialism emerges out of developments in quantified modal logic, wherein it became necessary to characterise modality in terms of possible worlds, and to allow quantification into modal contexts so as to provide truth conditions for certain modal claims. Accordingly, philosophers were led to distinguish between properties that a thing has in all possible worlds in which it exists, and properties that it has in only some possible worlds in which it exists. The former were taken to be essential properties, whereas the latter were taken to be accidental properties. So on this account, essential properties are designated by appeal to *de re* necessity, such that an object x will possess an essential property P just in case it is impossible that x lack P in any possible world in which it exists.[11]

An essential property, then, can be characterised as a rigid designator, since it designates a thing in all possible worlds in which the thing exists. The upshot of aligning essence with necessity is that drawing from a philosophical notion (necessity) that can putatively be made sense of independent of linguistic conventions, one can in turn make a case for essence that itself does not depend on some kind of conventionalism.[12] Modal essentialism

---

11. See, for example, Alvin Plantinga, *The Nature of Necessity* (Oxford: Clarendon Press, 1974), Chapters 4–5.
12. I say 'putatively' because the modal essentialist has the task of establishing the acceptability of *de re* necessity, and this independently of any essentialist considerations. For just such an attempt, see Plantinga, *The Nature of Necessity*,

then allows the philosopher to pull the rabbit of essentialism out of the hat of necessity.[13]

What is significant about this account is its property-based account of essence. Whereas on the Thomistic account essence is signified by the definitional content of the concretely existing individual, on the modal account essence is signified by the properties that a thing possesses in all possible worlds in which it exists. For the Thomist, problems emerge over how to characterise the concretely existing thing as a whole, that is, how to determine its *forma totius*, whereas for the modalist, problems emerge over precisely which properties one can ascribe to a thing in all possible worlds in which it exists.

It is difficult to make sense of modal essentialism insofar as it is difficult to hold that a thing has essential properties prior to taking into account what its essence may be. Modal accounts of essence characteristically trade on intuitions about which properties are to be taken as rigid designators and which are not; indeed, as has been pointed out (n. 12), one of the problems for the modal essentialist is to provide an acceptable account of *de re* necessity independent of any essentialist considerations. Such an account cannot be the result of any principled metaphysical considerations, because such metaphysical considerations will inevitably involve essentialist presuppositions. Thus, the modalist must account for *de re* necessity in some other way, and this is characteristically achieved by focussing on the usage of terms. But here there is a tension given that it is difficult to see how the use of terms could reveal anything significant about the nature of things. It is conceivable that a hardheaded philosopher might

Chapter 3. The paradigmatic anti-essentialist (modally speaking) is W. V. Quine, who denies *de re* necessity, but endorses *de dicto* necessity; though of course, support for the latter and not for the former is not in itself a commitment to any kind of real essentialism, see for instance Quine, 'Reference and Modality', in *From a Logical Point of View* (New York: Harper and Row, 1961), Chapter 8.

13. The metaphor is drawn from the picture on the dust jacket of Nathan Salmon's book, *Reference and Essence* (Princeton: Princeton University Press, 1982).

want to take a term to be used of a thing essentially, and with perseverance insist that such a term designates its object rigidly, even to the complete incredulity of his or her colleagues. Other than intuition about the use of terms, the only way to resolve such a disagreement is to appeal to the nature of the object—but this will undermine the modalist approach and sneak in a primitive non-modal notion of essence.

By contrast the Thomist, who believes that there are essential properties because things have essences, has a metaphysically principled way to deal with disagreements over essence: this is to observe the object and come to an understanding of its definitional content. To be sure, the latter procedure involves one in a whole host of epistemological quandaries, but the point is that metaphysically speaking the case is resolvable by focussing on an ontological principle of the thing distinct from linguistic conventions and usage.[14] In short, the Thomist sees as misguided any attempt to construe a thing's essence that does not begin with the essence in the first place, as is the case with the modal account.[15]

These substantive philosophical issues raise a second concern for modal essentialism, one that could be called the issue of methodological parsimony. The modal account looks for properties

14. On the epistemological issue, simply because it is difficult to grasp the essence of a thing does not mean it is impossible. Furthermore, whilst the thing's essence is independent of our thinking and speaking about it, it is nevertheless such that it is in principle capable of being understood and spoken of. Given his commitment to the intelligibility of being, Aquinas is not committed to the recognition transcendence of reality.

15. Gyula Klima, 'Contemporary vs. Aristotelian Essentialism', in *Mind, Metaphysics and Value in the Thomistic and Analytical Traditions*, ed. by John Haldane (Notre Dame, IN: University of Notre Dame Press, 2002), p. 179: 'Since [the modal approach] seeks to explain essence in terms of essential properties, rather than the other way around, it certainly cannot invoke essences in trying to cope with its primary task presented by anti-essentialist criticisms: to offer some reason why some common terms *have to* be regarded as essential to the things they are actually true of. So while the issues in this framework could not be settled on *logical* grounds, in the same framework they cannot be settled on principled *metaphysical* grounds either'.

possessed by a thing in all possible worlds in which it exists and characterises essence accordingly. But the notion of identity through possible worlds is a notoriously difficult one insofar as it appears impossible to consider an object x existing variously in all the possible worlds in which it exists and *then* to consider what essential properties x may have. Such a procedure seems either question begging or nugatory. It is question begging insofar as identifying x in the worlds in which it exists requires a primitive, non-modal appeal to the essence of x by which it is designated in its worlds and *then* an elucidation of its essential properties. It is nugatory because, given its appeal to a primitive non-modal notion of essence, there is no need to go on to elucidate the essential properties possessed by a thing in those worlds in which it exists, for if one can appeal to a primitive non-modal notion of essence, then why the appeal to possible worlds as in some way illuminative of our notion of essence?

By contrast, for the Thomist, the problem of transworld identity does not emerge, because in the Thomist account a thing has an essence by which it can be identified. So if one wants to locate a thing in other possible worlds in which it exists (a strange exercise for the Thomist indeed), then one can discern the thing's essential properties from its essence in this world before seeking to identify it in the other worlds in which it exists. Accordingly, the Thomist's methodological procedure seems much more parsimonious than the modalist's, because the Thomist need not appeal to possible worlds and all of their associated philosophical drawbacks. To be sure, the Thomist faces problems of a typically anti-metaphysical nature which have at their core the positivist's denial of the validity of any such metaphysical speculation, and which the modalist account was originally intended to address. But if the Thomist has these problems then so does the modalist—indeed more so, given that the modalist is working within a framework that is typically anti-metaphysical and yet tries to salvage the metaphysics of modality from within. The Thomist, on the other hand, can simply reject such a framework and refuse to play the positivist's game.

The modalist may object at this point and argue that I have misconceived possible worlds. Thus far, possible worlds have come across as real things, somewhat like foreign countries capable of being peered at through some kind of metaphysical telescope; the problem of transworld identification, then, is with how to locate the object in its various possible worlds so (mis) construed. The modalist may argue that when he is speaking of possible worlds, he does not have a foreign country-like conception in mind, but rather counterfactual situations, i.e., what the world might have been like but is not. Thus, one can quantify into modal contexts and thus be committed to possible worlds without thereby being committed to the reality of any worlds other than this, the actual world.[16] On this account, one need not take an object and peer at it in its various worlds so as to identify it; rather, one can look at the object in the actual world, determine its essential properties, and *then* determine what might have been the case otherwise.[17] If this is all the modalist is claiming, then I have no objections, except to point out that appeal to possible worlds as in some sense illuminative of essence is redundant, because this account, whereby rigid designation occurs prior to transworld identification, seems committed to a primitive non-modal account of essence, in which case essence can be

16. See, for example, Saul Kripke, *Naming and Necessity* (Oxford: Blackwell, 1981), p. 44. Actualists typically take this world to be the only world and conceive of possible worlds as all states of affairs (Plantinga), propositions (Adams), states of the world (Stalnaker), situations (Kripke), and scenarios (Salmon) signifying the way in which the world might have been.
17. Kripke, *Naming and Necessity*, p. 49: 'It is *because* we can refer (rigidly) to Nixon, and stipulate that we are speaking of what might have happened to *him* (under certain circumstances), that "transworld identifications" are unproblematic in such cases'; similarly pp. 52–3: 'Don't ask: how can I identify this table in another possible world, except by its properties? I have the table in my hands, I can point to it, and when I ask whether *it* might have been in another room, I am talking, by definition about *it*'.

known from the real essences that exist in the actual world.[18] The assertion that modal essentialism is redundant, however, is only in regard to an explication of essence. There are other uses to which modal essentialism can be put which are taken to illuminate deep philosophical problems, such as the truth conditions of our quantifying into modal contexts.

A third and final drawback for the modalist account is that it envisages objects as intrinsically bereft of but nevertheless still exemplifying properties. Indeed, it is just such a view that leads to the problem of transworld identity, because if one acquires an object's essential and accidental properties by observing it in all the worlds in which it exists, it follows that the object is really distinct from and not identified with those properties.[19] The object, then, is conceived as a kind of bare particular capable of supporting properties in possible worlds, but crucially not identified with any of those properties. Objects then, as intrinsically propertyless, are indiscernible from each other, and thus an elaborate scheme for discernability must be proposed that attempts to circumvent this problem.

18. Hilary Putnam seems to make a similar point to the effect that natural kinds and the usage of natural kind terms in the actual world are determined *before* drawing any conclusions about them in some possible worlds or counterfactual situations: see, for example, 'The Meaning of "Meaning"' in *Mind, Language and Reality: Philosophical Papers*, vol. II (Cambridge: Cambridge University Press, 1975), p. 233: 'Once we have discovered the nature of water, nothing counts as a possible world in which water doesn't have that nature. Once we have discovered that water (in the actual world) is H_2O, *nothing counts as a possible world in which water isn't H_2O*'; see also p. 241: 'If there is a hidden structure, then generally it determines what it is to be a member of the natural kind, not only in the actual world, but in all possible worlds. Put another way, it determines what we can and cannot counterfactually suppose about the natural kind'.

19. In an epistemic sense, the properties that the object exemplifies can serve as the means for identifying the object, just as in a football match the player's jersey and number can serve to identify the player, but in a metaphysical sense just as the player is not to be identified with his jersey and number, neither is the object to be identified with its properties.

ESSENCE | 51

But it seems that such a problem emerges only when a kind of Platonism about properties is assumed, such that properties are conceived of as abstract entities exemplified by their objects. This Platonic approach seems to be at the heart of modal essentialism, given that the latter's commitment to various possible states of affairs, propositions, or situations, all of which signify how the world might have been, is a commitment to abstract but non-instantiated properties.[20]

Now, the modalist might certainly protest that this is a gratuitous generalisation and that a more Aristotelian account whereby objects are viewed as substances, composite wholes of dependent parts, is consistent with modalism, and can indeed offer an interesting solution to transworld identity.[21] If the latter is the protest and the point is that an Aristotelian view of objects is simply not inconsistent with modalism, then I am in agreement. However, if the stronger point is made that (i) objects are envisaged as Aristotelian substances and (ii) essences are primarily accounted for on the basis of essential properties, then I must protest, for if objects are Aristotelian substances, then objects are composite wholes whose essence is in principle capable of being scrutinised in the actual world, in which case real essences are primary, and essential properties are discerned from these essences. Consequently, either (i) essences are acquired through essential properties and objects are Platonic instances of universal properties, or (ii) there are essential properties and objects are Aristotelian. One cannot have modal essentialism with Aristotelian objects unless one endorses the primacy of real essentialism, in which case one's modal essentialism is somewhat nugatory.

Perhaps at this point the modalist will argue that Platonism is an acceptable doctrine, because its alternative is a kind of

20. Indeed all of the actualists mentioned in n. 16 above seem to believe in the actuality of universal but uninstantiated properties, otherwise they cannot appeal to the ways in which the world might have been as ultimately significative of possible worlds.
21. My guess is that Kripke would be swayed by this view.

nominalism. The Platonist may so argue from semantic considerations of the following form. How is the truth of the sentence 'The chair is blue' accounted for? A natural reply is that it is because the chair has the property of being blue, or blueness. But in order to account for the truth of the sentence 'The chair is blue,' recourse is made to a universal property (blueness) exemplified by an object: the chair (similar considerations will entail that an object x is a chair if and only if that object exemplifies the property of being a chair). Now, lest one reverts to a sort of nominalism about properties, the property of being blue or blueness must be recognised as a real universal exemplified by the chair (and similarly being a chair is exemplified by some object). Thus, Platonism about objects and their exemplification of properties has some plausible reasoning behind it.

Whilst I admit that this reasoning has a lot to recommend it, I think that it is based on a certain semantic framework about universals that both the Platonic realist and the nominalist share and which can be respectably set aside, for it assumes that what our concrete common terms, such as 'blue', and their abstract counterparts, such as 'blueness', signify are things. Whereas the Platonic realist holds that the things signified by these terms are real universals, the nominalist holds that they are particulars, or that the sentence can be so parsed anew so as to commit us only to particulars. Whilst both the Platonist and the nominalist admit that such terms signify things, they differ precisely on what sort of things they are prepared to quantify over.

This semantic framework has conceptual connections with what has come to be known as the *via moderna* in medieval philosophy.[22] Its characteristic feature is that the signification of

---

22. For details of the *via moderna* and its contrast with the *via antiqua* a good introduction is offered by Gyula Klima in 'Ockham's Semantics and Ontology of the Categories', *The Cambridge Companion to Ockham*, ed. by Paul Vincent Spade (Cambridge: Cambridge University Press, 1999), pp. 118–43, as well as its associated references.

a term coincides with its reference, so that what the term signifies is what it is employed to denote, i.e., the actual thing in reality, be it a real universal (Platonism) or a concrete particular (nominalism).[23]

Contrast this semantic framework with the one employed by Aquinas and there is revealed a position midway between Platonic realism and nominalism. On this account, known as the *via antiqua*, concrete common terms ('blue') and their abstract counterparts ('blueness') are subordinated to the concept by means of which the particular colour in question is signified. When these terms are used in a propositional context they can be said to exist in the object about which the proposition makes a predication. So the sentence 'The chair is blue' is true when it expresses a proposition predicating blueness of a chair and the property of blueness exists in a concrete object which is a chair.[24] What crucially differentiates this account from the *via moderna* is that signification is not conflated with reference, supposition, or denotation. Terms have sense insofar as they can be used to express a concept by means of which we engage with reality; terms have reference depending on how they are used in a proposition. The *via antiqua* then escapes the semantic framework within which both the Platonic realist and the nominalist work, given that for both signification coincides with denotation.

Now, what is the payoff for our metaphysical discussion? In the *via antiqua* account, common terms are subordinated to concepts which are in turn subordinated to common natures

---

23. Of course the realist may hold that signification is independent of denotation and that the meaning of a term can be characterised independent of its reference; but then the realist moves closer to a kind of moderate realism about universals whereby the signification of a universal term need not require a referent that is itself a universal thing.

24. See Klima, 'Ockham's Semantics and Ontology of the Categories' for more in-depth details of this semantic framework and its endorsement of the inherence theory of predication.

by means of which objects are understood. Objects are understood by means of their common natures, but the common nature does not exist in the same way extra-mentally as it does mentally—that is, when one understands an object, it is understood as a particular of a kind, but this does not entail that the universality characteristic of understanding an object denotes the object itself as it exists in extra-mental reality. The object is a concrete particular whose common nature exists individually in the concrete particular and by means of which the object can be understood by the subject. To confuse the common nature existing extra-mentally and individually with the common nature existing universally and mentally is to confuse an *ens reale* with an *ens rationis*; this indeed is Aquinas's charge against the Platonists.[25] Provided that the latter confusion is not made, it can be asserted that things have a common nature by means of which they may be understood, from which concepts are formed; and common terms are subordinated to the latter. On this account, not only can the horns of Platonic realism and nominalism be navigated, since neither the real existence of universals nor their universal existence is denied, but it is also affirmed that objects are such that they *have* a common nature, and it is on the basis of this common nature that they display the universal properties that they have. Consequently, this position honours the desire to preserve some universality in reality without going to the extravagances of Platonic realism. But if this is the case, then objects are not propertyless bearers of properties, *pace* Platonism, but composite wholes made up of dependent parts constituting the object as a particular of a common type. And if the latter can be affirmed, then an object has a real essence which serves as the basis for the essential properties that are attributed to it.

25. *Summa Theologiae*, Ia, qu. 84, art. 1.

2.3 CONCLUSION

Aquinas understands the composite wholeness of a material object in terms of its matter and form, and such composition provides the object with the common nature that it has, existing individually as the concrete particular that it is. We have thus come full circle and returned to Aquinas's conception of essence as the definitional content of a thing signified by the composition of its matter and form. Given the problems with modalism and its seeming commitment to Platonism about objects, I submit that Thomistic essentialism, whereby objects are envisaged as having essences, is preferable. It is on the basis of its real essence that a thing can be said to have essential properties, and it is this essence that functions as the ontological co-principle of *esse* in the existing thing.

Therefore, Thomistic essentialism is significant not for the extravagances to which it goes, but rather for its moderation in refusing to be committed to elaborate schemes of determining the fundamental nature of essence. In short, Aquinas's view amounts to the rather unexciting thesis that real objects are structured in a certain way, and that such a structure can be intelligibly discerned and defined, with the definitional content thereby signifying the essence of the thing. Aquinas is not motivated to consider modal essentialism because he already has an account of essence focussing on real objects in the world. Thus, there is no need for Aquinas, and so no need for the Thomist, to characterise essence in terms of transworld identity across possible worlds. Indeed, as will be seen in the next chapter when examining Thomist *esse*, Aquinas has no need for the whole possible worlds framework, and so does not approach metaphysical questions on the basis of possible worlds. That being the case then, contemporary modal accounts of essence are not attractive for the Thomist, and indeed suffer from the several deficiencies outlined above.

So far one metaphysical principle of the finite thing has been considered: essence. But as is already clear from Chapter 1, essence is nothing unless united with a distinct act of existence, the term for which in Aquinas's thought is '*esse*'. Up till now the term '*esse*' has been untranslated, and I suggested in the previous chapter that this term could be read as 'existence', but with certain qualifications. In the next chapter the signification of Thomist *esse* will be unpacked and it will be shown that no philosophical account thereof, other than Aquinas's, can stand up to it. This indicates that Thomist *esse* is something both peculiar and novel to Thomism, so that any proof of God focussed on it will in itself be quite peculiar yet novel.

ESSE

AS HAS BEEN indicated, Thomist *esse* is a metaphysical principle of things more fundamental than any metaphysical principle that had been previously put forward—so much so that Aquinas's introduction thereof represents a definite development of his thought over that of his predecessors. *Esse* is the fundamental unifying principle of Aquinas's metaphysics, and here I will consider the nature of Thomist *esse* and contrast it with other, more contemporary, accounts of existence.

Accordingly, in what follows I shall consider (i) Thomist *esse* in itself and then (ii) Thomist *esse* in relation to other accounts of existence. Finally I shall conclude (iii) by considering how one ought to think of Thomist *esse*, given that no other philosophical position can match up to it, and this will in turn bring Part I of the book to a close.

3.1 *ESSE*

As has been discussed, essence and *esse* are really distinct for Aquinas, that is to say, they both signify realities of the finite thing, so that if essence tells us what a thing is, *esse* tells us that it is. It follows from this that essence as distinct from *esse* does not have the wherewithal for its own existence, in which case no essence exists that does not have *esse*. Consequently, all finite things have received *esse* from without, and this because they do not exist in virtue of their essences, but rather in virtue of something distinct from their essences. Whatever receives something from another stands in potency to that other in respect of what it receives; co-relatively, what is received in another is in another as actualising the potency in which the other stands to receive. Given the real distinction between essence and *esse, esse* is received in the entity and is thus possessed by that entity as an actualising principle; that is, it actualises the essence that stands in potency to it.[1]

At the heart of Aquinas's conception of *esse* is that it is act.[2] The co-relative potency of *esse*, that is, that which it actuates, is essence. So essence and *esse* are characterised by Aquinas as potency and act respectively, and their relation in the creature is a relation of potency to act.

The first point to be noted here is the rather non-Aristotelian nature of Aquinas's conception of *esse*. For Aristotle, the actualising principle of things is form and the co-relative potency is matter. Here one may observe Aquinas going beyond Aristotle in holding that form itself is not sufficient to account for the actuality of things; a further principle of actuality is required, and that is *esse*. This indeed reflects Aquinas's motivations in distinguishing between essence and *esse*; for as has been seen, he wants to show that there is an element of potency in immaterial substances without thereby rendering them material, and thus he envisages

---

1. *De Ente*, Cap. 4, p. 377:147–152: 'Omne autem quod recipit aliquid ab alio est in potentia respectu illius, et hoc quod receptum est in eo est actus eius; ergo oportet quod ipsa quiditas uel forma que est intelligentia sit in potentia respectu esse quod a Deo recipit, et illud esse receptum est per modum actus'. In this text Aquinas presupposes the existence of God as having been established, because it comes immediately after the proof for God's existence that is the subject of this study. Nevertheless, God's existence is not essential to Aquinas's point that *esse* that is received stands to its receiver as act to potency, that is to say, the essence that receives the *esse* is subject to the *esse*. Whilst here Aquinas describes *esse* as being received from God, he could just as well have adverted to the caused character of *esse* in order to make his point. See Wippel, *The Metaphysical Thought of Thomas Aquinas*, p. 150.

2. Aquinas, *In I Sent.*, d. 19, qu. 2, art. 2: 'Esse est actus existentis, inquantum ens est'; Ibid, d. 23, qu. 1, art. 1: 'Essentia dicitur cujus actus est esse'; *In II Sent*, d. 3, qu. 1, art. 1, ad. 4: 'Potentia tenet se ex parte quidditatis, et esse est actus ejus'; *Summa Theologiae*, Ia, qu. 76, art. 6: 'Primum autem inter omnes actus est esse'.

that the very thing that the immaterial substance is, is in potency to a principle of actuality even more fundamental than form. *Esse* is thus conceived by Aquinas precisely in order to account for the fact that there is anything rather than nothing; for without *esse* nothing other than God would actually exist.

Esse, then, is the principle by means of which things are not nothing. Therefore, without *esse* there is nothing. But if the latter is the case, then *esse* is subject to nothing, since there is nothing that is not subject to *esse*. It follows then that there cannot be an even more fundamental principle of actuality than *esse; esse* is most fundamental. Thence follows the important conclusion for Aquinas that *esse* is the act of all acts, the perfection of all perfections.[3] Far from being a nice catchphrase, the latter indicates that *esse* is the primary actuality of a thing, the basic principle by means of which a thing is differentiated from nothing; all other actualities of a thing flow from its having *esse*, and without *esse* a thing would be precisely nothing. Consequently, there is no principle of actuality more fundamental than *esse*.

Given the conception of *esse* as act and essence's relation to it as potency, the relationship between essence and its act of being, its *esse*, is one of participation. To be a participant in some reality is to possess that reality in a limited respect and non-essentially, that is, to participate is to take a part in some reality; correlatively, the reality that is participated in must be unlimited in itself and limited when realised in its participants.[4] Aquinas provides us

---

3. *De Potentia Dei*, qu. 7, art. 2, ad. 9; *Summa Theologaie*, Ia, qu. 4, art. 1, ad. 3.

4. Aquinas, *Expositio De Ebdomadibus*, lect. 2, p. 271:70–73: 'Est autem participare quasi partem capere; et ideo quando aliquid particulariter recipit id quod ad alterum pertinet universaliter, dicitur participare illud'; *Summa Contra Gentiles*, Lib. I, Cap. 22: 'Omnis res est per hoc quod habet esse. Nulla igitur res, cuius essentia non est suum esse, est per essentiam suam, sed participatione alicuius, scilicet ipsius esse'; *Summa Theologiae*, Ia, qu. 3, art. 5: 'Illud, quod habet esse, et non est esse, est ens per participationem'. William Norris Clarke, 'The Meaning of Participation in St Thomas', 93: 'The essential elements of any participation structure according to [Aquinas] are three: (1) a source which

with three examples in order to highlight the different modes of participation.

Firstly, when something receives in a particular fashion what pertains universally to another, it is said to participate in that other. For example, a species ('man') is said to participate in its genus ('animal') and an individual (Socrates) is said to participate in its species ('man') because they (the species and the individual) do not possess the intelligible content of that in which they participate according to its full universality (*secundum totam communitatem*).[5] Each subject takes a part in the received characteristic, but only to a certain degree: 'man' is not the only instance of 'animal' and Socrates is not the only 'man'. This mode of participation is concerned with the relation of the intelligible contents of things more or less universal. Thus, this first mode of participation signifies a logical participation, wherein a lesser extended intelligibility participates in a more extended one.

Secondly, a subject can be said to participate in accidental form, and matter can be said to participate in substantial form; for forms, whether accidental or substantial, are determined to their individual subjects. Thus, an accidental form is determined to the mode of the receiving subject and a substantial form is determined to the material component with which it is composed.[6] As in the first mode of participation so also in this second mode, to participate in something is to receive in a particular fashion something

possesses the perfection in question in a total and unrestricted manner; (2) a participant subject which possesses the same perfection in some partial or restricted way; and (3) which has received this perfection in some way from, or in dependence on, the higher source'. For this third point see also, Aquinas, *In II Met.*, Lect. II, n. 296: 'Omnia composita et participantia, reducantur in ea, quae sunt per essentiam, sicut in causas'.

5. *Expositio De Ebdomadibus*, lect. 2, p. 271:71–77: 'Et ideo quando aliquid particulariter recipit id quod ad alterum pertinet uniuersaliter, dicitur participare illud, sicut homo dicitur participare animal quia non habet rationem animalis secundum totam communitatem; et eadem ratione Sortes participat hominem'.

6. Ibid, p. 271:77–80.

that is in itself universal. However, notice that in this mode of participation there is composition of two real components: the subject and the form. Hence, in this mode, as opposed to the first mode, there can be said to be real or ontological participation.

Thirdly, an effect can be said to participate in its cause, especially when the effect is not equal to the power of that cause.[7] The effect particularises and determines the scope of the cause, for the effect acts as the determinate recipient of the power of the cause. The effect receives from its cause only that which is necessary for the production of the effect. In this way a cause is participated in by its effect. Notice again that in the participation framework, the participant (the effect) is somewhat less universal than the participated (what is derived from the cause).

Essence receives *esse* and in so receiving is caused actually to exist. But what is received is received according to the mode of the receiver, and this is especially true for the reception of *esse* by essence. So for example, consider some particular essence that has received *esse* and therefore actually exists: such an essence only exists according to its own mode of existence, that is to say, the existence of that essence is precisely *of* that particular essence and not of any other. So if the essence in question is that of a dog, its existence is that of a dog's existence and not a cat's or a horse's. What is brought into existence by *esse* in turn limits *esse* to a particular mode of existence, since the existence of any one individual signifies a particular way in which *esse* could be realised. It follows then that essence functions as a limiting principle of *esse*, and *esse* is in turn possessed individually by the essence that possesses it.[8] Given then that *esse* causes the essence to exist and that the essence in turn limits the *esse* in which it participates,

7. Ibid, p. 271:80–83.
8. *Summa Contra Gentiles*, Lib. 2, Cap. 52: 'Esse autem, in quantum est esse, non potest esse diversum: potest autem diversificari per aliquid quod est praeter esse; sicut esse lapidis est aliud ab esse hominis'; *De Potentia Dei*, qu. 1, art. 2: 'Esse enim hominis terminatum est ad hominis speciem, quia est receptum in natura speciei humanae; et simile est de esse equi, vel cuiuslibet creaturae'.

it follows that the participation relationship between essence and *esse* is according to the third mode outlined by Aquinas, that of cause–effect participation.

It follows from all this that essences which possess *esse* possess a participated *esse*, such that not only do they participate in the *esse* that they possess, but that *esse* itself, as limited, participates in and depends on something other than itself. The *esse* then that is common to all essence–*esse* composites (*esse commune*) is a limited and participated *esse*, which as distinct from the essence of each and every such composite is caused to be therein.[9] Participated *esse*, i.e., *esse commune*, is caused *esse* so that whilst a thing's individual *esse* causes that thing to be, its *esse* is itself caused to be in the thing. This enables Aquinas to set up a causal regress in the line of *esse*, a topic to be dealt with in the next chapter.

Thus far in discussing the participation relationship between essence and *esse*, these metaphysical principles have come across as quite thing-like. Such an impression poses the danger of conceiving of essence and *esse* as two distinct things, rather than two irreducibly distinct principles that are united within the single thing. As was noted briefly in Chapter 1, it is not the distinction between two separate things that Aquinas envisages between essence and *esse*, for then the obvious objection would be that

---

9. *In Librum Beati Dionysii De Divinis Nominibus Expositio* (Turin: Marietti, 1950), Cap. 5, lect. 2, n 660: 'Alia existentia dependent ab esse communi, non autem Deus, sed magis esse commune dependet a Deo . . . Omnia existentia continentur sub ipso esse communi, non autem Deus, sed magis esse commune continetur sub eius virtute, quia virtus divina plus extenditur quam ipsum esse creatum . . . Omnia alia existentia participant eo quod est esse, non autem Deus, sed magis ipsum esse creatum est quaedam participatio Dei et similitudo Ipsius'. Thus, things depend on their individual *esse* (*esse commune*) which in turn depends on God (the cause of *esse*). As the nature of *esse* is being clarified, God's existence here can be taken as putative. Furthermore, it should not be taken that *esse commune* is a subsisting reality in itself; rather, it refers to the collective totality of all the individual acts of existence possessed by essence–*esse* composites. See *Summa Contra Gentiles*, Lib. 1, Cap. 26, 'Adhuc' for explicit denial that *esse commune* is anything more than the abstracted totality of individual acts of existence.

essence has sufficient actuality to exist in itself without thereby needing a distinct principle—*esse*.

In depicting Aquinas's thought on participation, it is difficult to avoid a somewhat spatial conception of two things, with the one participating in the other. The examples of participation noted above, even including that of an effect's participating in its cause to which the participation of essence in *esse* is most closely aligned, suggests a thing-like conception of the two. At this point I would like to add a further layer to the Thomistic conception of *esse* and its actuating of essence, a layer that should, theoretically speaking, disassociate the 'thing-like' conception of the two from Aquinas's actual conception. As will be shown, if Aquinas's Platonic participation scheme suggests a distinction between essence and *esse* as distinct things, his Aristotelian compositional model of act and potency serves as a corrective. The fusion of the two models marks a unification of the Platonic and Aristotelian strands of Aquinas's thought.

Central to Aquinas's account of *esse* is its being a principle of actuality, the act of all acts. Considering *esse* as a principle of actuality and essence as a corresponding principle of potency permits us to envisage the relationship between the two as one of participation. But the same considerations will also permit us to see the relationship between essence and *esse* as one of composition, and this is because when one has a principle of act and a corresponding principle of potency, the un-actualised potency remains un-actualised, unless actualised by its principle of actuality coming into composition with it. Thus, if Aquinas's conception of *esse* and essence as act and potency permits him a certain Platonic outlook on their relationship, viz. participation, it no less permits him a certain Aristotelian outlook, viz. composition.[10]

---

10. *Tractatus De Substantis Separatis* (West Hartford: St Joseph College, 1962), Cap. 3, p. 46:26–35: 'Omne participans oportet esse compositum ex potentia et actu, id enim quod recipitur ut participatum oportet esse actum ipsius substantiae participantis; et sic cum omnes substantiae praeter supremam quae est per se unum et per se bonum sint participantes secundum Platonem, necesse

The existing thing is thus a composite unity of essence and *esse*, in which case its components, whilst unified in the thing, are not themselves identical.

Aquinas's account of composite unity straddles Aristotle's given that he takes any composite whatever to be a composite of potency and act. As was seen in the previous chapter, he adopts an Aristotelian view of material objects insofar as he views them as composites of matter and form. So material individuals are composed out of a formal principle which actualises the matter out of which it is made, thereby giving it its structural unity. Remaining with matter–form composition for the moment, the matter with which form is united is the principle of potency insofar as the form that the matter takes is not determined by the matter itself; rather, the matter is itself determinable and thus stands in potency to be formed. Form, then, is a principle of determination by which matter has the structure that it has, in which case form actualises matter's potentiality for assuming this or that structure. Whilst both matter and form as principles of potency and act, respectively, can be really distinguished in the material thing (matter is not form and form is not matter) nevertheless, unless the two were composed and unified in the thing, there would be no individual for consideration.

As has been seen, essence is the principle by which a thing is what it is, whereas *esse* is the principle by which a thing simply is. And given the argumentation outlined in Chapter 1, the two are known to be distinct. Thus, essence is that which is, whereas

est quod omnes sint compositae ex potentia et actu. Quod etiam necesse est dicere secundum sententiam Aristotelis'. It should also be noted that, while the pioneering studies into Aquinas's metaphysics of participation both stress the synonymy between participation and composition, they differ insofar as Geiger believes composition only to be a species of participation (the other being participation by formal hierarchy/similitude), whereas Fabro thinks composition to be the only species of participation. See Geiger, *La Participation*, Bk. 1, Pt. 1 (Participation by composition), and Pt. 2 (Participation by formal similitude); Fabro, *Participation et causalité*, pp. 63–72.

esse is that whereby a thing is. Now, essence of itself cannot exist, since *esse*, distinct from essence, is the principle by which it exists. Therefore, essence is united with *esse* and receives it in order to be.[11] Given that essence receives *esse*, essence stands in potency to *esse* and is therefore a principle of potency, whereas *esse* is its correlative principle of actuality. The finite existing thing is a composite unity of essence and *esse*; it is a unity insofar as it is not made up of two things constituting some third thing, but rather is a single thing of two components; it is composite insofar as it is made up of two principles, one of act and the other of potency, which unite to produce the individually existing thing.

The standoff between the Platonic and Aristotelian systems of thought is marked chiefly by Aristotle's rejection of Plato's notion of participation of individuals in some universal reality. Aristotle rejects such participation in favour of his more level-headed compositional model, whereby the form is composed with and individuated by the particular matter of the thing, and this as a species of act–potency composition. If Aquinas is prepared to follow Aristotle in regards to the essence of things, he is not prepared to side with Aristotle in his rejection of Platonic participation. Certainly Aquinas rejects independently existing Platonic exemplars functioning as causes of formed particulars (though he does grant a certain status to exemplars in the mind of God), but he does not reject participation *tout court*; rather, he sees a role for a participation framework in the articulation of the relationship between essence and *esse*, the latter being a metaphysical principle entirely novel to the Thomistic system. Only insofar as he distinguishes between essence and *esse*, with the former standing

11. This reception need not imply any temporal priority of receiver to thing received; as with matter–form composition, the two can be united instantaneously and yet be really distinguished. Indeed as we shall see in Chapter 7, Aquinas holds that the composite unity of essence and *esse* is brought into being by God in a single creative act. Thus God does not, in Demiurgic fashion, take an essence and then some existence and mix the two together; rather, God brings into existence a single composite unity of distinct metaphysical components.

in potency to the latter as act, can Aquinas maintain that the former participates in the latter. But, ironically, only insofar as he distinguishes between essence and *esse* as potency and act can Aquinas also adopt an Aristotelian compositional model for their relationship, so that Platonic participation and Aristotelian composition are seen to go hand in hand in such a way that neither Plato nor Aristotle would have recognised.[12] In doing so not only does Aquinas articulate his own personal metaphysical thought, but he also surpasses that of his predecessors and contemporaries, some of whom hold that in order to be distinct from God and in potency in some respect, all creatures, including immaterial creatures, must be material in some way. Whilst granting the distinction of all creatures from God, Aquinas has not been led to posit matter as *the* principle of potency for all things; rather, essence now enjoys that role, and essence can be either material or immaterial, yet stand in potency to the *esse* by which it exists. So much then for Thomist *esse*, the ontological co-principle of essence. Let us now contrast it with other accounts of existence.

3.2 CONTRAST WITH OTHER ACCOUNTS

In his monumental work on participation and causality in the thought of Aquinas, Cornelio Fabro, by way of introduction, contrasts Thomist *esse* with various other accounts of existence, and what are, by his lights, misinterpretations of Aquinas's position.[13]

---

12. Fabro, *La Nozione Metafisica di Partecipazione*, p. 5: 'In questo "sviluppo" dell'Aristotelismo S. Tommaso giugne all'*assimilazione*, non obbligata o fittizia, ma naturale per lui e reale del midollo speculativo, cioè dell'aspetto perenne, del Platonismo che è fatto convivere assieme all'Aristotelismo e, quello che più conta anche se può sorprendere, che questo fondo speculativo neoplatonico si sistiene quasi sempre nel Tomismo per principî aristotelici'. See also the telling text from *De Substantis Separatis* quoted in n. 10 above.
13. Fabro, *Participation et Causalité*, pp. 13–87.

One such account that he discusses later in the book is that of the doctrine of *esse essentiae* and *esse existentiae*, which figures in the metaphysical discussions of essence and *esse* in the immediate aftermath of Aquinas's death at the University of Paris, and seem to be of Avicennian origin.[14] The doctrine holds that there is a kind of actuality proper to essence (*esse essentiae*) and a kind proper to existence, such that essence is in itself actual, but not so much that it exists in itself. It requires another principle to exist: *esse existentiae*. Essence and existence then are two distinct things, each enjoying their own being, but with *esse existentiae* being required for the actual existence of *esse essentiae*. This doctrine suggests that there is a distinction between being and existence such that all things, existing or not, are in being enjoying a kind of *esse*, whereas only some of those things, those which have *esse existentiae*, actually exist.

Needless to say this doctrine is not like that of Aquinas, for whom the central distinction is that between essence and *esse*, not between *esse essentiae* and *esse existentiae*. Essence for him does not enjoy a less than full actuality to be perfected by something else; essence is precisely nothing without *esse*. Other than God, what exists for Aquinas are existing essences, those essences that possess *esse*. Thus, Aquinas does not envisage the distinction and composition of essence and *esse* as that between *esse essentiae* and *esse existentiae*.

One finds a similar distinction to that of *esse essentiae* and *esse existentiae* operative in the thought of Alexius Meinong, who postulates nonexisting objects in contrast with existing objects. These nonexisting objects, whilst not existing in themselves, enjoy a kind of being (*bestand*, "subsistence"), distinct from existence (*Existenz*).[15] At its core, Meinong's position represents a kind of philosophical thinking that seeks reference to nonexisting objects

---

14. Ibid, p. 282 *et seq.*
15. Alexius Meinong, 'The Theory of Objects', in *Realism and the Background of Phenomenology*, ed. by Roderick Chilsholm (Illinois: Free Press, 1960), §. 2.

in order to permit the veracity of propositions concerning such objects. Without appeal to the less than full actuality of nonexisting possibles, propositions concerning such nonexistents will prove troublesome. In this view, existence is a real property that existing things possess in distinction from nonexisting things. Nevertheless, both existing and nonexisting things enjoy some sort of very basic reality.

I shall consider accounts of existence that are characterised by their relation to this Meinongian view; such accounts come in various extremes, and I shall consider four of them: (i) the Frege-Russell-Quine view, which rejects the Meinongian position outright and does not conceive of existence in contrast to nonexisting possibles; (ii) Lewis's indexical possibilist account, which appears to accept that there is an important distinction between actual beings and merely possible beings; (iii) Salmon's indexical actualist account, which seeks to preserve Lewis's indexicalism, but rejects the possibilist basis of it; and finally (iv) actualist accounts, which along with (i) do not recognise the reality of non-existing possibles, but, in contrast with (i), hold that there is an important contrast between the way the world is (the actual world) and the way the world might have been (various possible worlds). Overall whilst each account has a number of important features that the Thomist can accept, none of them are capable of honouring Aquinas's position, in which case Aquinas's position presents an interesting and independent alternative.

3.2.1 The Frege-Russell-Quine View

Following the general issues surrounding the question of existence laid down by Hume and Kant, the Frege-Russell-Quine view denies that existence is a property that objects have, but along with Meinong it affirms that existence is nevertheless a property of sorts, albeit not a first order property. According to this view, rather than being predicated of things, existence is predicated of real predicates which are themselves predicated of things. So there are objects which have properties, and these properties exist in virtue of being instantiated by their objects. In this account, existence is a second order property, attributable to first order properties attributable to things.[16] This view posits that existence is reducible to instantiation, such that the statement of something's existing tells us that there are instances of some concept, set of properties, or cognate item. So if I say that a man exists, what I supposedly really mean is that there are men; or if I say that Pegasus does not exist, I mean there is nothing that answers to the concept of Pegasus. What this in turn assumes is that existence is wholly general and never singular, such that it cannot be said that individuals exist, only that there are instances of some general concept, properties, description etc.[17] To be, then, is to be the value of a bound variable.

16. Gottlob Frege, *The Foundations of Arthimetic*, trans. by J. L. Austin (Oxford: Blackwell, 1950), p. 65, §. 53: 'Affirmation of existence is in fact nothing but denial of the number nought. Because existence is a property of concepts the ontological argument for the existence of God breaks down'; Bertrand Russell, 'The Philosophy of Logical Atomism', in *Logic and Knowledge*, ed. by Robert Marsh (London: Allen and Unwin, 1956), p. 233: 'If you say that "Men exist, and Socrates is a man, therefore Socrates exists", that is exactly the same sort of fallacy as it would be if you said, "Men are numerous, Socrates is a man, therefore Socrates is numerous", because existence is a predicate of a propositional function, or derivatively of a class. When you say of a propositional function that it is numerous, you will mean that there are several values of x that will satisfy it, that there are more than one'; W.V. Quine, 'On What There Is', in *From a Logical Point of View*, p. 13: 'To be assumed as an entity is, purely and simply, to be reckoned as the value of a variable', 'Existence and Quantification', in *Ontological Relativity and Other Essays* (New York: Columbia University Press, 1969) p. 97: 'We found an explication of singular existence, "a exists," as "$(\exists x)(x = a)$"; but explication in turn of the existential quantifier itself, "there is", "there are", explication of general existence, is a forlorn cause. Further understanding we may still seek even here, but not in the form of explication'. For an in-depth critique of the view adopted by these three philosophers, see William Vallicella, *A Paradigm Theory of Existence: Onto-Theology Vindicated* (Dordrecht: Kluwer, 2002), pp. 108–22.

17. Peter Geach, however, working with both Fregean and Thomist principles, maintains a notion of individual existence whereby it is genuinely predicable of some individual thing. See 'Form and Existence', in *God and the Soul* (Indiana: St Augustine's Press, 1969), §. 2. If individual existence can be

The upshot of this account is that it provides a powerful logical tool for settling metaphysical disputes over what objects one is prepared to allow in one's ontology. Whatever one is prepared to quantify over, it will be precisely those things that one takes to exist and none other. However, quantification over possible entities is unnecessary for guaranteeing the truth value of some nonexistent yet possible entity, state of affairs, or situation, because in this account we can form any description we like, or in the worst case scenario verbalise a proper name, such as that which Pegasises, and quantify accordingly. Thus, retaining a robust sense of reality, existential quantifications can be limited to this, the actual world.

There is much in this account that the Thomist can accept. Undoubtedly, the Thomist is one in mind with Frege-Russell-Quine when they deny nonexisting possibles and assert that only actual things exist. For Aquinas, nothing exists that does not have *esse*, and nonexisting possibles are nonexisting precisely insofar as they lack *esse* (their possibility is accounted for in other terms). Moreover, if *esse* is that by means of which things are not nothing, then saying that something exists will include saying that there are instances of some concept, in which case quantification is involved in our articulation of *esse*.

Notwithstanding such agreement, Aquinas's account of existence (*esse*) does not confine it to the instantiation of some general concept, properties, description etc. For Aquinas, *esse* is really attributable to things such that if things did not possess *esse*, they would not be; objects primarily have *esse* whereas properties

defended on Fregean principles, then it would mark a contrast with the univocal account of existence that is often to the fore in his (Frege's) writing on such matters. However, in 'What Actually Exists', in *God and the Soul*, p. 65 *et seq*, Geach highlights a distinction in Frege's thought between existence expressed as quantification and existence expressed as actuality, the latter of which is predicable of individuals. Barry Miller, 'In Defence of the Predicate "Exists"', *Mind*, 84 (1975), 344–45 and '"Exists" and "Existence"', *Review of Metaphysics*, 40 (1986), 249–50, makes the same distinction.

participate in the *esse* of their objects. There is then a *prima facie* tension between the Thomist account and the Frege-Russell-Quine account, because in the former account individuals genuinely do have existence, whereas in the latter they do not.

Furthermore, the supposed exhaustiveness of this account is problematic for the Thomist, given that it entails that existence is univocal.[18] But for the Thomist there is more to existence than mere quantification, and in order to establish this, it must be shown that existence is not synonymous with instantiation, that is to say, saying that something exists *is not* the same as saying that there are instances of some concept.

One Thomist-inspired way of doing the latter begins by pointing out that just because the existence of something entails the instantiation of a concept, the instantiation of a concept does not entail the existence of that concept, which it would do if existence and instantiation were synonymous.[19] If I say that tigers exist, I am saying that there are instances of the concept 'tiger'. However, in saying this, I am not saying that the concept of 'tiger' (or 'tiger-hood') itself exists, because the nominalist would be quite happy

---

18. That this account is taken to be exhaustive is clear from Quine when he states in 'Existence and Quantification', p. 97: 'Explication in turn of the existential quantifier itself, "there is", "there are", explication of general existence, is a forlorn cause. Further understanding we may still seek even here, but not in the form of explication'. Moreover, Frege is explicit when it comes to the univocity of existence, holding that there is no difference between the attribution of singular existence and general existence. See Frege, 'Dialogue with Pünjer on Existence', in *Posthumous Writings*, trans. by P. Long and R. White (Oxford: Blackwell, 1979), p. 66: 'We can say that the meanings of the word "exist" in the sentences "Leo Sachse exists" and "Some men exist" display no more difference than does the meanings of "is a German" in the sentences "Leo Sachse is a German" and "Some men are Germans"'. See also Vallicella, *A Paradigm Theory*, pp. 108–12.

19. The core of this argument is due to Vallicella, 'A Critique of the Quantificational View of Existence', *The Thomist*, 47 (1983), 253 *et seq.* Objections based on similar reasoning, though obviously not explicitly Thomistic, are offered by Colin McGinn in *Logical Properties: Identity, Existence, Predication, Necessity, Truth* (Oxford: Oxford University Press, 2000), pp. 21–30.

to commit himself to the existence of tigers without thereby committing himself to the existence of the concept 'tiger'. On the other hand, to hold, as a Platonist would, that the concept 'tiger' exists does not entail that there are instances of that concept, in which case existence can be severed from instantiation.[20]

What seems to be at the heart of the assumption of synonymy between existence and instantiation is confusion between what Vallicella calls 'existence-*in*' and 'existence *simpliciter*'.[21] Tigerhood exists-*in* particular tigers, but this does not mean that tigerhood exists *simpliciter*. Tigers exist *simpliciter*, but they do not exist *in* anything. In the quantification account, existence is instantiation if and only if existence is taken to be existence-*in*. However, what about existence *simpliciter*? It seems that in order to have instantiation of a concept (say tigerhood), one must have an existing object that instantiates that concept. To say that there are tigers is indeed to say that there are things that instantiate the concept 'tiger', but it is also to say that there are things capable of being the things in which tigerhood is instantiated. The ontological value of the '*are*' in 'there *are*' is all important, because it cannot be reduced any further, and is presupposed for any affirmation of instantiation, and this is precisely what Vallicella terms existence *simpliciter*. So without existence *simpliciter*, i.e., without the existence of basic things that do not exist in other things, there can be no existence-*in*, that is, there can be no instantiation of concepts. But if existence *simpliciter* is the condition for the possibility of existence-*in* (instantiation of a concept), then existence *simpliciter* is not synonymous with instantiation. And if the latter

20. John Knasas makes the same point against Frege by arguing that simply because existence statements imply number statements, the reverse does not hold, i.e., number statements do not imply existence statements, since one can imagine a number statement, such as the length of a holiday, which nevertheless is never realised, in which case existence is severed from quantification. See Knasas, *Being and Some Twentieth-Century Thomists* (New York: Fordham University Press, 2003), p. 207.

21. Vallicella, 'A Critique of the Quantificational View of Existence', 253–54.

is the case, then the quantificational account of existence is not exhaustive, there is more to existence than instantiation.

Perhaps it might be argued that the absurdities that follow when one admits a non-quantificational account of existence supply the premises for a *reductio* in favour of the quantificational account. One such absurdity is that advanced by A. J. Ayer, amongst others, to the effect that if existence is attributable to things, then all positive existential statements are really tautologies, whereas all negative existential statements are just contradictions. This is so because, in Ayer's view, statements imply the existence of what they are about, so that when a statement is made about something to the effect that it exists (e.g., *x* exists), that statement commits us to the existence of what it is about, so that the former statement can be reparsed as 'the existing *x* exists'; saying that it has existence, then, is just an analysis of the original statement, and adds nothing new. On the other hand, to deny the existence of something—that is, to make a statement about something and then say that it does not exist—is to contradict oneself; so to reparse our former statement, 'the existing *x* does not exist'. On the assumption then that statements imply the existence of what they are about, our statement denying the existence of something implicitly commits us to its existence.[22] According to this view, in order to avoid absurdity, existence statements ought to be analysed without remainder into statements that are quantificational in scope.

If this analysis is correct, then there are good grounds for rejecting any account of existence that envisages it as something really attributable to things. This analysis, however, is incorrect. Ayer assumes that our statements commit us to the existence of what they are about; only on that assumption can he make his case. But that assumption is nothing more than the assumption that existence is the general existence captured by quantification, i.e.,

---

22. A. J. Ayer, *Language, Truth, and Logic* (London: Penguin, 2001), pp. 25–26.

that our ontological commitments can be gleaned from our true statements translated into quantified formulae. Thus, only on the assumption that existence is quantification will Ayer's criticisms have any bite, but it is precisely in opposition to the exclusivity of existence as quantification that the Thomist account stands. Any push of the quantificational account of existence against Thomist *esse* on the basis of an assumption that is only legitimate if the quantificational account has been antecedently assumed would be radically question begging.

Furthermore, one might question why Ayer (or anybody else for that matter) would actually assume that making a statement commits us to the existence of what that statement is about. After all, being committed to the existence of what a statement is about is not an intrinsic feature of the statement itself, but rather a feature of our use of a statement; that is to say, whilst language can be used to commit us to things, it can also be used noncommittally given the context of utterance.[23] Using language to refer to real existents is only a very small and contrived use of language, and unless one is willing to propose that such is the only proper use of language philosophically speaking, we should be permitted the indulgence of language as we please (so long as we remain meaningful), in which case our statements need not commit us to the existence of what they are about (if they did, no atheist, Ayer included, could deny the existence of God). If the latter is true, then it seems that Ayer has no case, because granted that the statement 'the existing x exists' is somewhat odd and uninformative

---

23. This point has been made by a number of philosophers. See, for example, Peter Strawson, 'On Referring', in *Logico-Linguistic Papers* (London: Methuen, 1971); Ludwig Wittgenstein, *Philosophical Investigations*, trans. by G. E. M. Anscombe (Oxford: Blackwell, 2001), I, n. 40; Gyula Klima, *Ars Artium: Essays in Philosophical Semantics—Medieval and Modern* (Budapest: Institute of Philosophy, Hungarian Academy of Sciences, 1988), pp. 51–52, and 'Existence and Reference in Medieval Logic' in *New Essays in Free Logic*, ed. by Alexander Hieke and Edgar Morscher (Dordrecht: Kluwer, 2001), pp. 197–226; Colin McGinn, *Logical Properties*, p. 34 *et seq.*

(replace *x* with whatever you like), the statements 'I exist', 'the mind exists', 'the world exists', and 'God exists', are all statements that express something of a philosophical interest about their subjects, statements that could be and have been doubted.

The account of existence here considered falls short of Thomist *esse* precisely because those thinkers who have propounded it have failed to think in a genuine metaphysical way. Frege, Russell, Ayer, Quine, and others have sought to engage in metaphysical discussions, whether positively or negatively, not from a context wherein the question of being is important, but from a context wherein meaning is important. Thus, the primary philosophical question for these thinkers is one of the meaning of terms, so that once the meaning of terms has been clarified, the task is to find out whether or not anything answers to those terms; and from the answering to our terms whose meaning has been clarified beforehand, the concept of existence emerges. But such a concept of existence will always be a rather emaciated concept, since if existence emerges out of a query of what answers to our terms, then existence will be nothing more than a statement of the fact that such terms convey reality in some way. To put things another way, existence becomes a statement of the fact that our concepts are instantiated. In that case, to be is to be the value of a bound variable, and since this is derived from a context in which meaning and not being is primary, there can be no other account of existence. But I submit that this mode of thinking signifies a failure to think metaphysically. What really matters in metaphysics is not whether there are beings that match up with our concepts, but being itself and coming to terms with that. Once the latter takes centre stage, all the concerns about what there is and the landscape of our ontology fall into place as derivative clarifications of the nature of being. The central question of metaphysics then is not meaning, but being and its truth. The latter will certainly lead to a consideration of what there is, but the 'is' is only explicable in terms of the question of being and not in terms of the question of meaning, so that in order to determine what there is, one must determine what it is to be. I do not think that the aforementioned philosophers have contributed anything to the question of what it is to be, yet they have contributed fruitfully to the question of what there is.

3.2.2 David Lewis's Indexical–Possibilist Account

Whilst those philosophers who developed the (i) account failed to think through the question of being and thus failed to think in a genuine metaphysical way, the same cannot be said for David Lewis. Lewis is a philosopher whose thinking, whilst influenced by the aforementioned philosophers, attempts to get to the very heart of being. To that extent, he seeks to think through the question of being and in turn to explicate the notion of existence. Frege-Russell-Quine offer what could be called a somewhat deflationary account of existence; it is deflationary insofar as it seeks to explain away existence in favour of the existing thing itself and its properties; it fails to consider existence as some positive reality. Lewis and the remaining thinkers to be considered do not fail to consider existence as a positive reality.

In contrast with the Frege-Russell-Quine account Lewis recognises, to some degree, Meinong's distinction between beings and existents, and this is due to his modal realism, by which is meant 'the thesis that the world we are part of is but one of a plurality of worlds'.[24] This world is the actual world and is distinct from all other so-called possible worlds, in which case there is something about this world making it actual. Lewis's approach to the question of existence then is to figure out just what it is about the actual world that makes it so. Given that his account recognises possible worlds as basic in the characterisation of actual existence, Lewis's view is a form of what Robert Adams has called 'possibilism'[25], and since Lewis offers an indexicalist account of

---

24. David Lewis, *On the Plurality of Worlds* (Oxford: Blackwell, 1986), p. vii.
25. Robert Adams, 'Theories of Actuality', *Noûs*, 8 (1974), 224.

existence, I call his an indexical-possibilist account, so as to distinguish it from other indexicalist accounts, notably Salmon's, which are actualist.

According to Lewis, terms such as 'actual', 'actuality', and 'actually' are indexical expressions whose index is the possible world in which they are expressed. So the actual world is the possible world in which the expression of actuality is made, and this is sufficient to contrast the actual world from all other possible worlds.[26] Possible worlds then that have subjects in them capable of affirming the actuality of their worlds are actual worlds. However, this does not entail that all possible worlds are actual worlds; for given that actuality is relative to a speaker in a world, the only world that is actual is the world relative to the speaker, and since no individual exists in all possible worlds, not all worlds are actual for some individual, in which case not all possible worlds are actual.[27] Actual existence then is context-relative, and the context is the possible world in which the individual speaker affirms its actuality.[28]

Whilst Lewis recognises that actuality is a special feature of the actual world such that existence is not to be interpreted fundamentally in terms of quantification, *pace* Frege-Russell-Quine, his account of actual existence nevertheless does not render it so special as to be some basic metaphysical principle of things, as *esse* is for Aquinas. Whilst there is something significant about actuality, not to be explained away in terms of quantification, such a distinction is not exactly a mark of perfection that the actual world has over possible worlds; the actual world is simply that of the subject's uttering the actuality of his world. Actual existence

---

26. David Lewis, 'Anselm and Actuality', *Noûs*, 4 (1970), 154 *et seq; On the Plurality of Worlds*, pp. 92–96.
27. *On the Plurality of Worlds*, p. 93: 'This is *not* to say that all worlds are actual— there's no world at which that is true, any more than there's ever a time when all times are present'.
28. Ibid: 'Given my acceptance of the plurality of worlds, the relativity is unavoidable. I have no tenable alternative'.

is robbed of all positive metaphysical significance; in its place are all the possible worlds in which subjects utter the actuality of the worlds they are in, so that what is metaphysically significant are possible worlds, not this here actual world.

Such an account may be offensive to one imbued with Lord Russell's robust sense of reality. But be that as it may, it is undeniable that Lewis offers an account of actuality that attempts to take actual existence seriously as a positive metaphysical phenomena, even though it robs it of all positivity. Whilst this is welcome for the Thomist, interpreting actual existence in an indexical fashion fails to get to the heart of the matter, and it carries with it a shadow of that philosophical methodology, ever present in Frege-Russell-Quine, that attempts to do metaphysics on the basis of meaning rather than on the basis of being.

The Thomist recognises that discussion of the actual world designates the subject's world, but he also recognises that the actual world would be actual irrespective of such talk. In other words, there is something about this world that makes it actual, even if there were no subject to utter its actuality. In proof, if the world were not the actual world without some subject to utter its actuality, then there would be no world into which the subject is born, grows up, learns the use of language, attains a grasp of philosophical concepts and thus realises that his world is the actual world. If the world were not the actual world without the affirmation of its being so, then there would be no world into which the subject could be born.

What is it that makes this world the actual world into which one is born and from which one will depart? What metaphysical feature of the world ensures that it has remained in existence before us and will remain in existence after us? What is it about the world that makes it a world for us? The indexicalist account maintains that it is us, subjects who affirm its actuality, but this is unsatisfactory, for it entails that without us the actual world is not so, in which case there is no world to be born into![29] The

---

29. A possible rejoinder is that the indexicalist account does not reduce existence to

indexicalist account thus confuses the semantic role of expressions of actuality with the metaphysical fact of such.[30]

Aquinas's notion of *esse* now makes itself felt; it is because things exist independently of us that there is a world into which one is born and a world that will remain after one departs. In other words, it is because things have actual existence (*esse*) that one can recognise the actuality of them and the world, not vice versa. Thus, whilst it is welcome that Lewis recognises something important about actuality not captured by quantification, the Thomist nevertheless cannot square Lewis's indexicalist account with *esse*.

3.2.3 Nathan Salmon's Indexicalist–Actualist Account

One concern with Lewis's indexialist account is that it makes actuality relative to some world-bound individual, in which case there is nothing particularly special about actuality—it is wholly relativized to the individual.[31] Adopting an indexicalist view, Nathan Salmon argues in line with Lewis that there is nothing

the utterances of the subject, but that it is only recognised as such by a subject; thus whilst the world actually exists prior to the subject, it takes a subject to recognise it as so. This would entail a considerably weaker indexicalism, one in which actual existence is not really explained but taken for granted and simply adverted to; it is such a weak form of indexicalism that Salmon proposes and with which I will deal in the next subsection.

30. Robert Stalnaker makes a similar point in *Ways a World Might Be: Metaphysical and Anti-Metaphysical Essays* (Oxford: Oxford University Press, 2003), p. 29.

31. Nathan Salmon, 'Existence', in *Philosophical Perspectives: Vol. 1—Metaphysics* (1987) p. 81: 'To say, then, that "actual" (in its primary sense) is indexical is to say that an utterance of it designates the possible world in which the utterance takes place, or the possible world in which the producer of the utterance exists, or something like that. But whereas it is perfectly legitimate to talk about the time or place of an utterance (in a given world) it is illegitimate to talk about the possible world of an utterance or its producer, since one and the very same utterance is produced by one and the very same speaker in indefinitely many different worlds'.

particularly special about actual existence, with expressions of actuality being indexed to the world in which they occur, but he nevertheless maintains that actuality is not relative to a speaker's viewpoint.[32] Just as the time of an expression, t, is not relative to the speaker uttering it at t but to a definite point in time at which the speaker utters it, so too is the actuality of the actual world not relative to the speaker uttering the actuality of that world, but that the speaker utters the actuality of that world because it is the actual world in which he is in.[33] Thus the referent of the indexical expression varies with the context in which the utterance is made, not with the utterer, so that the utterance may be transworldly, but the context of utterance which determines its extension is world bound.[34] There are no individuals then that do not exist, though there are individuals that might have existed; and this is enough to make Salmon reject possibilism and endorse actualism, albeit of a moderate kind.[35] Thus, Salmon proposes an account of actual existence that is (i) indexical but (ii) actualist.

There is much to recommend Salmon's position. By making the utterance of actuality transworldly but the context of utterance worldly, he avoids the absurdities of Lewis's view that would entail that all possible worlds with subjects in them are actual worlds and that no world is actual unless there is a subject in it to utter its actuality. Furthermore, there is a lot to recommend Salmon's view that just as the expression of a time is not relative to a speaker but to a definite point in time signifying its context of utterance, so too for actuality: the actuality of the world is not relative to the speaker but to the context of the speaker's utterance, i.e. the world in which it is uttered, so that actuality is a feature of the world and not the speaker's utterance. Having granted the latter, I wonder what could be left for indexicalism. If actuality is a feature of the

32. Salmon, 'Existence', §. 5 *et seq.*
33. Ibid, pp. 84, 88.
34. Ibid, p. 82.
35. Ibid, p. 91.

world in which the speaker utters it and thus not tied down to the speaker himself, then the world is actual in itself and the speaker simply recognises its actuality. If the speaker simply recognises the actuality of the actual world, then the indexical account simply amounts to this fact: the actuality of the world is recognised. But granting the latter, what exactly is being recognised?

Here I believe the indexicalist account fails, and retains a shadow of the methodology that would seek to interpret being in terms of meaning. Pointing out the recognition of the world as actual, and providing an acceptable semantic analysis of that position, does not tell us what existence is or what it is to exist. At best Salmon has presented indexicalism without possibilism, but I fail to see a positive account of what existence is. What is it in this world that the speaker of its actuality recognises? What makes this world actual and leaves other worlds merely possible? This has not been tackled on the indexicalist account, and it is precisely this that the Thomist seeks to account for in terms of *esse*.

3.2.4 Varieties of Actualism

Salmon presented us with an actualist account of existence that is indexicalist. Let us now turn to actualisms that are not indexical in scope. Actualism maintains that there is no distinction between being and existence. In other words, what exists are actual things and they and only they exist; there are no possible worlds. Nevertheless, contemporary actualists see the value of quantifying over *possibilia* so as to safeguard the truth value of counterfactual propositions. In order to allow for the latter without admitting the reality of the former, contemporary actualists interpret possible worlds as ways in which the world might have been but in fact is not.[36] Actual existence will be explicated, then,

36. Differences occur when depicting exactly how best to characterise the ways in which the world might have been, e.g., in terms of states of affairs (Plantinga), propositions (Adams), states of the world (Stalnaker), situations (Kripke), or scenarios (Salmon).

on the basis of determining some feature of the actual world that entails that it is the way it is and not any other way, e.g., its being true or obtaining.

The upshot of such actualisms is that they remain dedicated to the actuality of the world and only the world, yet they still retain quantification into modal contexts so as to preserve the truth value of our modal discourse. Thus, contemporary actualists retain the Frege-Russell-Quine sobriety with regard to the actual world, whilst enhancing the latter account with a developed quantified modal logic which permits quantification into modal contexts. This then permits a break from the exclusive quantificational account of existence found in Frege-Russell-Quine, and permits existence to be interpreted in terms of what it is that renders this the way the world is and not some other way.

As with the Frege-Russell-Quine account, the clearheaded commitment to the actuality of this world is something that the Thomist can appreciate. Moreover, conceiving of actuality as properly basic, from which possibility is interpreted, is also something that rings true to the Thomist. However, here is the problem. On the actualist account, whilst actuality is basic, it is interpreted in terms of something else and conceived of in terms of a contrast with possibility. That is to say, the actualist conceives of existence in terms of how it contrasts with possibility, so that the operative question is how to account for the fact that the world is the way it is and not some other way. Thus are presented accounts of what it is about the world that entails that it is this world and not some other world, such as its being true or obtaining, and existence is then explicated in terms of that.

Now, in interpreting existence in this fashion, the actualist could be doing one of two things: (i) he could be simply following the traditional Aristotelian procedure whereby what is better known in itself is approached via what is better known to us, and since one can come to a firm grasp of for example the truth or the obtaining of this world as opposed to other worlds without thereby appealing to actuality, one can then get a handle on actuality by first getting a handle on truth or obtaining; (ii) on the other hand, the actualist could be subjecting actuality to whatever he takes to be that by which this world is not some other world, so it is this that is metaphysically more basic than actuality, in which case a metaphysical account of actuality will essentially involve an appeal to something like the truth or obtaining of this world.

The first position, that is, (i), is harmless and simply represents a phenomenological approach to metaphysical realities that require one to think oneself into them, but, crucially, being led into the thought of some difficult philosophical reality by means of a simpler and more apparent reality is not the same as offering an explanatory account of the more difficult reality on the basis of the simpler and more apparent. The second position, (ii), is somewhat suspect for the Thomist because (ii) makes existence subject to something other than existence, and this the Thomist will reject. The question here is whether or not the actualist is offering (i) or (ii). I am inclined to think that he is offering (ii), since he is offering a metaphysical explanation of actuality in terms of how the world is as opposed to how the world could be. In that case, the actualist is not adopting a phenomenological method to guide us into thinking about obscure metaphysical realities, but an explanation of the metaphysical reality itself. Thus, in what follows I shall interpret actualism in the (ii) sense with the qualification that any actualist is free to reserve their actualism under the (i) interpretation, but of course in that case actualism will not be a metaphysical explanation of actuality, but an approach to thinking one's way into the metaphysical reality of actuality.

Actualism in the second sense outlined above is suspect to the Thomist because for him what renders the world the actual world as opposed to some other world is its possession of *esse*, and not some other feature such as its being true or obtaining. For Aquinas everything derives from *esse*, because without *esse* there is nothing. Thus in coming to terms with *esse*, it cannot be subjected to anything more basic, rather all things must be subject to it. Given that all things as derivable from *esse* must be subject to *esse*, there is nothing more basic that can be used to analyse *esse*; rather, *esse* will ultimately be involved in the analysis of everything else, and this represents the ultimate unifying principle of Aquinas's metaphysics. Given the latter, whilst the actualist's commitment to the basicality of actuality is welcome, it does not go far enough, since it takes as even more basic something, other than actual existence, by means of which the actual world is in fact the actual world, and seeks to interpret the actual world in terms of that. Thus, I submit that whilst actualism comes close to honouring Thomist *esse*, it nevertheless falls short.

Four contrasting accounts of existence have been considered, each of which is related in some way to the Meinongian distinction between being and existence. None of the aforementioned accounts can be adopted by the Thomist, given that all of them attempt to interpret existence in terms of something other than existence. I now offer some concluding remarks on Thomist *esse* and how one should think of *esse*, given that it cannot be considered in terms of the positions already outlined.

3.3 CONCLUSION

One cannot appeal to something other than *esse* in order to offer an account of it, because *esse* is more basic, more profound, more fundamental than anything else. In that sense all analysis is subsequent to *esse*, since there is nothing into which *esse* can be resolved. Given that there is nothing into which *esse* can be resolved, there is no conceptual grasp of *esse*. This is because one has a conceptual grasp of something either by virtue of the thing's immanent intelligibility or by virtue of the intellect's own inescapable conceptual framework; either way, a conceptual grasp is made on the basis of something more fundamental than the thing to be grasped. But given that there is nothing more fundamental than *esse*, there is nothing other than *esse* by means of which one can come to terms with it, conceptually speaking.

Nevertheless, *esse* is disclosed to us, albeit in a non-conceptual way, since it is a basic fact that whilst there can be an understanding of both existing and nonexisting things, such as a man or a phoenix, one can nevertheless recognise the difference between such things *qua* existing and nonexisting. So much is clear from the preliminary stages of the argumentation for real distinction explored in Chapter 1, wherein it was argued that existence does not enter into the understanding of a thing's essence or quiddity. But this does not entail that there can be no understanding of a thing's existence, only that such is not involved in our understanding of a thing's essence. Following Aquinas, let us take conceptual understanding to be involved with the understanding of a thing's essence, and judgment to be understanding of a thing's existence.[37]

This distinction is not primarily one between two intellectual contents, but between two intellectual operations. There is an intellectual operation that is directed towards the essence of a thing, and one towards the *esse* of a thing. The content of either is markedly distinct from the other, but this is because essence and *esse* are distinct *in re* (though not as *res*), thereby requiring distinct intellectual operations to grasp them; but the converse

---

37. Aquinas, *In Aristotelis Libros Peri Hermeneneias et Posteriorum Analyticorum Expositio* (Turin: Marietti, 1955), lect. 3, n. 31: 'Cognoscere autem praedictam conformitatis habitudinem nihil est aliud quam iudicare ita esse in re vel non esse: quod est componere et dividere; et ideo intellectus non cognoscit veritatem, nisi componendo vel dividendo per suum iudicium'. See also the distinction Aquinas makes elsewhere between the first operation of the intellect (understanding) and the second (judgment), *In De Trinitate*, qu. 5, art. 3, p. 147:89–102: 'Sciendum est igitur quod . . . duplex est operatio intellectus: una que dicitur intelligentia indiuisibilium, qua cognoscit de unoquoque quid est, alia uero qua componit et diuidit, scilicet enuntiationem affirmatiuam uel negatiuam formando. Et hae quidem due operationes duobus que sunt in rebus respondent. Prima quidem operatio respicit ipsam naturam rei, secundum quam res intellecta aliquem gradum in entibus obtinet. . .Secunda uero operatio respicit ipsum esse rei'. For commentary on these and related texts, see Joseph Owens, *An Interpretation of Existence* (Texas: Center for Thomistic Studies—University of St Aquinas, 1985), pp. 20–26.

inference from distinct intellectual operations to distinct meta-physical principles does not follow in my view (see the discussion in Chapter 1 on the *intellectus essentiae* argument).

In order to mark the contrast between understanding and judgment, consider the following two general types of question: (i) what is it? and (ii) is it?[38] Answers to the first type of question often involve an articulation of what the thing is, whether that be in terms of descriptions, essential properties, natural kinds etc, whereas answers to the second type of question are more directed toward whether or not the answer to the first type of question obtains in reality. At their most basic, answers to (ii) come in the form of 'yes' or 'no'. As Lonergan points out, one can ask the following (i)-type question: 'What is the logarithm of the square root of minus one?' It would be senseless to answer 'yes' or 'no' to such a question for with these types of question one is not concerned with whether or not something is the case, but with the case itself, i.e., with a possible suggestion as to what the square root of minus one is. Thus, an answer to (i)-type questions will inevitably involve an appeal to some sort of whatness, whatever one takes whatness to be. On the other hand, having proposed an answer to the question of the square root of minus one, in considering (ii)-type questions one is no longer concerned with a possible suggestion as to what the square root of minus one is, but with whether or not the suggestion made in answer to the (i)-type question is the case. Thus, answers to (ii)-type questions fundamentally differ from those of (i)-type questions, insofar as answers to (i) are concerned with the essence of the thing, whereas answers to (ii) are concerned with its *esse*, i.e., with whether or not the essence proposed as a possible answer to (i) is in fact the case. That is, does it obtain in reality? It is to the latter that judgment is directed.

38. Bernard Lonergan, *Collected Works of Bernard Lonergan vol. 3: Insight—A study of Human Understanding* (Toronto: University of Toronto Press, 1992), p. 297.

Given that judgment is directed to the *esse* of a thing, *esse* is disclosed to a thing in judgment. This is not to say that judgment signifies some sort of privileged access to reality; only that it is through judgment that one can distinguish between existing and nonexisting things. An ability to do this is so inbuilt to our natures that we don't even stop to think about it until the existence of the thing in question is something of such immense importance that acceptance or denial would have the power to fundamentally alter one's outlook on reality, e.g. the existence of the soul, the existence of the mind, the existence of God. One has a grasp of *esse* precisely insofar as one can see the difference between existing and non-existing things in judgment. But what exactly is thereby grasped?

The grasp of *esse* is not like that of some conceptual content made by understanding. When one grasps conceptual content, one is in a position so as to formulate a proposition that is representative of reality in some way. When it is affirmed in judgment that such a grasp is correct, it is realised that what has been understood is in fact the case, and to do so, one grasps that it is real, that it has *esse*. The grasp of *esse* then is the grasp of that whereby a thing whole and complete is presented before us for consideration by the intellect; in grasping it, one grasps that by which there is something other than us and present to us for consideration. To make use of a Kantian thought for a decidedly non-Kantian purpose, *esse* is not the concept of something, it is the positing of something, since without *esse* there would be nothing to form a concept of.

In holding that there is a non-conceptual grasp of *esse* in our true judgments about things, I am not thereby undermining what has been said above, viz. the basicality of *esse*. That is to say, the disclosure of a thing's *esse* in judgment does not render *esse* subject to judgment; rather it renders judgment subject to *esse*; for the thing has *esse* independent of the one who judges thereon, and one's judgment concerning the thing does not affect the thing's *esse* in any way. It follows then that judgment, in order to be true, aims to conform itself to the thing's *esse*, and not conversely; in which case the disclosure of *esse* to the subject in judgment does not entail that *esse* is somehow subject to judgment.

Owing to its distinction from essence, it has been argued by some that existence is the emptiest of all concepts—greatest in denotation, but least in connotation.[39] In this account, the diaphaneity of existence is, like the window to the outside world, what allows objects to be present to our minds; in this case it is most general, no object can appear without existence, for then it would be nothing. Thus, existence in itself says nothing of the nature of objects. It is empty of content, and in order to have content existence would have to be fattened, as it were, by the essence or nature of the things whose existence it is. It is fallacious to try to tease out some content for existence, since given the distinction of essence and existence, all content is bound up with essence; existence is empty.[40]

It is true that insofar as existence (*esse*) is distinct from essence, there is no conceptual content proper to *esse*. But this does not entail that *esse* is lacking in content, but rather only that it does not have a specified essence of its own. Rather than take the latter to show that *esse* has *no* essence and therefore wholly lacking in content, it can be argued that *esse*'s essence is that it actuates all other essences, causing them to be. In that sense, *esse* has a content of its own, and includes not only everything that was, is, or will be, but also everything that could be. In other words, *esse* is in itself pregnant with every possibility of being; for something

---

39. Donald Williams, 'Dispensing with Existence', *The Journal of Philosophy*, 59 (1962), 753: 'The reason that Existence must be empty, diaphanous, blank, neutral, and, in sum, *nil*, resides in its definitory contrast with Essence, by which all characters and their instances, all kinds and cases, and, hence, all that is conceivable or mentionable, must be ascribed to essences. There is no *nature* left for Existence, and it will be a metaphysician's miracle if he can assign anything affirmative to Existence that is not either quite inadequate to its known virtue or an error or both'.

40. Williams, 'Dispensing with Existence', 754 *et seq*.

is precisely a possibility of being insofar as it is capable of specifying *esse* in some respect, so that whilst *esse* is wholly lacking in conceptual content, because it is not intrinsically limited in any respect, it is not lacking in content per se.

The latter reasoning in turn militates further against any analysis of actuality in terms of its contrast with possibility. For Aquinas, possibility is not grounded in some ontologically independent entities, but (i) in the mind of God or (ii) in the potencies of actually existing entities; in both cases possibility is founded upon actuality. Consequently, Aquinas is not prepared to admit that possibility is more basic than actuality, with the actual world being just one of so many possible worlds; rather possibility is derivable from actuality, whether that be God's understanding of the imitability of His essence or in the potencies that an actual being displays.[41]

Thomist *esse* then is a profound metaphysical principle of all existing things. It marks the high point of Thomistic metaphysics and the development of Thomism over the various philosophical influences that Aquinas inherited. Ultimately, *esse* is the act of all acts, without which there is nothing, and so *esse* is unanalysable in terms of anything other than itself. In order to come to terms with *esse* one must think oneself into *esse*, not try to form some sort of concept of it. In order to think oneself into *esse*, one needs to advert to the kind of thinking that is done when one attempts to affirm that one's conceptual understanding of an object or state

<hr>

41. For details of this aspect of Aquinas's thought see Wippel, 'Thomas Aquinas, Henry of Ghent, and Godfrey of Fontaines on the Reality of Nonexisting Possibles', in *Metaphysical Themes in Thomas Aquinas Vol. I* (Washington: Catholic University of America Press, 1984). The view that there are alternate synchronic possibilities independent of the actual world and God's knowledge of the imitability of his essence seems to have emerged historically in the thought of John Duns Scotus. See Simo Knuuttila, 'Medieval Theories of Modality', *Stanford Encyclopaedia of Philosophy*, though the roots of it perhaps lie in the distinction between *esse essentiae* (essential being) and *esse existentiae* (existential being) which figures in the debates on essence and *esse* in the period after Aquinas's death.

of affairs is in fact the case. What one adverts to in true judgments is that by which something is or is not the case, i.e., a thing's existing, its *esse*; and in so doing one is able to think about *esse* without subjecting *esse* to oneself. There can be no analytical engagement with *esse*, precisely because there is nothing further into which *esse* can be analysed. There can only be advertence to the disclosure of *esse* in our true judgments about reality.[42]

In the build-up to his proof of God in *De Ente*, Cap. 4, Aquinas has put in place a certain metaphysical conception of objects that plays a vital role in his proof. He conceives of objects as composites of essence and *esse* whereby the former signifies the definitional content of the thing whereas the latter signifies that by which the thing is an actual thing. It is important to conceive of *esse* as a distinct actuating principle of the thing, for when it comes to the proof of God, it is precisely insofar as *esse* is distinct from essence that the thing need not exist but does in fact exist, and this calls for explanation in a causal manner thereby setting up a regress the termination of which is in a being that is pure *esse*. To the proof of God, then, let us proceed.

---

42. See my article 'Thomist Esse and Analytic Philosophy', *International Philosophical Quarterly* (2015) for development of the view that an analytic reading of *esse* is impossible.

PART **TWO**

THE PROOF OF GOD

IN PART I, Aquinas's views regarding the metaphysical constitution of objects were explored; it was pointed out that these views are presupposed by the proof of God in *De Ente*, Cap. 4 and play a key argumentative role. In Part II, Aquinas's actual proof of God will be explored. The text of the proof is as follows:

> [1] Whatever belongs to a thing is either caused by the principles of its nature (as the capacity for laughter in man) or comes to it from an extrinsic principle (as light in the air from the influence of the sun). [2] Now *esse* itself cannot be caused by the form or quiddity of a thing (by 'caused' I mean as an efficient cause), because that thing would then be its own cause and it would bring itself into being, which is impossible. It follows that everything whose *esse* is distinct from its nature must have *esse* from another. [3] And because everything that exists through another is reduced to that which exists through itself as to its first cause, [4] there must be something that is the cause of *esse* for all other things, because it is *esse tantum*. [3.1] If this were not so, we would go to infinity in causes, for everything that is not *esse tantum* has a cause of its *esse*, as has been said.[1]

---

1. Aquinas, *De Ente*, Cap. 4, p. 377:127–143: '[1] Omne autem quod conuenit alicui

Thomas reasons [1] that in observing a thing's features, one can observe that it has some of them as a result of its intrinsic nature, and others it has as a result of some extrinsic principle. And [2], *esse* cannot be caused by the intrinsic nature of the thing, because that would entail that a thing precede itself in existence, which is absurd. It follows then that *esse*, as it is distinct from the essence of a thing, must have an extrinsic cause of its being in the thing, that is, it must come from another. But [3] what comes from another is ultimately derivable from what is in itself, otherwise [3.1] an infinite regress of causes results. Thus [4], there must be something whose *esse* is not from another but which is *esse* itself, or pure *esse*.

Such is the argumentative framework of Aquinas's proof of God. The numbered sections indicate the breakdown of topics to be dealt with in Part II. First, in Chapter 4, Aquinas's causal principle [1] will be explored, including [2] how he applies it to composites of essence and *esse*. Chapter 5 will focus on the principle [3] that what is through another is reducible to what is through itself, and this because [3.1] a certain infinite regress of causes is impossible. In Chapter 6, the affirmation of the existence of *esse tantum* [4] will be considered. And as an addendum to the latter, Chapter 7 will consider the nature of *esse tantum* as the creator of all that is, as well as the particular metaphysics of creation that Aquinas adopts on the basis of the philosophical framework within which his proof of God in *De Ente* is elaborated.

uel est causatum ex principiis nature sue, sicut risible in homine; uel aduenit ab aliquo principio extrinseco, sicut lumen in aere ex influentia solis. [2] Non autem potest esse quod ipsum esse sit causatum ab ipsa forma uel quiditate rei, dico sicut a causa efficiente, quia sic aliqua res esset sui ipsius causa et aliqua res se ipsam in esse produceret: quod est impossibile. Ergo oportet quod omnis talis res cuius esse est aliud quam natura sua habeat esse ab alio. [3] Et quia omne quod est per aliud reducitur ad id quod est per se sicut ad causam primam, [4] oportet quod sit aliqua res que sit causa essendi omnibus rebus eo quod ipsa est esse tantum; [3.1] alias iretur in infinitum in causis, cum omnis res que non est esse tantum habeat causam esse sui, ut dictum est'.

4

THE CAUSAL PRINCIPLE

CHAPTERS 1 THROUGH 3 laid the preliminary groundwork for the proof proper for the existence of God. It was necessary in those chapters to sketch out Aquinas's metaphysical framework within which the proof of God will be offered. In that framework, Aquinas offers a causal proof for God's existence—that is to say, he sets up a causal regress and argues that there is a primary cause in the causal series that he initiates, and that this primary cause is what we understand God to be. In order to set up this causal series, Aquinas has recourse to a general principle of causality which he then applies to the metaphysics of *esse*. Thus, in the present chapter I shall consider Aquinas's causal principle and from there consider how he applies it to *esse*. Before doing so however, let us read what Aquinas has to say at this stage of the proof:

> Whatever belongs to a thing is either caused by the principles of its nature (as the capacity for laughter in man) or comes to it from an extrinsic principle (as light in the air from the influence of the sun).[1]

---

1. *De Ente*, Cap. 4, p. 377:127–31: '[1] Omne autem quod conuenit alicui uel est causatum ex principiis nature sue, sicut risible in homine; uel aduenit ab aliquo principio extrinseco, sicut lumen in aere ex influentia solis'. A formulation of the same principle, remarkably similar to the *De Ente* one. is found in *Summa Theologiae*, Ia, qu. 3, art. 4: 'Quidquid est in aliquo quod est praeter essentiam eius, oportet esse causatum vel a principiis essentiae, sicut accidentia propria consequentia speciem, ut risibile consequitur hominem et causatur ex principiis essentialibus speciei; vel ab aliquo exteriori, sicut calor in aqua causatur ab igne'.

Now *esse* itself cannot be caused by the form or quiddity of a thing (by 'caused' I mean as an efficient cause), because that thing would then be its own cause and it would bring itself into being, which is impossible. It follows that everything whose *esse* is distinct from its nature must have *esse* from another.[2]

The first quoted passage articulates Aquinas's causal principle, and the second applies it to *esse*; let us consider each in turn.

4.1 THE CAUSAL PRINCIPLE

In the first passage, Aquinas articulates a form of the principle of sufficient reason (PSR) to the effect that the properties a thing has require some reason or explanation, and the reason Aquinas provides is a causal one.[3] So a thing possesses the properties it has either (i) as a result of the principles of its nature, such as

2. *De Ente*, Cap. 4, p. 377:131–37: 'Non autem potest esse quod ipsum esse sit causatum ab ipsa forma uel quiditate rei, dico sicut a causa efficiente, quia sic aliqua res esset sui ipsius causa et aliqua res se ipsa in esse produceret: quod est impossibile. Ergo oportet quod omnis talis res cuius esse est aliud quam natura sua habeat esse ab alio'. A similar formulation of this *De Ente* text is found in *Summa Theologiae*, Ia, qu. 3, art. 4: 'Si igitur ipsum esse rei sit aliud ab eius essentia, necesse est quod esse illius rei vel sit causatum ab aliquo exteriori, vel a principiis essentialibus eiusdem rei. Impossibile est autem quod esse sit causatum tantum ex principiis essentialibus rei, quia nulla res sufficit quod sit sibi causa essendi, si habeat esse causatum. Oportet ergo quod illud cuius esse est aliud ab essentia sua, habeat esse causatum ab alio.' See also *In II Sent.*, d. 1, qu. 1, art. 1: 'Invenitur enim in omnibus rebus natura entitatis, in quibusdam magis nobilis, et in quibusdam minus; ita tamen quod ipsarum rerum naturae non sunt hoc ipsum esse quod habent: alias esse esset de intellectu cujuslibet quidditatis, quod falsum est, cum quidditas cujuslibet rei possit intelligi esse non intelligendo de ea an sit. Ergo oportet quod ab aliquo esse habeant '.
3. In stating that Aquinas endorses a form of the PSR, this is not to say that he adopts it as a principle, as some later arguments for the existence of God developed by other authors will maintain; rather, as will be seen, Aquinas offers reasons for his causal principle on the basis of the distinction and composition of essence and *esse*.

the ability to laugh in man, or (ii) as from an extrinsic principle, such as the light in the air by the influence of the sun.[4] As such these examples are quite innocuous. The ability to laugh in man is something native to man and does not require some extrinsic cause (though of course an extrinsic cause in the form of a comedian is often required to bring that ability into operation). On the other hand, air is not of itself illuminated, rather it must be illuminated by some source, and in this case that source is the sun.

Aquinas's reasoning can be put more formally as follows; if something, x, possesses some property, F, then x possesses F either as a result of the principles of its own intrinsic nature, its x-ness, or as a result of some extrinsic principle(s), y.[5] In both cases F is dependent on something other than itself for its being in x. At the heart of Aquinas's causal principle, then, is the notion that things have certain properties that they can be without which nevertheless belong to the thing, and their so belonging points to a reason in the form of a cause, such that without the cause the property would not belong to the thing.[6]

Those properties that depend on the principles of the thing's essence are accidents that are essential or proper to the thing (*accidentia propria*), since they happen (*accidit*) to the thing as a

---

4. By the principles of its nature, I here take Aquinas to mean those principles that are constitutive of its essence, i.e., matter and form for material creatures and form alone for immaterial creatures.

5. In order to facilitate the discussion, I shall henceforth speak of 'extrinsic principle', with the understanding that there could be more than one such principle and that some principled philosophical approach must be adopted in order to establish that the extrinsic principle which accounts for the property in question is the only principle that does so.

6. I here use 'property' to refer to any feature or characteristic of a thing, and not exclusively in the technical sense as something that is instantiable; in doing this I am not proposing a new account of properties, but rather facilitating the discussion of Aquinas's causal principle, because he will later argue that *esse* is something that a thing possesses but non-essentially, in which case it requires some extrinsic principle(s). Without recourse to a term to cover all the features or characteristics of a thing, including its *esse*, the ensuing discussion would become quite cumbersome.

result of the principles of the thing's essence. This, of course, is not to say that one who is without such proper accidents is a different type of thing than one who has them, given that, with regard to man's proper accident of being able to laugh, one can imagine a lot of men who are unable to laugh; rather, what it means is that the one who has them, whilst the same kind of thing as those which do not have them, is nevertheless characterised in a different way from one who is without them. The accidental nature of proper accidents consists in the fact that one need not have them to be the type of thing that one is, though the principles of one's essence entails that one has them at least *in potentia*; for no matter how deadpan a person is, they are still *qua* rational animal in principle able to laugh, even though in reality such a person is often referred to as one unable to laugh.

Those properties that depend on some extrinsic principle are wholly accidental to the thing in question, for they happen to the thing, and their so happening entails dependency on something other than the thing—that is, an extrinsic principle.

In both cases there is dependency on something other than the accident for the accident's so happening to the subject. In the first case, the accident is dependent on the principles of the essence of the individual substance, whereas in the second case it is dependent on some extrinsic principle. This entails, then, that what is distinct from the essence of a thing and is yet present in the thing is dependent on some principle for its being in the thing, whether that be the principles of the thing's essence or some extrinsic principle.

Underlying the foregoing account is the view that if things display properties, there must be a reason for their so doing, and the reason provided is a causal one. Thus, causality is aligned with the why of things; so to grasp the cause of something is to grasp why it is the way it is.[7] Causality in this respect is thus envisaged

---

7. *In Octo Libros Physicorum Aristotelis Expositio* (Turin: Marietti, 1954), Lib. 2, lect. 5, n. 176.

as a kind of derivation and dependence.[8] If there is some accidental property in a thing thereby dependent for its actuality, one in turn is motivated to ask why the thing in question possesses that property, and once a satisfactory answer to why it does so is offered, one in turn knows that on which it depends and from which it derives, which is its cause.

Now if one thing derives from and depends on another thing, the former stands in potency to the latter, since without the latter the former would not be. Thus, in Thomistic terms, causality is analysed in terms of act and potency, such that a cause is what actualises the effect and the effect thereby stands in potency to it.[9] The actualisation of some potency thereby signifies a causal relationship. This then allows Aquinas a very generous notion of causality, since different applications of causal dependency can be ascertained and thereby various classes of cause derived: (i) material, (ii) formal, (iii) efficient, and (iv) final. Therefore, causality can be conceived of in terms of causal properties, that is, properties that a thing possesses in a dependent and derived fashion whose derivation and dependence requires a cause of that property. There are thus as many causal properties as there are act–potency dependencies, so that there are as many causal contexts as there are causal properties.[10]

8. *De Potentia Dei*, qu. 5, art. 1: 'Effectum enim a sua causa dependere oportet. Hoc enim est de ratione effectus et causae'.
9. This accords with the more general definition of causality that Aquinas offers elsewhere, to the effect that the term 'cause', as opposed to 'principle', signifies some influence of the cause over the effect, whereas 'principle' signifies a priority in some order. Hence, the effect stands in potency to the influence of the cause, see *In V Met.*, lect. 1, n. 751: 'Hoc nomen causa, importat influxum quemdam ad esse causati', and lect. 3, n. 794: 'Potentia et actus diversificant habitudinem causae ad effectum'; *In II Phy.*, lect. 5, n. 183: 'Omnia ista habent unam rationem causae, prout dicitur causa id ex quo fit aliquid'.
10. See for instance *In V Met.*, Lect. 2, nn. 763–771, and Lect. 3, nn. 777–782. I think that in this sense a Thomist would simply bite the bullet and enlarge the applicability of causality in any case where there is act–potency dependence, rather than exclude such cases of dependence that intuitively appear as non-causal. See in relation to this point Jaegwon Kim, 'Causes and Counterfactuals', *Journal of Philosophy*, 70 (1973) reprinted in *Causation and*

Aquinas's account of causality is thus analysed in terms of act and potency, so that whilst it may be describable in conditional terms, that is only so because the actuality of the cause is the principle for the actuality of the effect, in which case the actuality of the effect is conditional upon that of the cause. This does not entail that the causal relationship is itself analysed in such terms, even though it may be describable thereby. Aquinas's statements elsewhere that would seem to imply a conditional analysis of causation, such as *Summa Theologiae*, Ia, qu. 44, art. 1, ad. 2: 'The effect would not be if the cause were not', merely highlight an essential feature of act–potency dependence, to the effect that what is in potency in a certain respect is only actualised by something that is in act in that respect. And as a consequence of *that*, the effect (the actualised potency) would not be if the cause (what actualises the potency) were not.[11]

To be in act is to be actual in some respect, and the primary mode of actuality for Aquinas is that of existing in act, being in possession of *esse*. Causality is primarily located in the causality of *esse* such that a thing can act as cause only insofar as it is in act through the *esse* that it has.[12] Amongst creatures at least, what has *esse* are essence–*esse* composites, and essence–*esse* composites are not events, changes, or states, but they nonetheless find themselves subject to events, changes, and states. Thus, for Aquinas, it

Conditionals, ed. by Ernest Sosa (Oxford: Oxford University Press, 1975), pp. 192–95.

11. This point is directed at Gabriele De Anna's Thomistic account of causal relations in terms of conditionals, in which she claims that Aquinas's account of causation is analysable in such terms. See 'Causal Relations: A Thomistic Account', in *Analytical Thomism: Traditions in Dialogue*, ed. by Craig Patterson and Matthew S. Pugh (Aldershot: Ashgate, 2006), pp. 79–101.

12. This is in effect Aquinas's principle that something acts insofar as it is in act— 'unumquodque agit secundum quod est actu'; for statements of this principle see *Summa Contra Gentiles*, Lib. 1, Cap. 16, *Summa Theologiae*, Ia, qu. 25, art. 1, ad. 1, IaIIae, qu. 55, art. 2, and *De Potentia Dei*, qu. 3, art. 8.

is things having *esse* that are primarily related in the causal relation and events, changes, or states only secondarily.[13]

As applied to the principle outlined at the beginning of the proof of God, things have certain properties; when inquiring as to why they are so, one is led to see that they can have these properties either as a result of their intrinsic nature or as a result of an extrinsic principle. An entity can have properties that are derived from and depend on its intrinsic nature, such that it would not have those properties if it were not of that nature.[14] An entity can also have properties that are derived from and depend on some extrinsic principle. In order to determine that a thing has properties dependent on some extrinsic principle, it must be antecedently determined that such a thing does not have those properties as a result of its intrinsic nature, i.e., that the property in question is distinct from the essence of the thing; and this, as has been seen, is the case for *esse*.

Immediately this causal principle raises two issues. Firstly, why can't x possess the property F non-intrinsically yet without F's having an extrinsic cause for its being in x? In other words, can't a thing have uncaused properties that it does not possess as a result of the principles of its nature? Secondly, and more fundamentally, this causal proposition embodies what is for some a strange account of causality, to the effect that what is involved in causality is the actualisation of certain properties in the patient which is subject of the effect, such that these causal properties are dependent on an extrinsic principle or are derived from the patient's intrinsic nature. Such a notion of causality certainly sits uneasy in a post-Humean philosophical climate, wherein causality

13. The qualification 'amongst creatures' is important, for later we will see that there is a type of causality applicable to pure *esse* and only to pure *esse*. This then is a type of causality that no essence–*esse* composite can engage in, but which is still analysable in terms of act and potency.
14. The coverse does not hold, i.e., that a thing would not be of that nature if it did not have those properties, since the properties in question, whilst derived from the thing's essence, are not the essence of the thing.

is principally associated with events and their regular succession. Thus, both these issues shall be dealt with in turn.

4.1.1 Can There Be Uncaused Non-Intrinsic Properties?

Dealing with the first issue, I shall put it forth in a manner specifically focussed on the metaphysics at the heart of the *De Ente*. The causal property that Aquinas has in mind is *esse*, and he wishes later to argue that with regard to composites of essence and *esse*, the causal PSR will lead us to inquire after a cause of the *esse* that such composites possess. But in assuming that things cannot possess non-intrinsic properties in an uncaused fashion, Aquinas assumes that *esse* can only be possessed by essence–*esse* composites causally—that is, *esse* is not uncaused in such things. The latter seems to be an implicit assumption that unless there is something that is just pure *esse*, which is the goal of the entire proof of God, then the *esse* of essence–*esse* composites remains unexplained. But, so the objection goes, it is the latter assumption, built in as it were to the causal PSR, that requires an explanation, and cannot be simply assumed for the purposes of the argument Aquinas wishes to make.[15] So what needs to be established is twofold: (i) that there cannot be any uncaused non-intrinsic properties of a thing, and, more specifically (ii) that there is no uncaused *esse* in essence–*esse* composites.

To begin with (i), that there are no uncaused non-intrinsic properties, it must be borne in mind that Aquinas applies his causal principle so as to account for a fact requiring explanation: that is to say, if one can ask and answer the question of why a thing possesses a certain property, then one can offer a causal explanation for the possession of that property. Now let us take the objection that Aquinas has not considered that a thing can

---

15. Alexander Pruss, *The Principle of Sufficient Reason: A Reassessment* (Cambridge: Cambridge University Press, 2006), p. 28.

possess certain properties that are neither (i) derived from the principles of its essence nor (ii) caused by some extrinsic principle. If such properties are neither (i) nor (ii), they are uncaused. But if such properties are uncaused, there is no explanation for why they exist in the thing, that is, there is no explanation of why they are there. Granted that it is a fact they are, such a fact is without explanation. If the possession of certain non-intrinsic properties that are uncaused is without explanation, then the burden is on the objector to establish how such properties can feature in a metaphysical analysis of objects at all. If the objector grants that there is an intelligible framework within which beings can be analysed and accounted for, then such uncaused non-intrinsic properties must be primitive. So in order to establish (i), it needs to be established that there are some primitive properties that a thing possesses non-intrinsically. In the previous chapter I granted that *esse* is primitive such that there is nothing more fundamental than *esse* that could offer an explanatory account of it. It could thus be objected that *esse* is just such a primitive, non-intrinsic property. This objection has some force, and it would entail that *esse* is a property not derivable from the principles of a thing's essence (thus distinct from it), and yet uncaused. So in order to answer this objection, one would have to show that there is no uncaused *esse* in essence–*esse* composites, which is (ii) above.

The upshot of the objection that there could be non-intrinsic, uncaused properties is that if correct, it would entail that one cannot move from the distinction of essence and *esse* to the caused character of *esse* in essence–*esse* composites, and because setting up a causal series in the line of *esse* is essential to the argumentation that Aquinas is making, the possibility that *esse* could be an uncaused yet distinct (non-intrinsic) property of a thing would undermine Aquinas's argument from the outset. Thus, the objection at this point is not arbitrarily suggesting that a cause can be expected in some cases and not in others; it is demanding that one can expect a cause when it comes to *esse*, especially when it has been conceded in the previous chapter that *esse* is primitive.

Why should there be a cause of *esse* simply because it is distinct from essence?

I think the resolution of the latter objection comes with an understanding of *esse* as act. *Esse* stands to essence as act does to potency, such that *esse* is what actualises essence and makes it exist. No essence would thus exist without *esse*. Given that essence would not exist without *esse*, why does some existing essence have *esse* in the first place? Even though *esse* is primitive and there is nothing more fundamental than *esse*, its being composed with some essence is not primitive; and since the essence with which it is composed does not possess such *esse* essentially, it possesses it from without. So, why does it thus possess *esse*? What is the cause of that essence's *esse*? These are not unreasonable requests, and so the burden of proof is on the objector to show how that in which essence and *esse* are distinct could have *esse* and thus actually exist without its *esse* being caused.

Given the above, I submit that (ii) can be rejected because insofar as *esse* is related to essence as act to potency, yet no essence–*esse* composite need ever exist, there is a cause for the *esse* that the essence enjoys. But this is just to say that the *esse* which is distinct from the essence of the thing it actuates depends on some principle extrinsic to the essence, and this is to say that the *esse* in essence–*esse* composites is a non-intrinsic caused property, which is to reject (i) as applied to *esse*. And this is all Aquinas needs to get his causal regress going.

Perhaps a more fundamental objection could be articulated as follows: seeking a cause of *esse* for essence–*esse* composites seems to assume that unless there were something that were pure *esse*, there would be no causal explanation for the *esse* of essence–*esse* composites, and such an assumption cannot be built into the premises of a proof the conclusion of which is that there is a cause of *esse* that is itself pure *esse*. Thus, it could be argued that Aquinas's reasoning here is circular.

In Aquinas's defence, he has not stated what the cause of essence–*esse* composites must be like; rather he has announced a principle which will permit one to look for the cause of things thus construed. So if a thing possesses some property, it either possesses it intrinsically or as the result of some extrinsic principle. In the case of *esse*, no essence–*esse* composite possesses *esse* intrinsically, in which case there is some extrinsic principle by means of which any essence–*esse* composite possesses *esse*. But this is not to assume that the only principle capable of accounting for the *esse* of such composites is something that is pure *esse*. The latter would be true if (i) it were also true that what has *esse* through another is reducible to what has it in itself (the *per aliud* principle), (ii) otherwise an infinite regress would result. However, it is Aquinas's task in the remaining stages of the proof to establish (i) and (ii), in which case in simply stating the causal proposition with which he begins the proof, Aquinas leaves it open for there to be an infinite regress of causes of *esse*, and thus no primary cause of *esse*. Nothing in the statement of the causal principle itself precludes an infinite regress of causes, though as will be seen, further philosophical considerations will show that such is contrary to right reason. But at this point, Aquinas has not assumed in stating his causal principle that there is a primary cause of *esse*.

One could, however, firm up the latter objection by fastening onto the fact for Aquinas that insofar as *esse* is absolutely primary, with nothing more basic in the thing all philosophical analysis stops with *esse*. But if this is the case, then the fact seems built into Aquinas's metaphysics of *esse* that when it comes to the *esse* of a thing, one must stop and cannot proceed any further. Coupling the latter with the fact that *esse* is that whereby anything at all actually exists, it would appear that nothing would exist unless there were some uncaused *esse* from which all things flow. So one need only understand *esse* to understand that there is an uncaused cause of the existence of things. In other words, it would seem that one can arrive at God simply through a proper understanding of the nature of God, pure *esse*, and this would be to repeat the ontological argument, such that the very concept of *esse* entails the existence of such.

This is certainly a pointed objection, and one that gets to the heart of the matter, because of course if God is *esse* itself, indistinct from His essence, God cannot fail to exist, whereas essence–*esse* composites can. And given that, as is obvious, things exist and thereby have *esse*, one need only engage in a conceptual analysis of the *esse* that things possess in order to arrive at the affirmation of God.

Whilst I think this is a strong objection, I think it is only strong because it misconstrues the nature of *esse*. Undoubtedly if one came face to face with pure *esse*, one could not doubt the existence of such. So, in coming face to face with God, one would be a fool to doubt His existence. However, adverting to the *esse* that things have is not adverting to God, so that a consideration of the *esse* of a thing is not a consideration of God and His necessary existence. Rather, in considering the *esse* of things, one is considering a principle of act in the thing—indeed the principle of act. And because such a principle is under consideration, one must consider that it is the act *of* that thing in question such that, as noted in the previous chapter, *esse* is individuated to the thing whose *esse* it is. In that case, one can reason that the *esse* in the thing, whilst in the thing, is not identical to the thing and thus has a cause. A causal regress is thus initiated, since either the cause is something that simply has *esse* (another essence/*esse* composite) or it is pure *esse*. But crucially, advertence to the caused character of a thing's *esse* is not advertence to the necessity of pure *esse* as a cause for that *esse*, since absent a denial of an infinite regress and an affirmation of the *per aliud* principle (to be established later), it is at least possible, at this stage of the argument, to hold that something that is not pure *esse* is the cause of the *esse* of the thing in question.

I do not think, then, that it can be stated that once one understands the metaphysics of *esse* one is led ineluctably to the affirmation of pure *esse* as that from which all things are derived, nor do I think that Aquinas loads the dice, as it were, in proposing his causal principle. The principle that he introduces comes across as a sober and quite parsimonious approach to our causal reasoning, such that if there are dependent properties one must ask what accounts for such properties.

4.1.2 Aquinas's Non-Humean Notion of Causality

The foregoing considerations more or less accepted Aquinas's general causal framework, and within that context challenged the exhaustiveness of the causal principle. Another promising way of challenging the causal principle is to challenge the very idea of causality involved therein, so that even if the principle is exhaustive, it is nevertheless ineffective, because supposedly causality does not work like that. A particularly promising way of challenging Aquinas's philosophy of causation is to be found in the thought of David Hume.

Hume approaches causality within what he sets forth as the science of man, that is to say, he wants to know how the ideas of cause and effect are formed and why causal inferences are made in the way that we often make them. Hume is thus primarily concerned with the ideas of cause and effect and how they come to be formed. In that case the necessary connection between cause and effect takes on the status of a logical necessity such that it would be contradictory to deny it.[16] And it is this that Hume seeks to demolish, arguing that it is not contradictory to deny the connectedness of cause and effect.

In his unpacking of the ideas of cause and effect, Hume argued that it need not be held that there is a particular cause for every effect; nothing in experience provides us with such universality. Indeed, all one can say is that as has hitherto been experienced, some particular cause has had a particular effect, but there is nothing in our experience that would justify the necessary connection between the two.[17] If Hume is correct, then causality is

16. Elizabeth Anscombe locates this shift to logical necessity in Thomas Hobbes: see 'Causality and Determination', in *Causation and Conditionals*, p. 64.
17. David Hume, *A Treatise of Human Nature* (London: Everyman, 2003), Bk. 1, Part. 3, §. 2, p. 52: 'Why we conclude, that such particular causes must

nothing more than the regular succession or constant conjunction of events with nothing necessarily connecting them.

What Hume seeks is a conceptual disassociation of one kind of effect from one kind of cause, such that the one is not necessarily bound up with the other; rather, the two are conceptually separable. Given such conceptual separability, it will not be absurd to think the one without the other, in which case it is not necessary to have the one always with the other. Thus, an effect need not always have a cause.[18]

As applied to Aquinas, one could argue that there is nothing that seems to mandate the universality of Aquinas's causal principle. It could be the case that certain properties thought to be caused by some extrinsic principle are in fact caused by some principle of the thing's nature; similarly, certain properties thought to be caused by the principles of a thing's nature, are in fact caused by principles extrinsic to the thing.

The problem here, however, is that one may doubt that a particular effect is derived from some particular cause and not another; this seems pretty innocuous, because such mistakes are made quite often. However, this does not mandate the move from the conceptual separability of one particular cause from a particular effect to the separability of cause and effect *simpliciter*. As per Anscombe's example, the ability to separate a rose from any particular colour it may have does not sanction the inference that

necessarily have such particular effects; and what is the nature of that *inference* we draw from the one to the other, and of the *belief* we repose in it?'.

18. Ibid, Bk. 1, Part. 3, §. 3, p. 53: 'All distinct ideas are separable from each other, and as the ideas of cause and effect are evidently distinct, 'twill be easy for us to conceive any object to be non-existent this moment, and existent the next, without conjoining to it the distinct idea of a cause or productive principle. The separation, therefore, of the idea of a cause from that of a beginning of existence, is plainly possible for the imagination; and consequently the actual separation of these objects is so far possible, that it implies no contradiction nor absurdity; and is therefore incapable of being refuted by any reasoning from mere ideas; without which 'tis impossible to demonstrate the necessity of a cause'.

the rose has no colour—for of course the rose has *a* colour—yet I am able to imagine its not having *that* colour (such as pink) but some *other* colour (such as yellow).[19] Similarly, I can imagine an effect's not having *that* particular cause, but this does not mean I can imagine an effect's having *no* cause, just not the cause that I previously imagined the effect to have. The Humean must provide us with stronger reasons as to why he thinks cause and effect, and not just particular causes and effects, are indeed separable notions.[20]

The Humean critique can be presented in another fashion. The foregoing presentation focussed on the separability of cause and effect, whereas one could focus on Hume's contention that there is nothing in experience that reveals to us the necessary connection of cause and effect, in which case it is not an idea drawn from experience and hence not an objective feature of the world. But to my mind this interpretation of Hume's critique fares no better than the previous, given that one can indeed discern a necessary connection between cause and effect, and this precisely because we can experience an actualised potency, in which case there is an experience of an effect dependent on its cause. Let us remain with Aquinas's examples and explore where the necessary connection lies. In both examples (the ability to laugh in man and the presence of light in the air) the properties in question need not belong to the thing, yet they do belong to it. The thing is required in which the properties belong, but insofar as the thing need not have the properties in question yet happens to have them, the thing is in potency to such properties. Now, given that a thing possesses such dependent properties, there is required a correlative principle of act, in virtue of which the thing actually

---

19. Elizabeth Anscombe, '"Whatever Has a Beginning of Existence Must Have a Cause": Hume's Argument Exposed', in *Collected Philosophical Papers Volume I: From Parmenides to Wittgenstein* (Oxford: Blackwell, 1981), p. 97.

20. Barry Stroud makes a similar objection to the effect that the separability of the notions of cause and effect is ill established in Hume's treatment thereof: see *Hume* (London: Routledge & Kegan Paul, 1977), pp. 46–50.

possesses the properties in question. Experience of dependent properties is experience of actualised potencies, which in turn points to a principle of actuality by which such potency is actualised. Thus there is an experience of an actualised potency, but an actualised potency is an effect that depends on its cause, in which case experience of an actualised potency is experience of causality such that without the cause (the principle of actuality), the effect would not be (the potency would remain unactualised).[21]

What is experienced in a causal relation is threefold: (i) a cause, (ii) an effect, and (iii) a relation connecting them. The three are not three experiences, and thus there is not revealed in the experience of causality three identical types of thing. Thus, whilst cause and effect are entities, the connection between them is not: rather, it is a relation. Only on the assumption that the connection between cause and effect must be the same type of thing as the things connected will it be true to say that such a connection is unobservable. Hume can make good on such an assumption if his empiricism is correct, in which case for one antecedently convinced of Humean empiricism there can be no observation of the causal connection. However, this does not show that the causal connection is unobservable, only unobservable once certain empiricist presuppositions have been made.[22]

21. See Knasas, *Being and Some Twentieth-Century Thomists*, pp. 219–21, for similar reasoning.
22. C. J. Ducasse, 'On the Nature and the Observability of the Causal Relation', *Journal of Philosophy*, 23 (1926) reprinted in *Causation and Conditionals*, p. 120–21: 'Hume's view that no connection between a cause and its effect is objectively observable would be correct only under the assumption that a 'connection' is an entity of the same sort as the terms themselves between which it holds, that is, for Hume and his followers, a sense impression . . . [But] the fact is that causal connection is not a sensation at all, but a relation'; see also Barry Stroud, *Engagement and Metaphysical Dissatsifaction: Modality and Value* (Oxford: Oxford University Press, 2011), p. 22: '[Hume's view] rests in large part on a completely general theory of perception according to which the most anyone can ever perceive is extremely limited in comparison with what we eventually come to think about the world on the basis of the "fleeting and momentary" impressions we receive'. See also William May, 'Knowledge of Causality in Hume and Aquinas', *The Thomist*, 34 (1970), 254–288 for an

Another objection of more recent, but nevertheless Humean, vintage is that causality trades in notions of necessity and dependency which in order to make sense cannot be understood in terms of entities in the world, but must be understood in terms of the way in which we humans think about the world at large. So causality will be seen to be a conceptual category by means of which we make sense of certain features of the world. Behind such interpretations lies a concern for sanitising what appear to be obscure notions at the heart of our picture of reality.[23] Thus, causal relations must be re-parsed in terms that do not invoke obscure unanalysable notions such as nomic necessity, for example—parsings that would have an exclusively extensional context for which an interpretation in terms of first-order quantification logic can be provided. Such an endeavour would remove much of the mystique surrounding causality and the necessary connection that appears to be involved therein.[24]

This certainly poses a challenge to Aquinas's causal realism, to the effect that for Aquinas causality is a real process operative in the world, in which case if one can locate a causal connection one can objectively say that something possesses some property because it is caused to by something else, in which case the cause is necessary for the effect in question such that without the cause there would be no effect. A rejection then of the foregoing reductionist objection is necessary for the viability of Aquinas's causal realism.

As noted, the motive behind the reductive re-parsing is to sanitise our causal notions so as to bring them in line with a more

in-depth treatment of the epistemological assumptions underlining the Thomist and Humean accounts of causality.

23. For statements of the need for such sanitation see Ernest Nagel, *Structure of Science: Problems in the Logic of Scientific Explanation* (London: Routledge & Kegan Paul, 1961), p. 52, and Richard Braithwaite, *Scientific Explanation* (Cambridge: Cambridge University Press, 1968), p. 294.

24. See for instance, G.H. Von Wright, 'On the Logic and Epistemology of the Causal Relation', in *Causation and Conditionals*, pp. 95–113.

acceptable picture of reality. But such a sanitary approach carries with it its own substantive philosophical commitments. When the reductive account is provided as the more acceptable and less obscure one, it must be asked, for whom? Certainly not for the scores of ordinary, non-philosophical language users who have no problem making use of causal notions in an often quite accurate sense. The reductive account is more acceptable and less obscure to those with antecedent philosophical commitments, without which a non-reductive account would be unacceptable and obscure. And it seems to me that those philosophical commitments are commitments that refuse to acknowledge certain modal features, such as necessity, as part of the furniture of reality.

I propose that the only way of establishing that modal notions such as necessity are not a feature of extra-mental reality is to be committed to some strict empiricist worldview, such that our epistemic access to reality is not to real objects but mediated by empirical counterparts, e.g., swathes of sensory contents, atomic sense data etc, from which thoughts are formed. On that view, whatever in our thought concerns the empirical counterparts reflects objective features of reality, whereas what is not reducible to such empirical counterparts is added by thought. In that case, necessity will be seen as an addition we make, not something that the world provides, in which case it must be analysed accordingly.

If such a conception of the mind–world relationship can be jettisoned, there need not be any constraint on thinking of the world in somewhat richer terms in which modal notions can play an important role. One problem with the empiricist position is that in reducing all objectivity to empirical counterparts, not only does it get rid of causal relations thought of in terms of the necessary connection between one thing acting as cause and another thing as effect, it also gets rid of things entirely. In other words, the very world of objects for the empiricist is really only swathes of sensory contents, atomic sense data etc, the objectifying and forming of which is an addition on our behalf. Objects cease to figure in our picture of the world on the empiricist account.[25]

Worse than that, such an empiricist account of our mental engagement renders impossible the notion of our thought's being answerable to the world of experience. This is because on the empiricist account, what is received in experience are the empirical counterparts of objects—such as patches of colour, waves of sound etc—which is conceptually naked; and as conceptually naked, such experience cannot inform a judgment about the reality thus experienced, nor can it function as a justification for any judgment about the reality thereby experienced.[26] Thus on the empiricist construal of the matter, experience can play no normative role in our engagement with extra-mental reality, and this undermines the very motivation for empiricism in the first place.

Given all of this, the philosophical commitments without which our modal notions are considered to be unacceptable and obscure are themselves quite unacceptable and obscure; if the latter is the case, then such commitments can be jettisoned, in which case it is not obscure to hold that the modal notion of necessity, at work in causality, is present in extra-mental reality.

A final position to be considered is one represented by Barry Stroud and is of a post-Kantian variety. Kant characteristically accepted but modified Hume's critique of causality by holding that the necessary connection between cause and effect whilst supplied by the mind is a necessary condition for the possibility of our thinking of the world at all. In that case, one cannot think of the world without our causal notions, in which case the idea of causality as involving necessity does have

---

25. This is a central criticism that Stroud makes of such reductive accounts in *Engagement and Metaphysical Dissatisfaction*, Chapter 2.
26. See John McDowell, *Mind and World* (Cambridge, MA: Harvard University Press, 1996), Chapter 1, for a presentation of this objection.

a respectable role to play in our interpretation of the world. However, as Stroud observes, simply because some conceptual category is indispensable for our thought does not entail that the world is so independent of thought, because whilst it may be that causality and thereby necessity are indispensable features of thought, it does not follow that in the absence of thought such features are present in the world. Furthermore, given that such features are indispensable to thought, no one is in a position to make an objective judgement on the independent reality of such features, given that those features are necessary for our judgments in the first place, in which case such judgments will be necessarily coloured by the indispensability of those features.[27] This objection has a lot to recommend it, for it does not go in for the reductionist tendencies of post-Humean thinking but recognises that there is something weighty about our modal concepts.

In response, I should like to point out that there lies a neglected alternative here. Whilst certain concepts may be indispensable to our thought, this does not entail that they are not objective features of the world, nor that the judgment cannot be made that they are. Rather, the judgment could be made that whilst such notions are essential to thought, if the world were not in itself as such it could not be thought, in which case these modal notions, whilst indispensable to thought, are revelatory of the world that is thought; the world's thinkability necessitates that it be so.

Furthermore, the necessity of certain concepts for thought does not entail that a positive judgment about the reality of such concepts is impossible; it could do so only if it were assumed that in order to make a positive judgement, thought must be free of any concepts, so that our minds become like empty receptacles,

27. *Engagement and Metaphysical Dissatisfaction*, Chapters 5–6.

ready to receive information from the world. Not only does that carry with it a rather curious commitment to a Cartesian conception of mentality, with the mind envisaged as a kind of receptacle into which thoughts enter, it also endorses the strange notion that in order for thought to be objective, it must not be tainted by thought, in which case to make the objective judgment that modal notions feature in extra-mental reality, modal notions cannot feature in our thought of such reality. But if the latter is the case, then in principle no objective judgment that modal notions are a feature of extra-mental reality could be formed, since to do so would be to think about and thereby include in thought such modal notions.

I submit then that a thing's properties can be observed, the inference made that a thing need not have some of those properties and still be the thing that it is, in which case an inference to a cause, whether intrinsic or extrinsic, of such properties can be made. It is certainly the case that when dealing with material essences we can be mistaken and take certain properties to be the result of an extrinsic cause but which are themselves really a result of the principles of the nature of the thing. This admission may bring about a certain uneasiness in applying Aquinas's causal principle. Such uneasiness is not a doubting of the principle, but a doubt in our ability to apply it correctly. The latter might be an issue for the Thomist given that, as has already been indicated, Aquinas applies the principle to the case of *esse*, and he will argue that insofar as *esse* is not the result of the principles of any finite thing's nature, and this because essence and *esse* are distinct in such things, *esse* is caused in such things. But given that mistakes occur as to what are and are not the properties caused by the principles of a thing's nature, can't the same be said about *esse*? If so, then the proof of God, beginning with the causal principle as applied to *esse*, will be of dubious probative force. Let us turn then to the case of *esse* and ascertain whether or not this is actually the case.

4.2 THE CAUSE OF *ESSE*

As noted, Aquinas's next move is to apply the causal PSR to the case of *esse*, and he argues that the *esse* of a thing cannot be caused by that thing's essence, for then it would be the cause of itself and bring itself into being, which is impossible. Hence, everything whose *esse* is distinct from its essence must have *esse* from another.

Needless to say, essence and *esse* must at this point have been shown to be really distinct principles of the thing, since if they were not, then I am at a loss as to how to determine whether or not *esse* is caused by the principles of the thing's nature or by an extrinsic principle. But in the passage quoted at the beginning of this chapter, Aquinas assumes that *esse* is caused in the thing by something extrinsic to the thing, in which case he assumes as established the real distinction between essence and *esse*.

Fortunately, in my interpretation, the real distinction is established prior to the proof of God and so this need not pose a problem for us. However, it will pose a problem for those Thomists who believe that the real distinction can be established only *after* a successful proof of God; at least in the *De Ente* this cannot be the case.[28] This point should also put to rest the objection of Van Steenberghen and those of like mind, to the effect that prior to the proof of God, essence and *esse* are only established as logically distinct, but the proof requires their real distinction, in which case it is invalid. At least on the interpretation I adopt, the real distinction is established prior to the proof of God, in which case

---

28. Joseph Owens is the main defender of the unreality of the distinction prior to the proof of God. He does, however, maintain that essence and *esse*, whilst not really distinct, are established as sufficiently distinct for a causal proof of God such as the one offered in the *De Ente: see An Elementary Christian Metaphysics* (Houston: Bruce Publishing Company, 1985), p. 77. I for my part cannot see how he can think they are sufficiently distinct unless they are really distinct principles of a finite entity; if they are not, then our causal reasoning about them may very well not point towards an extrinsic cause for the *esse* of the thing.

Aquinas does not enter the proof with only a logical distinction—he enters with a real one.[29]

Given that essence and *esse* are really distinct, such that no essence possesses *esse* as a result of its intrinsic nature, it follows that a thing's *esse* is derived from and depends on an extrinsic principle. *Esse* then is caused in essence–*esse* composites such that it is possessed by such things in a derived and dependent way; essence–*esse* composites would not exist without their *esse*, which as being the *esse* of a particular individual thing distinct from its essence is a caused *esse*. Thus, in the present context what is sought is a cause of *esse* of essence–*esse* composites.

In claiming that what is sought is a cause of the *esse* of essence–*esse* composites, the *esse* in question is the participated *esse* possessed by each and every essence–*esse* composite. Recall the metaphysics of participation outlined in the previous chapter: that is, essences participate in their individual *esse* (the collected totality of which is *esse commune*) which as a participated *esse* is itself caused.[30] So what is sought is a cause for the *esse* that essence–*esse* composites possess in a limited and participated fashion. In other words, we are looking for the source in which the individual *esse* of such composites (*esse commune*) participates. This is not to say that in being so dependent the *esse* of essence–*esse* composites is not most basic and fundamental in the thing; for even though it is caused it is yet most basic and fundamental—without *esse* there

29. See Fernand Van Steenberghen, *Le problème de l'existence de Dieu dans les écrits de s. Thomas d'Aquin* (Louvain-la-Neuve: Éditions de l'Institut Supérieur de Philosophie, 1980), pp. 34–42.

30. *De Substantis Separatis*, Cap. 3: 'Omne autem participans aliquid accipit id quod participat ab eo a quo participat, et quantum ad hoc, id a quo participat est causa ipsius . . . '; *Summa Theologiae*, Ia, qu. 44, art. 1, ad. 1: 'Ex hoc quod aliquid per participationem est ens, sequitur quod sit causatum ab alio'. For a discussion of these texts and others wherein the caused character of *esse* is established by means of its participated character and the dependence of that reasoning ultimately on the otherness of essence and *esse*, see Owens, 'The Causal Proposition—Principle or Conclusion', *The Modern Schoolman*, 32 (1955), 257–70.

would be no thing in question. Rather, such *esse*, whilst most basic and fundamental in the thing, is not most basic and fundamental *simpliciter*, and as such is caused.

In considering the cause of *esse*, a certain difficulty must be set aside; yet it is a difficulty that can only be set aside with a full account of God's creative causality. The difficulty is that when it comes to the possession of properties such as the ability to laugh in man or the presence of light in the air, the properties in question are caused to be in and thereby possessed by things that already exist (taking 'thing' here to be general enough as to be applied to any reality in which dependent properties exist, such as the atmosphere in which light exists). Often when considering causal relations, the effect is envisaged as coming to be present in something that already exists, as opposed to coming into being *simpliciter*, such that had it not been caused there would have been nothing. But this is exactly the case with *esse*, since insofar as a thing would not be without *esse*, a thing is not prior to its being caused to have *esse*. And if that is the case, it may be asked: in what was the *esse* caused? It has already been noted in the previous chapter that Aquinas rejects the reality of nonexisting essences: essences do not have any essential being by which they are somewhat real until they receive existential being. Essences without *esse* are mere ideas in the mind of God until God brings them into existence. So what is *esse* received in? The answer is that *esse* is received in nothing. There is nothing there for it to be received in, since without *esse* there is nothing. The causal context of *esse* then, whilst subject to the same analysis as other causal contexts, is nevertheless unlike all other causal contexts, for in no other causal context would it be the case that without the cause there would be nothing *simpliciter*.[31]

---

31. Owens, *An Elementary Christian Metaphysics*, pp. 72–73: 'The type of causality required for being is strikingly different. It is not a question of providing a ground upon which some property logically follows when both are already there in being . . . It is a question of making that basic nature be, when it is not already there in being'.

As indicated, this difficulty will not be fully resolved until an account of God's creative causality is offered, and this will only be forthcoming after a proof of God's existence. Nevertheless, it can be resolved to such an extent to allow us to proceed with the proof of God's existence. Whilst it is true that in no other causal context would it be the case that absent the cause there would be nothing *simpliciter*, whereas with *esse* this is precisely the case, it is also true that in *every* causal context the cause must be in act in the required respect in order to actualise the potentiality of the effect. The potentiality of the effect is often thought to be some part of the effect that pre-existed its actualisation, e.g., the potentiality of matter to undergo a change in quality. But not all potentiality is required to be a part of the effect pre-existing it, for potentiality is designated by a certain standing in relation to actuality, such that something is in potency with respect to a principle of actuality in relation to which it stands. Potency then can be subdivided into an active potency that is present in the cause signifying an ability of the cause to bring something about, and a passive potency present in some subject of the effect signifying an ability of that subject to undergo some change.

With these distinctions in place it can be said that active potency is a potency independent of the effect but not of the cause that brings the effect about, so that once the cause exercises such potency there comes to be an effect that, having been brought about, stands in a relation of (passive) potency to the cause.[32] And this indeed is the relative potency to which *esse* stands as act. In bringing the potentially existing essence into existence, *esse* is not received in some distinct pre-existing essence bringing about a change therein, but actuates the essence whole and complete.[33]

---

32. *Summa Theologiae*, Ia, qu. 25, art. 1, ad. 1: 'Potentia activa non dividitur contra actum, sed fundatur in eo . . . Potentia vero passiva dividitur contra actum'.

33. *In I Sent.*, dist. 42, qu. 1, art. 1, ad. 3: 'Divinum autem agens agit in eo quod dat esse non per motum; unde potentia activa est principium operationis in aliud in effectum productum, non sicut in materiam transmutatum'. The references to divine causality in this quote can be taken as putative and thereby at this stage overlooked in favour of the point that is being made to the effect that in

In other words, the existing essence would not exist without *esse*, and the potentiality of the essence that stands in relation to the *esse* that actuates it simply signifies a possibility of being that could be actual and is indeed actualised through *esse*. The ontological foundation of such possibility is nothing independent of God's ideas, so that when God creates, He brings into existence the essence–*esse* composite all at once. But for now it suffices to proceed with the proof of God by pointing out that when the causal context is that of *esse*, the essence in which *esse* is received and inhabits as principle of act cannot pre-exist the reception of *esse*; what pre-exists the reception of *esse* is the cause of *esse*.[34]

Given the applicability of Aquinas's causal proposition to the case of *esse*, Aquinas has effectively set up a causal regress. Take any essence–*esse* composite you like and inquire after the cause of its *esse*: such a cause is either pure *esse*, that is, something that is not an essence–*esse* composite, in which case the causal proposition is not further applicable, or another essence–*esse* composite; if the latter, then the same again, and so on. Thus, Aquinas begins his proof of God in *De Ente* Cap. 4, by setting up the causal regress in which *esse* is the causal property. Decisive importance, then, will be attached to the next stage of argumentation, to the effect that such a causal regress cannot proceed to infinity, but terminates in a primary cause which is pure *esse* itself.

the context of *esse* causality is not a change in some pre-existing subject capable of undergoing such change, but a bringing of something whole and complete into existence so that the potency for such is not any passive potentiality in the patient but an active potency in the agent (the cause).

34. Owens, *An Elementary Christian Metaphysics*, p. 76: 'The basic dependence of existential act is not upon the subject it actuates. It may inhere *in* that subject, in the sense of actuating it. Nevertheless, it is accepted as prior to it. The substance on which the act of being depends is not the substance that it makes be. It is prior to the substance in which it is found, is presupposed by that substance. It must depend upon another substance. This means that a sensible thing's being is dependent upon something else . . . Accordingly, everything whose being is other than its nature is produced by an efficient cause other than itself'.

Aquinas's causal principle is remarkable not for what it says but for what it does not say. Aquinas does not hold that every existent requires a cause of its existence. This would be quite a global principle. Rather, Aquinas is committed to the very meagre principle that for anything whose essence is other than its *esse*, its *esse* is caused therein: call this a narrow principle. Within the overall strategy of argumentation for God's existence, it would be self-immolative for Aquinas to affirm the global principle, precisely because he wants to argue for God as the cause of all other things but Himself uncaused. If Aquinas were to affirm the global principle in order to get the causal series going, he would have to deny that principle when he affirms the existence of God. By affirming only the narrow principle, Aquinas can consistently hold that essence–*esse* composites require a cause for their *esse*, but that when it comes to the primary cause, which is pure *esse*, and hence not composite, the causal principle does not apply. Thus, Aquinas does not doom his proof to absurdity before he even gets it off the ground.

Furthermore, it must be observed that the causal principle is not for Aquinas co-extensive with contingency. For Aquinas, a contingent being is a corruptible being, whereas a necessary being is incorruptible,[35] but this does not entail that there are no dependent necessary (incorruptible) beings, because for Aquinas angels and the heavenly bodies, whilst incorruptible, are themselves dependent on something else for their *esse*. But in so depending on something else such beings are caused, in which case their *esse* is a participated and thereby caused *esse*. Thus, the argument from the *De Ente* is not an argument from contingency, even though an argument from contingency, such as the

---

35. See Cornelio Fabro, 'Intorno alla Nozione 'Tomista' di Contingenza', *Rivista di Filosofia Neoscolastica*, 30 (1938), 145: 'Nel vocabolario tomista il termine "contingens" . . . non ha l'ampiezza originaria che aveva in Avicenna, ma serve solo . . . ad indicare i corpi corruttibili, ed oggi possiamo dire i corpi in genere'.

third way, might share many of the traits of the argument from the *De Ente*.

Having set forth his causal principle and established that when applied to the case of *esse* a causal regress is inaugurated, it remains to establish that the causal regress is not infinite but has a primary cause; and this is the topic of our next chapter.

5

THE *PER ALIUD* PRINCIPLE AND

INFINITE REGRESS

IN THE PREVIOUS chapter I articulated Aquinas's thought on the causal principle and how he applies it to the case of *esse*, thereby setting up a causal regress. In this chapter I focus on the related issues of the affirmation that what is through another (*per aliud*) is reducible to what is through itself (*per se*) and the denial of an infinite regress, and these as applicable to the causal regress that was explicated in the previous chapter. The truth of these related issues is crucial for Aquinas's whole argument for the existence of God, such that if these were not true, the argument would fail.[1] In addressing these issues, let us first read what Aquinas has to say. He begins by stating what I call the *per aliud* principle:

> Everything that exists through another is reduced to that which exists through itself as to its first cause.[2]

---

1. It is therefore odd that when dealing with the proof of God in *De Ente*, Cap 4, Anthony Kenny in *Aquinas on Being* (Oxford: Oxford University Press, 2002), pp. 40–45 offers no treatment of these crucial stages in the proof.
2. *De Ente*, Cap. 4, p. 377: 137–139: 'Omne quod est per aliud reducitur ad id quod est per se sicut ad causam primam'. See also *De Potentia Dei*, qu. 5, art. 3, where Aquinas articulates a similar principle attributing it to Avicenna: 'Cum enim esse sit praeter essentiam cuiuslibet rei creatae, ipsa natura rei creatae per se considerata, possibilis est ad esse; necessitatem vero essendi non habet nisi ab alio, cuius natura est suum esse, et per consequens est per se necesse esse, et hoc Deus est'.

He then states that there must be a first cause of being from which all being flows, otherwise one would be led into an infinite regress of causes since everything that is not its own *esse* has a cause of its *esse*:

> If this were not so [i.e. if there were no first cause], we would go to infinity in causes, for everything that is not *esse tantum* has a cause of its *esse*, as has been said.[3]

This is quite a tangled web of argumentation that needs straightening. To begin with, what is the order of explanation? Is the *per aliud* principle sufficient to ground the conclusion that there must be a primary cause, whereas the possibility of an infinite regress is simply an unsavoury accompaniment to a denial of the *per aliud* principle? Or is there a more profound connection between the two? Clearly, even on the simple hermeneutical level, this is a decisive stage of argumentation and must be considered carefully. Thus, I begin with the hermeneutical problem concerning the order of explanation, and then I shall go on to defend Aquinas's argumentation.

5.1 THE HERMENEUTICAL PROBLEM

Aquinas's text clearly indicates that if the *per aliud* principle is true, then one can arrive at a primary cause of *esse*. So, establishing the *per aliud* principle ought to be his primary concern. However, Aquinas also states that if the *per aliud* principle were not true, there would be an infinite regress of causes; so how are these two issues related?

Two competing interpretations can be offered. One is that the *per aliud* principle is analytic and distinct from the assertion

---

3. *De Ente*, Cap. 4, p. 377: 141–143: 'Alias iretur in infinitum in causis, cum omnis res que non est esse tantum habeat causam esse sui, ut dictum est'.

of the undesirability of an infinite regress; such is Joseph Bobik's interpretation. He holds that if one can prove God's existence on the basis of the *per aliud* principle alone, then appeal to the undesirability of an infinite regress is irrelevant to the proof; whereas if God's existence can be proved on the basis of the undesirability of an infinite regress, then, in the context of the *De Ente*, God's existence has not been established.[4] What is clear is that Bobik takes the *per aliud* principle to be something distinct from the undesirability of an infinite regress, so much so that to focus on one is to interpret the argument differently than one would by focussing on the other. On this view, the *per aliud* principle can be established analytically, without recourse to the impossibility of an infinite regress.

On the other hand, a differing interpretation is adopted by Wippel, who believes that the critical step is the elimination of the possibility of an infinite regress. He contends that Bobik's attempt at establishing the *per aliud* principle analytically is unsuccessful.[5] Thus for Wippel, one of the truth conditions for the *per aliud* principle is that an infinite regress of causes be eliminated.

As I see it, the *per aliud* principle is independent of the elimination of the possibility of an infinite regress if the truth of the latter is independent of the truth of the former. That is to say, if the *per aliud* principle can be established without appeal to the

4. Joseph Bobik, *Aquinas on Being and Essence: A Translation and Interpretation* (Notre Dame: University of Notre Dame Press, 1965), p. 175: 'Does the argument . . . conclude that God exists because an infinite regress of causes is impossible? . . . Or, does the argument . . . conclude that an infinite regress of caused causes is impossible because God exists [as inferred from the *per aliud* principle]? If the latter alternative is the case, then this concern with an infinite regress appears to be irrelevant to the proof of God's existence. If the former alternative is the case, then it appears that the existence of God has not been established here'.

5. Wippel, *The Metaphysical Thought of Thomas Aquinas*, p. 408: 'The most critical phase in this step in Aquinas's argument is his elimination of the possibility of one's appealing to an infinite regress of caused causes of *esse*'. See p. 409, n. 25 for his rejection of Bobik's attempted defence of the *per aliud* principle.

impossibility of an infinite regress, then the *per aliud* principle is analytic and distinct from the denial of an infinite regress, as Bobik would have it. But this interpretation seems to be undermined by Aquinas's use of the term 'otherwise' [*alias*] in connecting the *per aliud* principle with the undesirability of an infinite regress. The most straightforward interpretation is that if what is *per aliud* is not traced back to what is *per se*, and there is not a being that is *esse* itself from which everything comes, then there would be an infinite regress of causes. The latter reading seems to me to be a clear case of material implication: if the *per aliud* principle does not obtain, then an infinite regress of causes does obtain.

It could be suggested that, in accord with Bobik, the *per aliud* principle can be established analytically, and yet lead to and thereby be connected with a denial of an infinite regress, in which case they would be mutually entailing. However, in that case the onus is on the defender of the *per aliud* principle as analytic to show not only that it is analytic, but that it can be shown to be so irrespective of a consideration of the impossibility of an infinite regress. Bobik defends the analyticity of the principle by arguing that the extrinsic cause of what is *per aliud* is *all* on which it (i.e., what is *per aliud*) depends for its existence, thereby ruling out any essence–*esse* composite as the cause of the *per aliud*, because such a composite would itself depend on another, in which case it would not be all on which the *per aliud* depends for its existence.[6] However, this reasoning seems, implicitly, to presuppose the impossibility of an infinite regress, since it holds that insofar as no essence–*esse* composite can be the cause of *esse* of the *per aliud* there has to be a cause of the *per aliud* that is not itself *per aliud*, but is primary and therefore *per se* in some causal series. But if the impossibility of an infinite regress is implicit in a defence of the *per aliud* principle, then surely that principle is not analytic,

---

6. Bobik, *Aquinas on Being and Essence*, pp. 177–78.

but its truth depends on the impossibility of an infinite regress, in which case the one does not just lead to the other, rather the truth or falsity of one is bound up with the truth or falsity of the other.

In order to untangle the philosophical nature of the *per aliud* principle and its relationship to the undesirability of an infinite regress, I shall use symbolic form. Consider the following bi-conditional: P ↔ −Q, where 'P' stands for the *per aliud* principle and 'Q' stands for an infinite regress of causes. Let us take one half of the bi-conditional: P → −Q, further, let us negate the consequent and assume that an infinite regress does obtain. By *modus tollens* then the negation of the antecedent can be inferred, in which case there is obtained the negation of the *per aliud* principle (−P). Thus, if an infinite regress does indeed obtain, then the *per aliud* principle does not obtain. But if the *per aliud* principle does not obtain, then Aquinas has no means for establishing the existence of God, because the *per aliud* principle is instrumental in establishing God's existence. Thus, it would seem that the truth of the *per aliud* principle is bound up with the truth of the impossibility of an infinite regress, as the bi-conditional shows. If an infinite regress of causes can be shown to be a real impossibility, then the *per aliud* principle can be seen to be established. Thus, I take it that the real impossibility of an infinite regress of causes brings about an affirmation of the principle that what is *per aliud* can be traced back to what is *per se*. Given that he does not actually argue against the possibility of an infinite regress in the *De Ente*, but such an impossibility is itself bound up with the truth of the *per aliud* principle, I see it as valid to read into Aquinas's thinking in the *De Ente* his later argumentation against the possibility of an infinite causal series.

Before doing so, however, it will be helpful to bear in mind some of the philosophical undercurrents of the *per aliud* principle. With regard to this principle, Aquinas's thought will become clear by recalling his distinction between properties a thing displays as a result of the principles of its nature and those it displays as the result of an extrinsic principle. No essence–*esse* composite exists in virtue of the principles of its nature, since the *esse* of all such composites is something other than the nature. Thus, every essence–*esse* composite depends on some extrinsic principle for its existence, in which case every such composite exists *per aliud*. Now, Aquinas's reasoning in stating the *per aliud* principle is that no being whose *esse* is the result of some extrinsic principle, that is, no being that is *per aliud*, can sufficiently account for the existence of another being of which it is the cause. If essence–*esse* composites were solely to account for other essence–*esse* composites, then no real account of *esse* would be offered. What is at issue here is the origination of *esse*. To endorse a closed chain (finite or infinite) of essence–*esse* composites causing other essence–*esse* composites is to envisage *esse* as something to be passed amongst finite entities, with no real explanation for the actual origination of *esse* within that system. Thus, unless there exists some being that exists *per se*, the origination of *esse* in a chain of composites itself remains unexplained and quite mysterious.[7] And the existence of a being that exists *per se* is affirmed through a denial of an infinite regress of essence–*esse* composites causing other such composites.

5.2 THE INFINITE REGRESS

Whilst the foregoing clears up the interpretation of this part of the argument, it in no way indicates why Aquinas thinks an infinite regress of causes of *esse* is unacceptable. There is a suggestion that such is unacceptable insofar as it was the existence of things

---

7. I see here an implicit recognition by Aquinas of the need to account for the being of beings as beings; see Lawrence Dewan's discussion of Aquinas's recognition of such in his (Aquinas's) argumentation against infinite causal regression and for further references to the same in the writings of Aquinas in 'St. Thomas and Infinite Causal Regress', in *Idealism, Metaphysics, and Community*, ed. by William Sweet (Aldershot: Ashgate, 2001), p. 122 (p. 127, n. 28 for references to Aquinas).

having *esse* but not being pure *esse* that motivated the regress in the first place; if there is not something that is *per se*, i.e., something that is not one of the things motivating the causal regress, then the causal regress remains motivated and the existence of essence–*esse* composites remains unexplained. Thus, an infinite regress of causes of *esse* must be denied.

Whilst the latter might have some intuitive appeal, it is not a metaphysically tight argument against a regress. Therefore an argument against such a regress is required, but unfortunately, Aquinas did not offer any such argumentation in the *De Ente* itself. As it stands, this is a major lacuna in the argument from the *De Ente* and perhaps represents Aquinas's context and motivations for writing the *De Ente*. Nevertheless, this gap can be closed through appeal to argumentation offered by Aquinas elsewhere, so that whilst the historical argument in the *De Ente* remains inconclusive without the argumentation against an infinite regress, by 'fixing' it as it were with later argumentation, the argument from the *De Ente* can be set forth as a conclusive argument for God.

The denial of an infinite regress of causes in a proof of God, whilst significant in itself, calls upon some quite profound and fundamental metaphysical views on the nature of causal series. In order to draw out the complexity of the issues involved, consider the following. Imagine a beginningless series whose members are such that at some point they pass away so that earlier members in the series successively give way to later members. Such a series is without a beginning and could potentially stretch to infinity in the future, but such an infinity will never be actual, since the earlier members of the series will pass away at some point, with later members coming in to replace them. Thus, the series is actually finite but potentially infinite, that is, it is without a beginning and can go on and on. So one issue that must be dealt with in regard to infinite causal series is whether or not the infinity in question is a potential or actual infinity.

Now imagine a series of fathers producing sons, and imagine that such a series has no beginning, with fathers continually generating and being generated, so that as the earlier fathers pass away the children themselves become parents and soon pass away and so on and so on. Potentially this could be an infinite series, and since every member of the series has a cause of its existence in its own parents, there is no conceptual absurdity in positing an infinite such series. In the Middles Ages, such a series was known as a *per accidens* series.

On the other hand, imagine a series in which a fire heats a pot which heats the contents of the pot. The heat in the series is caused by the fire and is such that to remove the fire as the cause of heat without providing a suitable alternative would also be to remove the ability of the pot to heat its contents; in other words the first cause in this series is the cause of the causality of the pot (whereas in the fathers–sons series the fathers *qua* fathers were not the causes of the causality of the children—it is not in virtue of his father that a son is himself a father but in virtue of his own biology and finding of a suitable mate). It seems that in this series at least, with regard to heat as a causal property, one must stop upon some primary cause of heat. In the Middle Ages, such a series was known as a *per se* series, and the logic of this series was such that it was taken to be necessarily finite, and was thus often utilised in proofs for God's existence.[8] So another issue to be dealt with is the type of causal series at work in the proof of God.

8. Even though in the per se series the fire is uncaused with regard to heat, this is not to say that there is no cause of the fire, since the fire itself may be caused in some other respect, for example it may have a cause of combustion, e.g., oxygen in the air, but is not itself caused in respect of causing heat, because the generating of heat is just one of those things that fire does of itself. So even granting that the per se series has a primary cause, it must be considered whether or not that cause is absolutely uncaused, given that as Paul Edwards has pointed out, it is one thing to show that a cause is primary and another thing to show that it is uncaused. See Paul Edwards, 'The Cosmological Argument', in *Philosophy of Religion: A Guide and Anthology*, ed. by Brian Davies (Oxford: Oxford University Press, 2000), pp. 202–13, note in particular p. 203 *et seq* for this particular objection. What the defender of a proof for God

In what follows I shall: (i) articulate Aquinas's thought on infinity and causal series, (ii) offer a model of Aquinas's *per se* series that draws out the logic of such a series indicating its necessary finitude, and (iii) apply that series to the case of causes of *esse* thereby showing that there is a primary cause of *esse* in which case the *per aliud* principle will be established and a cause of *esse* which is *esse tantum* is affirmed; as a corollary to the latter I shall argue that a primary cause of *esse* is both primary and absolutely uncaused, thereby dealing with Edwards's objection.

5.2.1 Aquinas on Infinity and Causal Series

In the *De Veritate* (1256–1259), qu. 2, art. 10, Aquinas makes several distinctions pertinent to his analysis of infinity, and the position that he elucidates therein, aside from a certain reluctance to commit himself on the issue of an actual *per accidens* infinity, is one that he held for the rest of his career. Therefore, it shall be my template in the following discussion with amendments in later works alluded to in the footnotes.

He begins by stating that there is a twofold distinction to be taken into account when analysing infinity: (i) the distinction between (i.i) an actual infinity and (i.ii) a potential infinity; (ii) the distinction between (ii.i) a *per se* infinity and (ii.ii) a *per accidens* infinity (the same distinctions were made above in the introductory remarks to this section).

Aquinas tells us that a potential infinity is one that consists in universal (*semper*) succession such that one member can always be taken after another to the effect that the series so construed is subject to infinity. Aquinas offers the examples of generation, time, and the division of a continuum.[9] There is thus a certain

wants to establish is both (i) that there is a primary cause of existence and (ii) that the latter is caused in no respect.

9. In his commentary on Aristotle's *Metaphysics*, Bk. 11, lect. 10, he states that (i) number, (ii) magnitude, and (iii) time are potentially infinite because they can be (i) constantly added to, (ii) constantly divided, or (iii) a mixture of both.

successiveness, whether that of addition or division, that is characteristic of the potential infinity.[10] An actual infinity, on the other hand, has nothing to terminate it, and in this respect he offers the example of a line without ends.

Having distinguished between the potential and the actual infinite, Aquinas then distinguishes between the *per se* and the *per accidens* infinite. In order to draw out this distinction, he explains the nature of infinity somewhat. The *ratio* of the infinite is congruent with that of quantity, and quantity is primarily used in reference to discrete quantities rather than continuous quantities; that is to say, quantity is primarily characterised by discrete items that can be enumerated, rather than some continuous item that can be measured and thereby quantified. Given the latter, the metaphysics of the *per se* and *per accidens* infinity can be explicated through understanding how multiplicity is sometimes *per se* and sometimes *per accidens*.

A *per se* multiplicity is required when there are causes and effects ordered to one another such that the one has an essential dependency on another. Aquinas proceeds to offer probably his favourite example of such a series: the soul animates the body which moves the hand which moves the stick which moves the stone.[11] Aquinas tells us that in this series, the posterior members have a *per se* dependency on the prior—that is to say that if

10. See also the following for the affirmation that a potential infinity involves succession or division: *In II Sent.*, dist. 1, qu. 1, art. 5, ad. s.c. 3: 'Ad tertium dicendum, quod infinitum actu impossibile est; sed infinitum esse per successionem, non est impossibile. Infiniti autem sic considerati quodlibet acceptum finitum est: transiens autem non potest intelligi nisi ex aliquo determinato ad aliquod determinatum'; *Summa Theologiae* Ia, qu. 7, art. 4: 'Esse multitudinem infinitam in potentia, possibile est. Quia augmentum multitudinis consequitur divisionem magnitudinis, quanto enim aliquid plus dividitur, tanto plura secundum numerum resultant'.

11. I have adapted this somewhat, though my adaptation is not at odds with Aquinas's actual example, which is: the soul moves the natural heat which moves the nerves and the muscles which move the hands which move the stick which moves the stone.

some prior member of the series were removed and not replaced, the causal efficacy of the series itself would be removed; and ultimately, if the primary member of the series were removed, the whole series would be lost. What I take to be significant about this series is that the causality of the posterior causal relata is not something that they possess of themselves but in virtue of some prior cause (the soul in this case) which not only actuates the posterior causal relata but also allows them to participate in its own activity; in this case the soul not only brings about the motion of the body, hand, stick, and stone, but also in virtue of the body, hand, and stick's participation in its own causality the soul can be said to cause the movement of the stone primarily, whereas the body, hand, and stick cause the motion of the stone in a secondary sense.

A *per accidens* multiplicity is found when all things contained in the multitude are placed as if in one position, with no proper relation to one another. It matters not in such a multiplicity whether there are many or few, more or less. Aquinas gives the example of a builder building a house, who successively goes through many saws. The number of saws used in the building of the house is unimportant, and indeed, the replacement saws are not properly related to their predecessors. The multiplicity of saws is accidental to the building of the house—what is essential is the work of the builder and his use of the saw (any saw). Hence, the successive saws have no dependency on one another, and this is juxtaposed to the *per se* causal series wherein the posterior members of the series do indeed depend on the prior members thereof. The hand is not related to the stick in the same way that the first saw is related to its replacement saw when the first is worn out. There is no proper causal relation between the first and second saw, merely succession, hence such a series of causes is an accidental series.

Having made these clarifications, Aquinas puts them together in accord with what previous philosophers hold. He begins with the ancient philosophers, and he claims that some of them believe that there could be an actual infinity of both the *per se* and the *per accidens* series. Thus, the ancient philosophers are committed to the following:

Infinity:	In act
Per se	✓
Per accidens	✓

Others hold that a *per se* infinity is impossible both in act and in potency, but a *per accidens* infinity is not only possible but actual. Aquinas claims that this is the position of Algazel and Avicenna.[12] They hold to the impossibility of an actual *per se* infinity, because in a *per se* series the effects have a dependence on their causes, in which case if the series were infinite, the ultimate effect would be dependent on an infinite chain of causes; and since an infinity cannot be traversed, the being of such an effect would never be explained. However, they believe in an actual *per accidens* infinity, because in such an infinity there is no dependency amongst the multitude, in which case an actual infinity need not be traversed in order to sustain the being of one of the multitude. The example used in this respect is the immortal souls of men in an eternal universe. Assuming that men's souls are immortal and the universe eternal, there is an infinity of immortal human souls, but they are not dependent on each other as causes and effects are in a *per se* series. Thus, there is an infinity of immortal souls accidentally related, in which case there is an actual *per accidens* infinity.[13] Algazel and Avicenna, according to Aquinas, thus believe in the following:

12. He only mentions Algazel in *De Veritate*, but in *Summa Theologiae*, Ia, qu. 7, art. 4 and in *Summa Contra Gentiles*, Lib. 2, Cap. 80, he mentions Avicenna.

13. The most succinct presentation of this reasoning is in *Summa Contra Gentiles*, Lib 2, Cap. 80: 'Quidam vero, omnia praedicta vitantes, dixerunt non esse inconveniens animas separatas actu existere infinitas. Esse enim infinitum actu in his quae non habent ad invicem ordinem, est esse infinitum per

Infinity:	In act	In potency
Per se	X	X
Per accidens	✓	✓

Finally, Aquinas tells us that some thinkers hold that there cannot be an actual infinite, whether *per se* or *per accidens*. There can only be a potential infinite that consists in succession; this was the position of Averroës and Aristotle.[14] Thus, Averroës and Aristotle held the following:

Infinity:	In act	In potency
Per se	X	X
Per accidens	X	✓

At the end of this article, Aquinas is unclear as to his own position on the matter. He notes that an infinity can be impossible for two reasons, either (i) because the infinite *qua* infinite is impossible or (ii) because of something else prohibiting its actuality, as when a lead triangle cannot be lifted, not because

accidens: quod ponere non reputant inconveniens. Et est positio Avicennae et Algazelis.' Aquinas is not immediately critical of this position in the *Summa Contra Gentiles* nor in the *De Veritate*, however in the *Summa Theologae* Ia, qu. 7, art. 4, he holds that an actual *per accidens* infinity is impossible arguing that every multitude is contained within some species of multitude, and that a species of multitude is such according to a certain species of number. But no species of number is actually infinite, because every number is a multitude measurable by the unit. But the actually infinite is what is not measurable, since it has no ends, in which case number is only potentially infinite.

14. It is notable that Aquinas holds that the potential infinite is characterised here as consisting in succession. Above when discussing the *per accidens* series,

it is a triangle, but because it is lead. Aquinas concludes that an infinite in act is impossible if it is repugnant to the very nature of the infinite to be in act, but it is not impossible if there is simply some other reason preventing it from being in act. But at least in this instance Aquinas offers us nothing further on whether or not it is repugnant to the very nature of infinity to be in act.[15]

It is not my goal here to settle the vexed issue of whether or not Aquinas believes there could be an actual *per accidens* infinity. Certainly he always denies the possibility of an actual *per se* infinity, but he is less sure regarding the possibility of an actual *per accidens* infinity. Whilst it was the strategy of later thinkers first to establish that an actual infinite is impossible and then to apply that reasoning to some causal series in order to establish that there is a primary cause which we call God, this is not Aquinas's strategy.[16] Aquinas does not move from a prior commitment to the impossibility of an actual infinite causal series to the necessity of there being a primary cause of that series; rather he focuses on the causality of that series itself and thence infers the necessity for a primary cause. Thus,

it was noted that the multitude in that series were successive. Now, when stating that these thinkers believe in a potential infinite, they do so because it consists in successiveness of its members. Though he is not explicit about it, I take Aquinas to mean that the potential infinite is to be correlated with the *per accidens* series, and this because the multiplicity involved in both is one of successiveness.

15. Despite his reticence in the *De Veritate*, in *Quodlibet* 9, qu. 1, he produces the same schema of opinions as above, but this time he tells us that the opinion of Averroës, to the effect that it is repugnant to the infinite to be in act, is the more true.

16. I have in mind John Duns Scotus and William of Ockham. Both outlined the logic of per se causal series, denied that they could be actually infinite, and thence inferred the existence of God, with Scotus focussing on efficient causality and Ockham on conserving causality; see Scotus, *Opera Omnia* Vol. II (Civitas Vaticana: Typis Polyglottis Vaticanis, 1950), *Ordinatio* I, dist. 2, pars. 1, qu. 2, nn. 48–54, and Ockham, *Opera Theologica* Vol. II (New York: St Bonaventure, 1970), *In I Sent.*, dist. 2, qu. 10, 342:17–354:14 [Contra Opinonem Scoti], and 354:15–357:9 [Responsio Auctoris].

in what follows I shall consider his thought on the nature of the causality involved in the *per se* and the *per accidens* series, and leave the issue of the actual *per accidens* infinity to further scholarly discussion.

5.2.2 The Causality of the Causal Series

Something of the metaphysics behind the two different kinds of causal series has already been highlighted. The *per accidens* series is one characterised by succession or division, such that there is no essential dependency amongst the members of the series, rather simply succession. Thus, in the fathers-sons series, whilst a father is necessary for the existence of the son, the father is not necessary for the causality that the son is able to wield to bring about his own son, thereby continuing the series. Thus, the causality of the father is not essential to the succession of the series, only to the generation of the son. On the other hand, in a *per se* causal series, the causality of the later members of the series is essentially related to some prior member, because in such a series there is some cause without which the causality of the series would not begin, such as the fire heating the pot which heats its contents or the mind moving the hand which moves the stick which moves the stone. Thus, the succeeding members of the series would be causally inefficacious without the causal influence of some prior cause in the series.

So what seems to be essential to the *per accidens* series is that the causal relation in the series obtains between a single cause and a single effect (father-son); causal transitivity does not pass from a single cause to a multitude of effects (mind-hand-stick-stone). Thus a *per accidens* series is a one-one causal series, since causal transitivity passes from one cause to one effect. On the other hand, in the *per se* series the very opposite is the case: causal transitivity passes from a single cause to a multitude of effects, and it is in virtue of such causal transitivity that the effects can themselves act as (secondary/intermediate) causes for an ultimate end, as in the mind-hand-stick-stone series. Therefore, the *per se* series is a one–many series, since causal transitivity passes from one cause to a multitude of effects. In constructing a model for these distinct causal series, I shall take as my guiding theme the one-one and one-many relations that characterise the *per accidens* and *per se* series respectively.[17]

Taking the examples already mentioned, the series can be modelled as follows:

(i)   One-one: A son (z) is begotten by his father (y) who is begotten by his father (x) who is begotten by his father (w) and so on. Hence (. . .)→(w→x)→(x→y)→(y→z).

(ii)   One-many: The stone is moved by a stick which is moved by the hand which is moved by the mind. Hence: (w→(x→(y→z))).

Notice that in (i) each father–son relationship is a closed causal unit, capable of generating the prior member of the succeeding causal unit, but nevertheless a unit enclosed within itself. Take for instance w; w is the father of x and thus his immediate causal activity as father of x is discharged in relation to x; w is also the grandfather of y, but not the cause of y, since x, as y's father, is the cause of y. Thus, the causal activity of w is related immediately to x and only mediately or derivatively to y, in which case w and x (as father and son) can be understood in isolation from y. In simpler terms, w can father x, and having done so cease to exist without thereby impugning the ability of x to go on to father y. In the latter sense, the causal duty of w does not interfere with the causal duty of x in relation to y, in which case the causal relationship of w and x as father and son is captured in a one-one causal relation.

---

17. I first put forth this model of the different causal series in 'Essentially Ordered Series Reconsidered', *American Catholic Philosophical Quarterly*, 86 (2012), 541–55.

In (ii) the case is a little different. The causal activity of y with regard to z cannot be isolated from the more encompassing causal activity of x, which in turn cannot be isolated from the even more encompassing causal activity of w. Thus, in the example, we cannot isolate the stick's moving the stone from the movement of the hand, which in turn we cannot understand in isolation from the mind. The series of causes that go to produce the overall effect, z, act as one so as to produce z. What is fundamental then to the one-many relationship is that there is some prior cause that accounts for the causal activity of the posterior causes in question and naturally terminates the series. So, in the example, the stone does not move without the movement of the stick, which in turn does not move without that of the hand, which in turn does not move without the urging of the mind. But here there is a natural stop; for assuming the absence of psychological coercion, the mind is capable of inducing motion to its members without thereby being induced itself.

The example can be modified somewhat to the case of Dr Smith on the golf course. Dr Smith induces motion to his arms which swing the club which moves the ball, and all this for no other reason than sheer indulgence. It seems that in this scenario there is a natural stop: 'Why did you go to the golf course Dr Smith? Because I just wanted to knock balls about'. Now, of course, one could inquire after Dr Smith's desire to knock balls about. Perhaps he wanted to improve his swing because he works in a department whose dean is an avid golfer whom he wants to impress. Such considerations would be inquiries into Dr Smith's desires, and whilst relevant to why he chose to start knocking balls about the golf course, the knocking of the balls about the course can be explained without recourse to Dr Smith's motivating desire to impress the dean; but they cannot be explained without Dr Smith himself and his swinging of the clubs.

Given the dependence of posterior causes on some prior cause in a one-many relation, the causal transitivity in such a series moves down a descending scale (or conversely, up an ascending scale) of generality. Thus, the mind can move more than just the hand, the hand can move more than just the stick, and the stick can move more than just the stone.[18] Given the latter, one cannot remove any of the prior causes of the particular series and yet hope to sustain the effect. Thus, in the series in question, the stone cannot move without the stick, which itself cannot move without the hand, which itself cannot move without the mind.

I submit that the one-many causal relation cannot be cashed out in terms of isolatable causal units interacting with each other, as in the one–one relation; for one cannot understand the motion of the stone without that of the stick, nor the motion of the stick without that of the hand, and so forth. But one can understand the father-son relation between y and z without appealing to the relation of x to y and in turn w to x. Whilst the previous members of the series may be relevant to the presence of y and thereby z in the series (like Dr Smith's desires in the above example), the causal relation between y and z can be understood without appeal to the previous members (just like Dr Smith's desires), whereas the same cannot be said for the stick's moving the stone; for in order to understand the stick's moving a stone, one must inquire after the movement of the stick, whereas in order to understand a father begetting a son, one need not inquire after the grandfather's begetting the father.

Furthermore, in the one-one relation, it was noted that a prior cause in some distinct causal unit can discharge its causal duty and thence cease to exist without thereby its effect ceasing to exist. So, w can father x and thence cease to exist without

---

18. The same sentiment is expressed by Aquinas when discussing the priority of efficient causes, amongst which, as is clear from the *secunda via*, there is an order; so he writes *In Librum de Causis Expositio* (Turin: Marietti, 1972), prop. 1, n. 34: 'Manifestum est enim quod, quanto aliqua causa efficiens est prior, tanto eius virtus ad plura se extendit; unde oportet ut proprius effectus eius communior sit. Causae vero secundae proprius effectus in paucioribus invenitur; unde et particularior est. Ipsa enim causa prima producit vel movet causam secundo agentem, et sic fit ei causa ut agat'.

x's ceasing to exist, and also without preventing x's going on to father y. In the one-many relation the case is wholly different. Should the stick begin to move and then all of a sudden cease to move, say just before hitting the stone, then the stone would not move. Similarly, should the mind urge the hand to move the stick, and in the act of doing so suffer some irreparable damage such that it can no longer urge the hand to move, then the motion of the series would be lost. In other words, in a one-many relation, not only do the posterior causes depend on some prior cause for some causal characteristic (motion in this example), that causal characteristic is itself sustained in the series by the presence thereto of the prior cause.

The one-many series is not a successive series, but rather a single action constituted by a number of causal relata related as outlined above. Thus, the mind's movement of the hand is not a single event, nor is the hand's movement of the stick, nor the stick's movement of the stone. Rather, the single event is the mind's movement of the stone by means of the hand and the stick. On the other hand, the one-one series is a series of successive acts: namely, acts of procreation in the fathers-sons series.

Given the participation of the posterior causal relata in the efficacy of the primary cause in the *per se* series, the primary cause both causes and sustains the members of that series, such that without the presence of the primary cause to the members of the series (the hand-stick-stone in our example) those members would be causally inefficacious. On the other hand, in the one-one series, the cause simply causes and does not sustain, since its causality is exercised and terminated in a single act. Thus, in the example, the father procreates and thus causes his son, but *qua* biological father, as opposed to guardian, he does not sustain his son in existence.

I think that the foregoing model of the distinct causal series has thus far honoured the metaphysics of those series as Aquinas depicts them. Furthermore, insofar as they model typical and uncontroversial types of causal series (assuming of course the correctness of Aquinas's causal realism), they model real features of the world.[19] Let us now consider the infinity of such causal series, bearing in mind the clarifications that Aquinas has made with regard to infinity.

In the one-one series it was pointed out that the causality exercised in the series is exercised and terminated in a single cause and effect, so that there is a succession of distinct causal acts being constantly added. In such a series, every effect has a sufficient explanation if an immediate cause of its existence can be located, e.g. the cause of the son in his father, and the father, being in turn somebody's son, himself caused by his father. Furthermore, the cause in such a series can exercise its causal role and cease to be without its effect thereby ceasing to be. Thus, fathers can cease to be without their sons ceasing to be (though of course other factors accidental to the fatherhood of the father can affect the survival of the son). It follows then that there is no conceptual absurdity involved in a beginningless one-one series, that is, a series without a terminus *post quem*, because in such a series: (i) every effect would have a cause, and (ii) previous causes can pass away successively giving way to current causes, in which case an infinity of causes and effects need not be traversed to get to the present.[20] A one-one series, such as fathers begetting sons, can thus be potentially infinite, but this does not entail its actual infinity, since previous causes can give way to present causes in which case there is actually a finite series without a beginning and going on indefinitely into the future, in which case whilst finite it is potentially infinite.

---

19. I think that insofar as Kenny fails to consider the fact that the distinction between the causal series is one derived from the metaphysics of causality inherent in each of them, he is led to the absurd conclusion that the distinction between the series is based on medieval astrology. See Anthony Kenny, *The Five Ways* (London: Routledge & Kegan Paul, 1969), pp. 41–44.
20. David Hume, *Dialogues Concerning Natural Religion*, ed. by R. Popkin (Cambridge: Hackett, 1985), Part 9, p. 56: 'Did I show you the particular causes of each individual in a collection of twenty particles of matter, I should think it very unreasonable should you afterwards ask me what was the cause of the whole twenty. This is sufficiently explained in explaining the cause of the parts'.

In the one-many relation, the posterior causal *relata* depend on some prior cause for their ability to act. Thus, in (ii), the hand, stick, and stone all depend on the causal efficacy originated and preserved in the series by the mind; remove the mind's causal activity and you remove the efficacy of the series. Now let us explore a causal regress of such a series and ascertain whether or not it can go to infinity. It is not difficult to add to the symbolic formulation of the one-many series and cash it out accordingly; any number of further antecedent causes can be added and suitably interpreted as applying to real causal processes. Thus, the symbolic formulation of the series will be (n . . . $\rightarrow(w\rightarrow(x\rightarrow(y\rightarrow z)))$ . . .), where n stands for however many previous causes it takes to get to w. The question then is whether or not n is finite or infinite.

One peculiar aspect of the one-many relation is that, unlike the one-one relation, it cannot be broken up into basic units of causal relation; $y\rightarrow z$ (the stick's moving the stone) cannot be understood in isolation from $x\rightarrow(y\rightarrow z)$ (the hand's moving the stick which thereby moves the stone), and so on. The bracketing in the symbolic formulation captures this aspect. Thus, as noted, in the one-many series there is a cause on whose causal activity depends the activity of the subsequent causes: remove that cause, and you remove the activity of the posterior causes. In an infinite series of causes there is no primary cause, because if there were, it would *ipso facto* be a finite series. This is because a finite series is necessarily a series that has an origin out of which (*ex quo*) it proceeds, in which case an infinite series is precisely a series without such an origin.[21] Hence, an infinite series has no primary cause. So considering a supposed infinite one-many series, there will be no primary cause in such a series. But if this is so, then the causes in the series will have no

---

21. This does not entail that finite series cannot go indefinitely forward, only that there is a terminus *ex quo*, that is, a point from which the causal activity of the series originates.

causal efficacy, because, as has been noted, causal efficacy in the one-many series is originated and preserved therein by a primary cause. Therefore, to deny a primary cause of the one-many series (i.e., to affirm the possibility of an infinite such series), is precisely to remove the causal efficacy of the causes within the series, which is in effect to deny the causal series itself. So the believer in an infinite one-many series has to face the following contradiction: (i) in a one-many series the causes are causally inefficacious without some primary cause on which the causal efficacy of the series depends and which naturally terminates the series, and (ii) in an infinite series there is no primary, naturally terminating cause, in which case there is no cause for the causal efficacy of the series. Thus, a believer in an infinite one-many series denies any causal efficacy to that series, in which case he or she denies the possibility of that series precisely as a causal series. The one-many series is thus finite, otherwise it is not a one-many series. *Per se* causal series then are necessarily finite series.

5.2.3 Cause of *Esse*

The necessary finitude of the one-many series may be uncontroversial when it comes to such straightforward series as the mind-hand-stick-stone or the fire-pot-contents, because in both series there is a natural stop at the mind or fire as the primary causes of the causality of the series. However, such primary causes are only conditionally primary, that is, they are primary with regard to that series of which they are the causes of causality, but secondary in regard to some other series in which they depend on another for their causality. Thus, even granting the necessary finitude of the one-many series, the case is not easily made for the theist to infer the existence of some primary *uncaused* cause, because, as Edwards has argued, something's being a primary cause does not entail that it is uncaused. Or as I have put it, something's being a primary cause with respect to some one-many series does not entail that it is uncaused with respect to any other series.[22] Thus, the theist needs to make the argument that there is some primary cause that is not conditionally primary but absolutely primary—and at this point I shall return to the *De Ente* argumentation.

The argument in the *De Ente* focussed on the *esse* possessed by essence-*esse* composites and inaugurated a causal series by taking *esse* as the causal property of that series, holding that *esse* is caused in all such series. Aquinas denies that there can be an infinite series of causes of *esse* and thereby affirms the principle that what is through another (*per aliud*) is reducible to what is *per se*. Thus, essence-*esse* composites exist through another, i.e. each such composite's *esse* is caused, and so, if the *per aliud* principle is correct, the cause of its *esse* is something that is *per se*, that is *esse tantum*. So in what follows the following need to be established: (i) that *esse* is a causal property of a *per se* causal series which, as necessarily finite, has a primary cause of that series; and (ii) that *esse* is a causal property leading to a primary cause that is *esse tantum*, a cause that is not conditionally primary, but rather is absolutely primary.

Let us begin by ascertaining whether or not *esse* as a causal property is locatable in a *per se* or *per accidens* series. When *esse*

22. Paul Edwards, 'The Cosmological Argument' p. 203: 'Aquinas has failed to distinguish between the two statements: (1) A did not exist, and (2) A is not uncaused. To say that the series is infinite implies (2), but it does not imply (1) . . . [T]he believer in the infinite series is not "taking A away". He is taking away the privileged status of A; he is taking away its "first causeness". He does not deny the existence of A or of any particular member of the series. He denies that A or anything else is the first member of the series. Since he is not taking A away, he is not taking B away, and thus he is also not taking X, Y, or Z away. His view, then, does not commit him to the absurdity that nothing exists now'. Interestingly, Aquinas himself recognizes the principle behind Edwards's objection: that within some domain there can be a first cause without its being absolutely first, i.e. uncaused in itself, see *Summa Theologiae*, IaIIae, qu. 6, art. 1, ad. 1: 'Sed tamen sciendum quod contingit aliquod principium motus esse primum in genere, quod tamen non est primum simpliciter sicut in genere alterabilium primum alterans est corpus caeleste, quod tamen non est primum movens simpliciter, sed movetur motu locali a superiori movente'.

is referred to as a causal property, what is meant is the *esse* that essence–*esse* composites possess, but not of themselves, in which case *esse* is caused in such composites. Now if *esse* were a causal property in a *per accidens* series, a single cause would be the cause of a single effect with regard to *esse*; thus a single cause would bring about the *esse* of a single effect. This appears promising, for when one takes the paradigmatic case of things coming into existence one thinks of parental generation, and it is such generation that has figured prominently in the explication of the *per accidens* series above. However another factor of the one-one series must be borne in mind, and that is to the effect that in the one-one series the cause can discharge its causal duty and cease to be without its effect ceasing to be. Now the latter cannot be the case for the cause of *esse* in essence-*esse* composites. Such composites do not exist of themselves, but in virtue of a distinct act of existence (*esse*) that is caused therein. Given that such composites do not possess *esse* essentially, it must be caused in them, they participate in it, for as long as they have *esse*; that being the case, *esse* is not a causal property locatable in a one-one series, since in the latter series the cause of the effect can cease to be without its effect ceasing to be—that is, the being of the effect can outlast its cause, whereas with *esse*, the being of the effect (the essence/*esse* composite) cannot outlast its cause (of *esse*), since if its cause of *esse* were to cease, then its effect, the *esse* of the essence-*esse* composite, would itself cease, in which case, given that the *esse* of the composite is its cause of existence, the entire composite itself would cease. It follows then that *esse* is not a causal property locatable in a one-one series.

The fact that *esse* is not only caused but also sustained in essence-*esse* composites entails that it is a causal property located in a one-many, that is, *per se* series, because in such a series, the posterior causal relata possess the causal characteristic of the series for as long as they are caused to do so by some prior cause; that is, the prior cause in the series both causes and sustains in one and the same act of causing. Thus, *esse* as a property caused in essence-*esse* composites is caused in a series of such composites by some prior cause that itself causes and sustains *esse*. If such a series were to lack a *terminus post quem*, that is, if it were to be an infinite series lacking a primary cause, not only would there be no cause of *esse* in the series, but there would be no subsequent causal relata, since as is evident from the logic of the one-many series, the causal relata in such a series only have causal efficacy in virtue of some primary cause. Given that in the case of *esse*, the causal property is that whereby something is said to exist, if there were no primary cause of *esse*, nothing would exist. But this is absurd, in which case there is a primary cause of *esse*. Not only that, the primary cause of *esse* is not caused in respect of *esse*, because, as is evident from the logic of the one-many series, the primary cause of that series from which the causality of that series is derived is uncaused in respect of the causality of the series.

So given that *esse* is a causal property locatable in a one-many causal series and that in such a series, given the causal dependency of the posterior causal relata, there must be some primary cause of the causality of the series, otherwise the posterior causal relata would not emerge as causal relata in that series, there is a primary cause of *esse*. The latter, as the cause of the causality of the series, cannot be an essence-*esse* composite for two reasons: (i) as is clear from the previous chapter, all essence/*esse* composites are caused in respect of their *esse*, whereas the primary cause of *esse* is not caused in respect of *esse* (whether it is caused in some other respect remains to be seen); and (ii) as the cause of the causality of the series, the primary cause of *esse* does not have its causality caused, given that the cause of the causality of the one-many series is necessarily a type of thing capable of causing the causality of the series in virtue of what it is, e.g., the mind with regard to motion or the fire with regard to heat, but the causality of the series in question is that of *esse*, in which case the primary cause of *esse* is capable of causing *esse* in virtue of what it is, and not through another (*per aliud*). If the primary cause of *esse* is capable of causing *esse* in virtue of what it is, it is capable of causing *esse* through itself (*per se*), in which case those whose *esse* it causes have their *esse* through another (*per aliud*), and because in the one-many series the posterior causal relata have their causality through the primary cause of that series and are thus reducible thereto, with regard to *esse*, that which possesses *esse* through another (*per aliud*) is reducible to that which possesses *esse* through itself (*per se*); hence what is *per aliud* is reducible to what is *per se*, and the *per aliud* principle is established.

Aquinas's initial move from a consideration of essence-*esse* composites to a primary cause of *esse* from which all such composites receive *esse* is thus legitimated. Causing *esse* through itself, such a cause of *esse* is not an essence-*esse* composite, but is simply *esse* itself or *esse tantum*. Thus, the primary cause of *esse* is *esse tantum*, and this is what we understand God to be. But here Edwards's objection emerges with full force. Granted that there is a primary cause of *esse*, all that has been established is that there is a primary cause relative to the causal series whose causal property is *esse*; arguably, it has not been established that such a cause is absolutely primary, that is, uncaused in respect of any other series. Unless it is established that the primary cause of *esse* is absolutely primary, it cannot be said that this is what we understand God to be.

In response I argue as follows. The primary cause of *esse*, *esse tantum*, is uncaused with regard to *esse* and is the cause of *esse*. According to Edwards, such a cause could be first insofar as it would be the first cause of *esse*, but this cause would not necessarily be uncaused, because even though it may be the first cause of *esse* and thereby uncaused in that respect, it may be caused in some other respect, just as the mind or the fire in our other *per se* series are first with regard to the causality of their series but secondary with regard to the causality of some other series. But at this point I would like to confront Edwards or those of like mind with the following question: in what respect could a first cause of *esse* be caused? If a first cause of *esse* is successfully established, then it is the cause of everything other than itself that has *esse*.

To suggest that such a first cause of *esse* could be caused in some respect would be to suggest that it is caused by what it itself causes; for insofar as it is the first cause of *esse*, anything that in any way exists other than itself is an effect of it, in which case any candidate for the role of the cause of the first cause of *esse* (whatever role that might be) will itself be an effect of the first cause of *esse*. But no cause is caused by its effect, in which case a first cause of *esse* cannot be caused by anything that itself has been caused to exist; but what has not been caused to exist is either uncaused or nothing. Assuming that the proof is successful and there is a first cause of *esse*, that cause is not nothing, in which case it is an uncaused first cause of *esse*. What is here established is a counter example to Edwards's proposal that one can consistently think of a first cause yet deny that it is uncaused. In the order of *esse* at least, a first cause of *esse* is absolutely uncaused, otherwise it would not be the first cause of *esse*, it would depend on another for its *esse*.

5.3 CONCLUSION

The conclusion that there exists a cause of the existence of all things has now been established, and in so existing such a cause does not merely have *esse*, but is *esse* itself or pure *esse* (*esse tantum*). That is, the cause of *esse* of things is not another one of the things that has *esse*, or in which essence and *esse* are distinct, things that motivated the causal regress in the first place; rather, it is a cause that is such that it terminates the regress of causes of *esse* in *esse* itself.

The chapters leading up to this conclusion have been at pains to depict Aquinas's metaphysical framework and to defend the steps by which he arrives at his conclusion. Often such close attention to the fine details of an argument occludes its central thrust. Thus, I will complete this current chapter with a brief summary of Aquinas's argument, bearing in mind the defence of each stage up till now.

It will be remembered that Aquinas begins his argument for God's existence armed with the real distinction and composition of essence and *esse* in things. Such distinction and composition entail that such things are not self-existing, but depend on another for their existence. Aquinas thus opens the proof with a statement of his causal principle, to the effect that if a thing has some characteristic, it possesses it either as a result of the principles its nature, or as a result of some extrinsic principle. Given the real distinction of essence and *esse*, such composites do not possess *esse* of themselves, that is as a result of their intrinsic natures, in which case each and every such thing has a distinct cause of its *esse*. For obviously no such thing could be the cause of its own *esse*, because it would then have to precede itself in existence, which is absurd. A causal series is thus inaugurated whose causal characteristic is *esse*, and the question then is whether or not this causal series proceeds to infinity. Aquinas states that insofar as what exists from another—that is, has *esse* from another—is reducible to what exists in itself, there must be a primary cause for the *esse* of all things that exist *per aliud*, otherwise an infinite regress would follow. *Esse tantum* is just such a cause.

Aquinas does not offer any reasons in the *De Ente* for holding that what is *per aliud* is reducible to what is *per se*, nor for the inappropriateness of an infinite series of causes. Nevertheless, the argumentation in the *De Ente* can be buttressed by appeal to argumentation that he offers elsewhere and which is in harmony with the thought in the *De Ente*. So elsewhere Aquinas distinguishes between an essentially ordered series of causes and an accidentally ordered series, where in the essentially ordered series some primary cause is cause of both the existence and the causality of the posterior causal relata, whereas in the accidentally ordered series, there is no need for a primary cause to account for the causality of the posterior causal relata. It was observed that it is possible to go to infinity in the accidentally ordered series, but not so in the essentially ordered series, for that would entail that there is no cause for the causality of the posterior causal *relata*, in which case such a series would fail precisely as a causal series. Given such buttressing, it was concluded that Aquinas legitimately arrives at the conclusion that there is a primary cause of the *esse* of things, and this is what we understand God to be.

In the next two chapters I shall focus on Aquinas's conception of God as *esse tantum*. In Chapter 6 I shall consider whether or not this is an altogether coherent notion, and in Chapter 7 I shall consider the metaphysics of creation that is entailed by this conception of God.

6

ESSE TANTUM

IN THE PREVIOUS chapter it was concluded that there is a primary cause of *esse: esse tantum*. This is what we understand God to be. In the present chapter I shall explore this conclusion by first unpacking the notion of *esse tantum* and then considering some objections to it. The objections I shall consider fall into two general categories: (i) that the very notion of *esse tantum* is unintelligible; and (ii) that this is not what we understand God to be. Concerning (i), I shall consider the objection that the notion of something that is pure *esse* is incoherent and reflects a confused understanding of what existence is. Concerning (ii), I shall consider two objections. First, that *esse tantum* signifies something abstract which is instantiable, whereas God is a concrete individual, uninstantiable and incommunicable, in which case this is not what we understand God to be. Second, that whilst *esse tantum* does reflect man's understanding of God as the cause and Lord of all things, it does not express man's experience of God as a warm and loving father figure—an experience of God that was not lost on the saintly friar Thomas.

6.1 *ESSE TANTUM*

In his conclusion to the proof of God in *De Ente*, Aquinas simply states that this is what we understand God to be. He does not unpack this assertion any further, and this no doubt is because of his intended audience. But not only must this assertion be unpacked, it can be unpacked, and indeed it is unpacked by Aquinas himself throughout his writings. So in this section I would like to consider the notion of *esse tantum* with a view to the later objections to be considered.

The first thing to be noted about *esse tantum* is that it resists the modes of multiplication highlighted earlier in *De Ente*, Cap. 4, when establishing the real distinction between essence and *esse*. Recall that Aquinas outlined three modes of multiplication: (i) genus to species, (ii) species to individual, and (iii) absolute property to received property. In that argument, Aquinas takes the hypothesis of a being whose essence is its *esse* and establishes that it resists multiplication in the first two ways, with the third way being set aside because what is absolute is not itself actually multiplied in what receives it. Aquinas's goal is to establish that, insofar as the aforementioned modes of multiplication are inapplicable to that whose essence is its *esse*, anything that is in turn multiplied is not something whose essence is its *esse*. So in my interpretation (following Wippel), not only does this argumentation show that that whose essence is its *esse* cannot be multiplied, it also establishes the real distinction between essence and *esse*.

When dealing with this argument for real distinction, I emphasised that the being whose essence is its *esse* comes into such argumentation only as a hypothesis; whilst considering that position, it remained to be seen whether such a being actually exists. Having now established that *esse tantum* actually exists, it has been therefore established that there exists a being that does not possess *esse* through another (*per aliud*) but through itself (per se). Insofar as *esse tantum* is something that does not possess *esse* through another, it must be pure subsistent *esse*. In other words, in not possessing *esse* through another, it cannot possess *esse* as a result of some more fundamental intrinsic nature (such as man's ability to laugh possessed as a result of his rational nature). Hence, *esse* cannot be a proper accident of *esse tantum*, and this is clear from the following.

A proper accident depends for its being on the nature of the subject of which it is an accident. However, *esse* cannot depend on the nature of the subject of which it is supposedly the accident. Given that *esse* is the act of all acts, it cannot be derived from any more fundamental nature, in which case it cannot be a proper accident of some nature. If it were, the subject of whose nature it is the proper accident would pre-exist that very property without which the subject would not exist, which is absurd. Consequently, *esse tantum* cannot possess *esse* as some proper accident.

But if *esse tantum* possesses *esse* neither as a proper accident nor as the result of some extrinsic principle, then *esse tantum* can be nothing other than pure subsistent *esse* (*ipsum esse subsistens*). As such *esse tantum*, which is now known to exist, is that very hypothetical being whose essence is its *esse*, which figured in the multiplication argument for real distinction earlier in *De Ente*, Cap. 4.

Given that *esse tantum* is the subsistent *esse* considered in the multiplication argument, the same reasoning that established that subsistent *esse* is one and immaterial will establish that *esse tantum* is one and immaterial. Recall that subsistent *esse* resists multiplication in terms of (i) genus to species and (ii) species to individual, because in both there must be some addition made, whether of differentiating characteristic or matter, and such an addition would entail that the nature being multiplied is no longer subsistent *esse*, or *esse tantum* in the present case. Behind this reasoning is the insight that for multiplication to occur, there is required some plurifying principle which, when added to the nature in question, results in multiplication of that nature. So (i) the nature of the genus is multiplied into its species through some differentia that specifies it, and (ii) species are multiplied into individuals through being received in distinct clumps of matter. But there can be no principle distinct from *esse tantum* that could plurify it, because whatever is distinct from *esse tantum* is either (i) subject to *esse tantum* or (ii) nothing. In neither case, (i) and (ii), is *esse tantum* subject to anything, in which case there is nothing, neither differentiating characteristic nor matter, to which *esse tantum* is subject that could plurify it.[1]

Given that there is nothing distinct from *esse tantum* that could plurify it, *esse tantum* is not an individual of any nature, that is to say, it does not instantiate a nature; for if it did, even though there might only be one *esse tantum*, it would still be of a nature capable of being multiplied. But *esse tantum* is not, by its nature, capable of being multiplied, in which case it is not simply an instance of some nature: it is *esse tantum* itself. Thus, nature and individual are not distinct in *esse tantum*, but identical.[2] Whatever then is predicable of *esse tantum* does not signify any nature other than *esse tantum*; in other words, *quidquid in Deo sit Deus est*—God is utterly simple and not identified with anything other than Himself.

Strictly speaking, then, *esse tantum* is incommunicable, because if (*per impossible*) the *esse* of *esse tantum* were communicated to others, they would be other than *esse tantum* and thereby subject to it. Thus, the *esse* of things caused by *esse tantum* is not *esse tantum* but a caused *esse*, which in being caused and thereby composed with a distinct essence, is limited and somewhat lesser than *esse tantum*. The *esse* then of creatures, as will be recalled from Chapter 3, is an *esse* common to all creatures (*esse commune*) which is caused by *esse tantum* and is dependent thereon.

1. *Expositio De Ebdomadibus*, Lect. 2, p. 273:252–258: 'Si ipsum esse nichil aliud habet admixtum preter id quod est esse . . . impossibile est id quod est ipsum esse multiplicari per aliquid diuersificans, et, quia nichil aliud preter se habet adiunctum, consequens est quod nullius accidentis sit susceptiuum. Hoc autem simplex, unum et sublime est ipse Deus'.
2. In medieval terms, nature and supposit are identical in *esse tantum*, see *Summa Theologiae*, Ia, qu. 3, art. 3 for the same conclusion but arrived at via a consideration of God's immateriality. The difference between the reasoning based on multiplication and that based on immateriality is that the reasoning based on immateriality shows the unicity of both God and immaterial creatures, i.e. angels, whereas the reasoning based on multiplicity shows the unicity of God alone.

In being so dependent on *esse tantum, esse commune* participates in *esse tantum*, but in the very act of so participating, is somewhat other than *esse tantum*. Thus, *esse tantum* is per se, whereas *esse commune*, along with the individual being whose essence it actuates, is *per aliud*, or what amounts to the same in this context, *per participationem*. So whilst the third mode of multiplication, as what is absolute is multiplied in its diverse instances, might seem to be applicable to *esse tantum*, it is not, because *esse tantum* is not really *in* creatures: what is in creatures is *esse commune*, and *esse commune* in turn participates in *esse tantum*.[3]

Given that pure *esse* is subsistent *esse* it depends on nothing. As dependent on nothing, *esse tantum* does not stand in potency to anything, in which case it is not perfectible by anything. It follows that *esse tantum* is complete in itself and everything is incomplete in relation to it, because everything is lacking in *esse* unless granted *esse* by *esse tantum*, whereas *esse tantum* is lacking in nothing. But if *esse tantum* subsists and is complete in itself, then it is a subsisting individual. Given that *esse tantum* is an individual that subsists, *esse tantum* is also an *ens*, a 'that which is'. *Esse tantum*, then, whilst signified in the abstract in terms of *esse*, is indeed a concrete individual. But the *ens*-hood of *esse tantum* is not like the *ens*-hood of any other being, since every other being is an *ens* because (i) it has some principle of individuation and (ii) it has *esse*. *Esse tantum* has neither (i) nor (ii), rather, it is an individual because it is impossible for anything to be like it, and it exists not in virtue of having *esse* but in virtue of being *esse* (this will be developed further in dealing with some objections below).

Finally, not only is *esse tantum* a single, immaterial, subsistent, individual, it is also utterly transcendent. Yet the transcendence of *esse tantum* is not founded upon any kind of spatial

---

3. Recall a text already considered in Chapter 3 when considering *esse commune*, *De Divinis Nominibus*, Cap. 5, lect. 2, n. 660: 'Omnia alia existentia participant eo quod est esse, non autem Deus, sed magis ipsum esse creatum est quaedam participatio Dei et similitudo Ipsius'.

distance, but on its metaphysical unlikeness to everything else. Everything else is such that it is a composite of essence and *esse*, and as such is wholly other than *esse tantum*. There is nothing that it is like to be *esse tantum* other than being *esse tantum*. In having *esse*, creatures are not like *esse tantum* because their *esse* is a limited and participated *esse*. Nevertheless in having *esse*, creatures can be said to be close to *esse tantum*, because if they did not participate in the *esse* (*commune*) that they have—an *esse* which in turn depends on and participates in *esse tantum*—creatures simply would not be. Thus, in the very depths of their being, creatures are close to *esse tantum*. This closeness is like no other closeness; for whereas fundamental physical realities (such as the environment and nutrition, to give a couple of examples) will contribute towards one's remaining in existence, it is all for nothing without the primary causality of *esse tantum* both causing and sustaining one's existence. Nothing can take the place of the primary cause of *esse*, because everything else is an effect of such a cause. The closeness, then, of creatures to *esse tantum* is like no other closeness and is thus of the most fundamental kind. So whilst *esse tantum* in being such is utterly transcendent and unlike everything, it is also close like no other thing is close, given that it is the very cause and sustainer of our being.

Theoretically the reasoning here can be followed, but usually when one arrives at a rational affirmation of joint conclusions that seem intrinsically to repulse each other, such as the joint affirmation of transcendence and immanence, there is a concern that one has gone astray. With that in mind, John Knasas offers an illuminating (not to mention down to earth) analogy of the nature of being which highlights the transcendence and immanence of *esse*. Consider a donut: a donut is a circular pastry with a hole in the centre. Without the hole in the centre the donut is not a donut but some other pastry. The hole is essential for the very being of the donut, yet the hole is nothing of the donut; it is wholly other than the donut, such that if it were not wholly other there would be no donut. Thus, the hole in the donut is utterly transcendent, but in being utterly transcendent is so fundamentally immanent to the donut that without it there would be no donut.[4]

Having explicated the nature of *esse tantum*, let us now consider some objections offered against this peculiar notion of God.

6.2. *ESSE TANTUM* AS AN ABSURD NOTION

Anthony Kenny has argued that it is impossible to make sense of Aquinas's notion of *esse*; it is an aspect of his metaphysics that is fundamentally confused and should be rejected in a post-Fregean climate. With regard to *esse tantum*, Kenny latches onto the 'existence' signified in 'subsistent existence', and inquires after its possible meanings. He argues that in this case 'existence' could have one of two significations: it could signify (i) specific existence or (ii) individual existence. Kenny takes specific existence to be what instantiates a given species (horse, dog, human), so that one would be in a position to say: 'there is a horse/dog/human'. Specific existence for Kenny, therefore, is akin to Frege's quantificational account. Kenny takes individual existence to be the existence possessed by an individual horse, dog, or human, which, as noted in Chapter 3, Peter Geach takes to be a notion defensible on both Thomistic and Fregean grounds. In neither interpretation does it make sense to say that God is subsistent existence (or in the language of the *De Ente, esse tantum*).

If one were to say that God is subsistent-specific-existence, then the nature of specific existence has been misunderstood, for specific existence is what instantiates a species. However, in the present case it is maintained that God simply is specific existence, with no species to instantiate. Thus, the notion that God is subsistent-specific-existence is absurd, since specific existence

4. John Knasas, *Being and Some Twentieth Century Thomists*, p. 196.

must instantiate some species. If one were to posit that God is subsistent-individual-existence, then existence is an essential attribute of God, so that for God to exist is for God to be God. However, such a position does not entail that God in fact exists, because for a unicorn to exist is for a unicorn to be a unicorn, but that does not entail that unicorns exist. So the notion of subsistent existence (*esse tantum*) is absurd in Kenny's reading.

In response, I suggest that the notion of subsistent existence is indeed absurd in Kenny's reading, but this is because Kenny's reading is a poor reading, rather than because there is something intrinsically wrong with Aquinas's notion of subsistent existence. It has been noted that in dealing with Aquinas's metaphysics of *esse*, Kenny reads Aquinas with a Fregean straightjacket and refuses to accept that Aquinas could have a distinct vision of existence other than Frege's; rather, Kenny subjects Aquinas to a Fregean critique of existence and finds Aquinas wanting.[5] But of course Aquinas does not fit into a Fregean straightjacket, because Aquinas has his own non-Fregean notion of existence which recognises some of the Fregean categories, but also has some of its own.

Perhaps however Kenny's point is that whilst Aquinas does not have a Fregean framework within which to approach issues of existence, he should have. This suggests that for Kenny, Frege's account of existence is the preferred account, to be wielded against any other account as a mark of its veracity. If this is Kenny's intention, then his case against Aquinas is rather weak, because in his treatment of Aquinas he offers no reason for taking the Fregean account as the true account. And, as noted in Chapter 3, there are problems with the Fregean account of existence, specifically concerning the existence of individuals, that the Fregean account cannot handle, but the Thomist can.

5. This is the central thrust of Klima's critique in, 'On Kenny on Aquinas on Being: A Critical Review of *Aquinas on Being* by Anthony Kenny'.

Turning then to God's being, *esse tantum*, let us consider Kenny's objections and determine whether or not the *esse* here is that of specific existence or individual existence.

To begin with specific existence, this is Frege's account: a statement of existence is analysable in terms of the denial of the number zero, so that to say that humans exist is to say there are humans. As indicated in Chapter 3, Aquinas does not recognise as exhaustive such a quantificational account of existence, because, delving deeper, Aquinas focuses on the ontological value of the 'is' in such existential statements and holds that they only express the fact that something has existence, and the existence that the thing has is something more fundamental. Aquinas holds that a thing's existence, its *esse*, is an ontological co-principle of essence without which a thing could not be said to be. Thus, *esse* is a principle of actuality by which an essence can be said to exist. Consequently, without an account of the ontological value of the existence of the object that is an instance of the species, the specific existence signifying the instantiation of the species would have nothing to ground it. In which case, without Thomist *esse*, there would be no specific existence. Thus, in holding that God is pure *esse*, (that without which nothing would be), Aquinas cannot mean specific existence.

Turning then to individual existence, Kenny's argument has some bite, because if God's being subsistent existence means that God is individual existence such that God's existence is God's existence and none others' (call it divine existence, or *esse divinum*), then it follows that for God to exist is for God to be God, but this does not entail that God does in fact exist. Thus far, Aquinas would agree that holding that for God to exist is for God to be God is possible without thereby being committed to the actual existence of God; such is the typical Thomistic response to the Anselmian argument for God. But, as per the argumentation considered in previous chapters, it is clear that God does exist, given the denial of an infinite regress of causes (something that Kenny does not consider when considering the *De Ente* proof), and because the only being that could terminate that regress is one whose essence is its *esse*, such a being, known to exist, is pure or subsistent *esse*. If individuals have *esse* such that their *esse* is their own and belongs to no other, and bearing in mind that God does not just have *esse* but is pure *esse*, then the notion of God's individual existence is intelligible, bearing in mind the qualifications made above on God's individuality. Kenny in fact concedes that if this is what Aquinas holds, then there is no problem;[6] rather, he takes issue with the inference to the actual existence of God. But given that the inference to God is made on the basis of the affirmation of the *per aliud* principle and the denial of an infinite regress (something that Kenny does not consider in this respect), then Kenny's problem need not arise.

Granting the lack of absurdity in the identity of essence and *esse* in God, Kenny goes on to question the intelligibility of their distinction in creatures. He argues that one cannot conceive of the distinction of essence and *esse* in terms of being able to have one without the other. So for an entity, *x*, to go on being that entity is for the entity to possess the essence that it does.[7] But this entails that the existing of some entity is tied in with its essence and does not require a metaphysical principle distinct from its essence.

It seems that Kenny's problem here is that he is intent on reading the real distinction as one between two things, such that essence is one thing and *esse* another. In that case, it is certainly absurd to hold that they are distinct; for then the essence would be without a distinct principle to actuate it. The issue here of course is that Aquinas does not distinguish between essence and *esse* as two distinct things, but as two distinct principles of the one thing, just as Aristotle distinguished between matter and form, potency and act (distinctions that Kenny does not find unintelligible). So,

---

6. Kenny, *Aquinas* (Oxford: Oxford University Press, 1980), p. 54: 'If we take essence and existence in this way, there is no longer anything clearly absurd about the doctrine that in God essence and existence are not distinct'.

7. *Aquinas*, pp. 54–56.

just as potency and act can remain distinct but united in the concrete entity, so too does Aquinas argue that essence and *esse* are distinct yet united, and this because an essence considered in itself does not have the wherewithal to be, and requires a distinct (though not separate) principle in order to be. Thus whilst Kenny is right to say that for some entity to be is for it to go on being the type of entity that it is, his focus is entirely wrong; for it is not in being a *type* of thing that a thing exists, but it is in *being* a thing of some type, that a thing exists, and the *being* of a thing of some type is not attributable to its essence but to a distinct principle by which it is: namely, *esse*.

In arguing then that God is subsistent existence, or *esse tantum*, Aquinas is claiming that God is pure subsistent actuality without which nothing would be. God is known to exist given the denial of an infinite regress of causes of *esse*, and the notion of *esse tantum* certainly makes sense within Aquinas's own metaphysical framework of *esse*. Thus, Kenny's objections would seem to rest on misunderstandings of Aquinas's actual thought. But let us consider one final objection offered by Kenny, to the effect that if God is pure *esse*, then God is at best a minimal property that everything that in any way exists has, so that the identification of essence and *esse* in God is rather uninteresting and uninformative, not to mention absurd, because it amounts to stating that God is simply that minimal reality that even the barest of existing things must have in order to be anything at all.[8]

The problem here is that Kenny's reading fails to take seriously a distinction that Aquinas makes and of which Kenny is aware (*Aquinas*, p. 58): the distinction between the *esse* that is common to all things such that it is *de facto* without any addition—*esse commune*—and the *esse* that is such that it in principle admits of no further addition, being complete and perfect in itself—*esse divinum*.[9] This distinction is made by Aquinas precisely in order to

8. Ibid, p. 58.
9. Aquinas makes this distinction in the following places: *In I Sent.*, dist. 8, qu. 4, art. 1, *Summa Contra Gentiles*, Lib. 1, Cap. 26, *De Potentia Dei* qu. 7, art. 2,

distinguish between the *esse* that all things have, and the very *esse* that is God. The *esse* that is common to all things, signifying the individual distinct acts of existence of each and every creature, is fundamentally distinct from *esse divinum* insofar as the latter is the cause and source of the former in which the former participates. Aquinas's view amounts to the fact that created *esse* is not identical to divine *esse*, so that whilst in both cases *esse* signifies act, in the case of created *esse* it is the act *of* some essence from which it is distinct, whereas in the case of divine *esse* the act is the divine essence itself. Consequently, *esse divinum* cannot be identified with the common *esse* that all things have, and so is not the most minimal property that anything that in any way exists has.

Given that Kenny grants that Aquinas makes a distinction between *esse commune* and *esse divinum*, it is odd for Kenny to argue:

> If the 'esse' which denotes God's essence is like the 'esse' which is predicable of everything, except that it does not permit the addition of further predicates, then it is a predicate which is totally unintelligible.

It is not clear why Kenny, having taken into account Aquinas's distinction, would argue that God's essence is like the *esse* predicable of everything (*esse commune*), when Aquinas is explicit in noting that God's *esse* is *not* like the *esse* predicable of everything. Perhaps Kenny is of the view that his clarification that the *esse* of God admits of no further predicates suffices to distinguish between *esse commune* and *esse divinum*, but unfortunately this does not bring out the transcendence of God's *esse* in relation to *esse commune*.

ad. 4, *Summa Theologiae*, Ia, qu. 3, art. 4, ad. 1, *De Divinis Nominibus* Cap. 5, lect. 2. For commentary on several of these texts see Kerr, 'The Meaning of *Ens Commune* in the Thought of Thomas Aquinas', *Yearbook of the Irish Philosophical Society* (2008), 32–61.

God's *esse* is the cause of the individual acts of existence which taken together signify *esse commune*, in which case the inapplicability of addition to *esse divinum* is not simply some arbitrary condition that Aquinas stipulates for God's *esse* (something of which Kenny seems unaware), but a characteristic of viewing God as the primary cause of all that is. In other words, as the primary cause of all that is, *esse tantum*, God's *esse* is complete in itself insofar as it signifies the fullness of being without which there is nothing. God's *esse*, then, is not simply a minimal predicate that everything must at least have before it has anything else; God's *esse* is a maximal reality that includes within its power anything that in any way exists, for if anything is independent of God's power it is precisely without *esse* and thereby nothing. Thus, *esse commune* participates in *esse divinum* as an effect in its cause, in which case *esse divinum* transcends *esse commune* as a cause does its effect. This is what Kenny has failed to grasp in Aquinas's doctrine of the identity of essence and *esse* in God, and it goes hand in hand with his various other confusions regarding Aquinas's metaphysics of *esse*—so much so that he fails to comprehend Aquinas's actual thought in this regard.

Given that Kenny has failed to present any objections that are actually applicable to Aquinas, nor has he criticised Aquinas's causal reasoning to the existence of God, we may move beyond Kenny to consider some further objections to this aspect of Aquinas's philosophical thought.

6.3 'THIS IS GOD'

6.3.1 A Personal God

Whilst the notion of subsistent existence or *esse tantum* may not be absurd, it is arguable that this is *not* what we understand

God to be. Many people, when they conceive of God, especially the Israelites, conceive of a loving person, a father figure, who is involved with His people. Thus, it has been argued that conceiving of God as some abstract property, pure *esse* in this case, is absurd because something abstract cannot be a person nor can it be wise, all knowing, or powerful. Only a concrete being, an *ens*, an *id quod est*, can be such things, in which case God cannot be pure *esse*.[10]

Arguing against Alvin Plantinga, Eleonore Stump concedes that to consider God exclusively in terms of pure *esse* does present a challenge to the classical notion of God, and part of her response is motivated by the work of some Thomists who seek to conceive of God as *esse* alone, denying that He is an *ens*.[11] Stump argues that seemingly contradictory predicates can be attributed to God if it is recognised that there is a more fundamental reality of which those predicates are predicated and the predication in which may entail that they are not contradictory. Thus, Stump refers to the debate in quantum physics over the interpretation of light as a wave or a particle, and points out that there are good reasons for holding that light is both and can be interpreted as both in different respects. Analogously, God can be envisaged as pure *esse*, and this especially so when He is considered as that from which all being flows. Nevertheless, God can be considered as an entity (an *ens*), and this especially when He is considered in Himself. Thus, just as in the wave-particle dispute, there is recognised that there

10. This objection has been pushed particularly by Alvin Plantinga in *Does God have a Nature?* (Milwaukee: Marquette University Press, 1980), pp. 37–61, note in particular p. 47: 'No property could have created the world; no property could be omniscient, or, indeed, know anything at all. If God is a property, then he isn't a person but a mere abstract object; he has no knowledge, awareness, power, love or life'. Eleonore Stump has responded to this objection in 'Simplicity and Aquinas's Quantum Metaphysics' forthcoming in *The Reception of Aristotle's Metaphysics in the Middle Ages*, edited by Gerhard Krieger, see also 'God's Simplicity', in *The Oxford Handbook of Aquinas*, ed. by Brian Davies and Eleonore Stump (Oxford: Oxford University Press, 2012).
11. Stump refers to Leo Elders and David Burrell in this respect.

are good reasons to hold that light is both a wave and a particle, thereby indicating that there is a more fundamental unifying reality in which the opposition of wave and particle can coexist. Similarly there are good reasons to think of God as both pure *esse* and an *ens*, thereby signifying that there is a deeper reality that can be said to be both and in which the opposition of *esse* and *ens* is dissolved.

In Stump's account, care must be taken in our predications about God and the context kept clear. So God can be thought of in terms of pure *esse* perhaps when thinking of Him as creator, but He can be thought of in personal terms, as an *ens*, when thinking of Him in Himself. If one accepts that when faced with two opposing characteristics of a thing for which there are good reasons to predicate them of that thing, there must be a deeper reality within which such opposition is dissolved, then Stump's response to Plantinga certainly has a lot to commend it. However, even granting that when it comes to God, our attributions cannot come close to approaching the divine mystery, one can evade Plantinga's objection without holding that the opposition between conceiving of God as pure *esse* and an *ens* may be dissolved at the deeper level of the divine mystery of God's hidden life.

One reason for not fully endorsing Stump's response is that it entails that being pure *esse* is just another divine attribute like simplicity, perfection, or goodness, behind all of which is the divine essence itself; whilst I do not intend to diminish the other divine attributes as somewhat lesser than *esse*, I do think it is correct to say that for Aquinas *esse* could be said to be most proper to God, since *esse* is the act of all acts, without which nothing would be in act, in which case only what is wholly independent of all else on which everything depends, i.e. God, could be pure *esse*. Furthermore, it is clear from Aquinas's mode of procedure elsewhere that in considering the divine attributes, God's being *ipsum esse*, pure act, or primary cause from which all things come is often employed in deriving the various other attributes, thereby signifying the primacy for Aquinas of this conception of

God.[12] Not only that, Aquinas frequently refers to God simply as *esse* rather than any of the other divine attributes that he assigns to God.[13] Therefore, God's being pure *esse* is fundamental to the Thomistic conception of God, such that any conception of God that would downgrade it loses sight somewhat of the Thomistic conception of God. For these reasons, a different response to Plantinga is required.

It seems that Plantinga's objection turns on a mistaken view of the type of properties envisaged in the current case. Certainly properties like the state of being a specific colour, height, weight, or age, cannot subsist in themselves, but must subsist in some subject. And, given that a person does not subsist in a subject but is itself a subsisting thing, a person cannot be identified with any such properties. However, the foregoing properties are unlike *esse* precisely because their existence is rooted in the existence of the subject in which they are instantiated. *Esse* on the other

12. See, for example, *Summa Theologiae*, Ia, qu. 3, art. 7 (God's simplicity), qu. 4, art. 2 (God's perfection), qu. 6, art. 3 (God's goodness), qu. 7, art. 1 (God's infinity), qu. 8, aa. 1–2 (God's omnipresence), qu. 9, art. 1 (God's immutability), qu. 10, art. 2 (God's eternity), and qu. 11, art. 4 (God's unity),

13. Note for example the following unqualified assertions that God simply is *esse: Summa Contra Gentiles*, Lib. 3, Cap. 19: 'Esse habent omnia quod Deo assimilantur, qui est ipsum esse subsistens'; *Summa Theologiae*, Ia, qu. 4, art. 2: 'Cum Deus sit ipsum esse subsistens, nihil de perfectione essendi potest ei deesse'; Ibid, qu. 11, art. 4: 'Est enim maxime ens, inquantum est non habens aliquod esse determinatum per aliquam naturam cui adveniat, sed est ipsum esse subsistens'; *Quaestio Disputata De Anima* (Turin: Marietti, 1927), art. 6, ad. 2: 'Si sit aliquid quod sit ipsum esse subsistens, sicut de Deo dicimus, nihil participare dicimus'; *Quaestio Disputata De Spiritualibus Creaturis* (Turin: Marietti, 1927), art. 1: 'Unde dicimus, quod Deus est ipsum suum esse', *De Malo*, qu. 16, art. 3: 'Deus enim per suam essentiam est ipsum esse subsistens'; *Quaestiones Quodlibetales* (Turin: Marietti, 1927), Quod. 3, qu. 1, art. 1: 'Cum autem Deus sit ipsum esse subsistens, manifestum est quod natura essendi convenit Deo infinite absque omni limitatione et contractione'; *De Divinis Nominibus*, Cap. 5, lect. 1: 'Sed solus Deus, qui est ipsum esse subsistens, secundum totam virtutem essendi, esse habet'; *De Causis*, lect. 7, n. 182: 'Causa autem prima non est natura subsistens in suo esse quasi participato, sed potius est ipsum esse subsistens'.

hand is not such a property, because as the act of all acts *esse* is that without which there would be no subject in the first place, and thus does not itself require a subject in which to be instantiated. Furthermore, given that *esse* as act is the cause of the existence of things, to insist that *esse* cannot be in itself but, like other properties, requires some subject is to insist that a cause (*esse* in this case) cannot exist without its effect, the subject in this case; but this is to invert the understanding of cause and effect and to suppose that an effect can be a cause of its cause, which is absurd. Thus, once Aquinas's understanding of *esse* as existential act is brought to the fore, it is not absurd to hold that *esse* can be itself without some subject in which it is instantiated.

Turning then to the objection that what is pure *esse* could not be a person since a person is an *ens*, it has been seen that *esse tantum*, as both subsistent and complete in itself, is an individual *ens*. To be sure, the *ens*-hood of *esse tantum* is not like the *ens*-hood of any other individual, but this does not entail that *esse tantum* is not an individual being, only that it is an individual unlike any other, in which case it can be a person unlike any other (a conclusion to which I think Plantinga is not averse). Given then that *esse tantum*, in Aquinas's account, is a subsisting individual, the objection to conceiving of God as pure *esse* is somewhat undermined, because that objection was to the effect that pure *esse* is something that could not in principle be a person. It has not here been established that God is a person, that is, an individual substance of a rational nature, but it has been established that God is a subsisting individual and not just some abstract property that stands to be instantiated. Thus, conceiving of God as pure *esse* is not in itself a barrier to conceiving of God as a person.

6.3.2 A Biblical God

Conceiving of God as pure *esse* permits us to arrive at a God that has many of the characteristics of the God of classical theism;

for example, such a God is the primary cause of all that is, without this God there is nothing, such a God is Lord of all things and all things stand under this God. In other words, Aquinas's conception of God as *esse tantum* seems to arrive at the transcendent God of classical theism. Moreover, as has been seen, given that nothing would be unless it were present to God for its *esse*, God is at the heart of all things, and is thus immanent. *Esse tantum* is both transcendent and immanent, and thus not a deist watchmaker.

Even so, Aquinas's notion of God does not seem to fit into any of the scriptural categories of the revealed books that Aquinas himself took to be inspired. Aquinas was first and foremost a devout Catholic, a member of the Order of Preachers whose spiritual life centres on preaching true doctrine to those who had either fallen from the faith or had none. First and foremost in Aquinas's mind was to preach the truth of the Gospel. But where in the revealed books do we find God referred to as *esse tantum*? Nowhere, it seems: the only definition of God offered in the New Testament is in the first letter of St John, who identifies God with love (1 Jn. 4:8); the Old Testament offers us a smorgasbord of images of the divine, none of which seems to match up to *esse tantum*. Indeed, the God of the Bible is a loving fatherly figure, not the cold, clinical Thomistic *esse tantum*. Perhaps then one might want to argue that interesting as Aquinas's vision here is, he has not reached God.

Above I pointed out that the only definition we have of God in the New Testament is that He is love, and that nothing comparable is found in the Old Testament. But there is something promising in the Old Testament, something that gives us an insight into Israel's evolving conception of what God is. When Moses meets God and receives his divine mission to free the Hebrews from Egypt, he asks God whom he should say is sending him. God's response is somewhat startling: 'I Am Who Am. This is what you will say to the sons of Israel: "I am sent me to you"'. God thus reveals Himself as He Who is.[14] Philologically speaking, the text places God's answer not in the nominative, but in the verbal form. Thus God's revelation of Himself is not that of a name, but an action, one that expresses a kind of dynamism or causality at the heart of God. God as understood by the scriptural author is not just some being but that by which any being is at all, such is what is implicit in the verbal form of the divine name.[15]

The Mosaic conception of God envisages God as He Who is ('I am Who Am'). God is thus not a great warrior, or a great animal, or a great natural force. Doubtless God's interventions in human history justify such attributions, provided that the manner of attribution is strictly defined. But when it comes to God's revelation of His very self—the self that is the God of the Hebrews, whom the Hebrews would know as their God—God reveals Himself as 'I am Who Am'. If a metaphysical insight into God and His relation to creatures is not intended by this passage, it is certainly contained therein.[16] God reveals Himself as He Who is; no composite of essence and *esse* could proclaim itself as such.[17] Only that which is pure *esse* could be He Who is. No individual essence simply having *esse* could be such, because every such individual is something of a kind, (a man, horse, dog, etc), so that an essence-*esse* composite could only truthfully answer Moses with 'I am a man/ horse/dog etc'. *Esse tantum* simply is; everything else is in relation to it. Thus, whilst one cannot immediately move from *esse tantum* to its identification with He Who is, one can move from He Who

---

14. Ex. 3:13–15. Josef Cardinal Ratzinger (later Benedict XVI) holds that this episode is central to the biblical conception of God. See *An Introduction to Christianity* (San Francisco: Ignatius Press, 1969), p. 116.

15. For the philological details of the name of God see *New Jerome Biblical Commentary*, ed. by Raymond Brown, Joseph Fitzmyer, and Roland Murphy (London: Burns & Oates, 1990), p. 47.

16. For an articulation of the metaphysics of Exodus, see Étienne Gilson, *The Spirit of Medieval Philosophy* (Notre Dame: Notre Dame University Press, 1936), Chapters 1–4.

17. Assuming of course that God was not lying to Moses.

is to *esse tantum*. It follows then that with this understanding in place, Aquinas's conception of God is contained implicitly within the Mosaic scriptural tradition as Aquinas interprets it.

Aquinas the preacher, then, can rest content with his metaphysical conception of God as *esse tantum*, knowing that whilst such a conception does not authorise a direct inference to 'I am', a prior commitment to 'I am' does authorise an inference to *esse tantum*. Aquinas has thus provided the philosophical resources for those who are committed to 'I am' to affirm the existence of *esse tantum* without having to rely on their prior commitment to 'I am'. And since Aquinas's role as a preacher was to preach not only to those who had faith and were thus committed to 'I am', but also to those without faith and thus without a commitment to 'I am', Aquinas has fulfilled his role as a preacher by showing that one can be committed to the existence of what Catholics understand God to be; the move from *esse tantum* to 'I am', then, will be no leap at all, but rather a recognition that the activity of God in the Bible is the activity of *esse tantum*.

A further reflection on the congruence between the Mosaic and Thomistic conceptions of God is worth considering. The author of the biblical text was no trained philosopher; he did not display that characteristic flair of reasoning necessary in philosophical matters. So his statement that the God of the Hebrews is He Who Is is not a conclusion made on the basis of philosophical reasoning. But consider the latter along with the fact that the Mosaic conception of God as He Who Is had no known predecessor of which we can tell.[18] So it seems that without any deep metaphysical insight nor with any explicit prior determination as such, the author of the biblical text has managed to offer an expression of God that just happens to be in accord with some of the most profound metaphysical reasoning about the nature of God and His relation to the world in the history of Western thought.

18. Ratzinger, *An Introduction to Christianity*, p. 120.

This certainly raises the awareness of one dedicated to thinking through such things in a serious manner, and it no doubt raised the awareness of Aquinas as it ought to do for us today.

Aquinas obviously thinks that the revelation of the divine nature to Moses was precisely that—a revelation. In contemporary biblical interpretation the existence and role of Moses in the freeing of the Hebrews from Egypt is often cast in doubt, as is God's revelation of the divine essence to him. Whilst having no desire to enter into the historical dispute here, I think it is worth bearing in mind that a conception of the divine essence with no known antecedents or philosophical reasoning adduced in its favour is expressed in the biblical text, and this conception just happens to be in accord with what I submit the best philosophical reasoning tells us about the nature of God. Whilst the historical veracity of the biblical text may be cast in doubt, I think that when it comes to the revelation of God's very nature these considerations lead us to take seriously the possibility that the divine nature was revealed to someone, and that this revelation has found its way into the biblical text. Otherwise we have to admit that a conception of God with no known antecedents, and which just happens to coincide with a profound philosophical approach to these matters, just happened to be thought up by a biblical author. The coincidences do not establish divine revelation, but they urge us to take its possibility seriously.

One final issue I would like to address is the worship of God. It has been noted that Aquinas was a man who worshipped God profoundly, and is now considered a saint. Indeed, a central feature of man's conception of God is that God is a being to be worshipped. In the Catholic tradition to which Aquinas contributed, God is not to be worshipped because he is almighty and commands respect, but because he is love, and in being love, loves us so that our response is to love Him back.[19] God then is not like the

---

19. 1 Jn. 4:8.

ancient pagan gods who stand aloof and expect humanity to find them and worship them; rather, God in this account goes looking for humanity, His people.[20] Can it be said that any of this is consonant with Aquinas's conception of *esse tantum*?

I believe that something of this biblical context shines through in Aquinas's conception of *esse tantum*, and it is precisely in considering the relationship that *esse tantum* has to creatures. In the next chapter the nature of creation per se will be considered, but for now I will consider briefly something to which Aquinas is committed in thinking of God as *esse tantum* and creatures as things simply having *esse*.

Creatures ultimately exist out of dependence on God, Who is *esse tantum*. What creatures are in themselves is precisely nothing unless granted *esse* from God, without which they would not exist. Creatures thus do not naturally exist, but exist only in dependence upon God, from Whom they receive *esse*. *Esse* then is what brings creatures from a state of nothingness to a state of being, such that *esse* is the first act and perfection of the creature without which nothing. Because creatures were nothing before they existed, they could not have earned their existence in any way; it follows then that the bringing of creatures into existence is utterly gratuitous; there was no necessitation on God's part to bring creatures into being. It follows then that the being that creatures enjoy is a gift from God, and it is a gift such that without it there would be nothing.

In the *Summa Theologiae*, after he has established that God exists, Aquinas argues that God is the good itself and as such is motivated by the good in anything that He does, so that what He does is always out of love.[21] I have not addressed those aspects of Aquinas's thought here, but taken hand in hand with his thought on *esse tantum* it offers us a philosophical conception of God that

---

20. Jn. 10:11 *et seq.*
21. *Summa Theologiae*, Ia, qu. 6 (God's goodness), qu. 20 (God's love).

accords nicely with what has been revealed about God. God is a person Who is love and Who loves us first so that our loving is only a response to God's love. It is in the latter sense that we can understand the gratuity of God's bringing creatures into existence; God brings creatures into existence out of love for them, and He wants them to love Him in return. Creation then is not primarily characterisable as an act of sheer power, but as one of sheer love, wherein God brings things into being so that they may love. And understood as such, God's being *esse tantum* represents God as a being supremely worthy of worship, because no other being has acted out of such gratuitousness than has God in bringing us into being. With that in mind, let us now consider that very act by which God brings things into being: creation.

7

CREATION

UNTIL NOW I have focussed quite closely on the steps by which Aquinas arrives at the conclusion that *esse tantum* does indeed exist. In the previous chapter I began to explicate what *esse tantum* actually is, and considered some of the more religious issues surrounding the affirmation of *esse tantum*. One conception of God that is almost unanimous in Western thought, and certainly explicit in the proof of God defended in this work, is that God is the creator of all that is, such that there is nothing not subject to God's creative power. It is fitting then that this study concludes with an account of creation endorsed by the conception of God demonstrated in the *De Ente*. Whilst this takes me outside of the strict confines of the proof of God in the *De Ente*, I will not be moving outside of the metaphysical framework that endorses it. Therefore, this chapter works as a natural extension of the proof of God.

First, I shall consider a contemporary unreflective notion of creation that envisages the creative act as something that occurred at the beginning of the universe, giving the universe its first nudge into existence. Second, I shall consider Aquinas's metaphysics of creation, and then, third, contrast that account of creation with the more contemporary unreflective account, thus bringing this book to a close.

7.1 CREATION AND BIG BANG COSMOLOGY

Nearly all contemporary scientists accept big bang cosmology as offering the best account for the beginning of the universe.[1] It is often assumed on the back of big bang cosmology that the question of the creation of the universe and its dependence or otherwise on the activity of a creator can be settled if one can settle what happened before the big bang. An inference is often made to the effect that if there is a beginning of the universe, there must be a cause of the universe. And the latter goes hand in hand with the wider assumption that to be created is to have a beginning of existence.

Stephen Hawking is one scientist who endorses the assumption that to be created is to have begun to exist. In his highly popular work, *A Brief History of Time*, Hawking claims that in the classical theory of gravity, there are only two possible ways in which the universe can behave: either it has existed for an infinite time, or it has a beginning with a singularity at some finite time in the past. However, in the quantum theory of gravity, there arises a third possibility: space–time could be finite, yet have no singularities that form a boundary or edge signifying its beginning.[2] In this model, space–time would be like the surface of the earth: finite, but with no boundary (at least horizontally speaking) beyond which one can go. Given the latter, one could not, hypothetically speaking, go back to the starting point and observe the boundary between the universe and nothingness, just as one cannot walk off the face of the earth. Given that in

1. For a dissenting voice see E. Lerner, *The Big Bang Never Happened: A Startling Refutation of the Dominant Theory of the Universe* (New York: Random House, 1991). Being a philosopher, I am not qualified to adjudicate on the scientific integrity of Lerner's work; I merely bring it to the attention of the reader as a divergent viewpoint.
2. Stephen Hawking, *A Brief History of Time* (London: Bantam Press, 1998), p. 154.

this account there is no boundary to space-time, there is no question of its boundary conditions. Consequently, the universe is a self-contained system; one need not look for an explanation of the universe by asking what conditions were in place before the big bang in order to cause it.

Understanding the particular details of Hawking's physics is not primarily important for understanding the more philosophical point he is trying to make. His point is that given the lack of boundary conditions, and the very lack of a beginning for the universe, it is inferred that, whilst finite, the universe is neither created nor destroyed, it just is.[3] And given the lack of a beginning of the universe, Hawking infers the lack of a need for a creator. Thus, for Hawking, a finite beginningless universe is a finite uncreated universe.

Hawking's position quite naturally has implications for the question of God's role in creation. As he states:

The idea that space and time may form a closed surface without boundary also has profound implications for the role of God in the affairs of the universe. With the success of scientific theories in describing events, most people have come to believe that God allows the universe to evolve according to a set of laws and does not intervene in the universe to break these laws. However, the laws do not tell us what the universe should have looked like when it started—it would still be up to God to wind up the clockwork and choose how to start it off. *So long as the universe had a beginning, we could suppose it had a creator* [my emphasis]. But if the universe is really completely self-contained, having no boundary or edge, it would have neither beginning nor end: it would simply be. What place, then, for a creator?[4]

3. Ibid, p. 155.
4. Ibid, pp. 160–161.

As is clear from this quoted text, Hawking associates closely the beginning of the universe with its creation, such that the creation of the universe is signified by its beginning in time, its being started off by God. But if a model of the universe can be presented that is self-contained such that it is without a beginning, then, according to Hawking, the role of the creator of the universe is radically reduced. Hawking thus clearly connects the beginning of the universe with its being created; and this is a theme that is found in several important instances throughout the book.[5]

It is always perilous when a specialist in one field, say metaphysics or theology, attempts to enter another field, say physics, and lay down authoritative conclusions for the newly entered field. It is equally perilous for a physicist to enter a field such as philosophy, metaphysics in particular, and lay down authoritative claims for that field.[6] As an indication of the peril of a physicist entering metaphysics, note that Hawking connects the question of the beginning of the universe with the question of the creation of the universe—so much so that if the universe has no beginning, then it has no creation, in which case, what role for a creator?

For those with a background in metaphysics, the question of a thing's beginning and the question of a thing's creation are two formally distinct types of question. The beginning of a thing signifies the time at which it came into existence, but the creation of

5. For example, p. 7: 'It was generally accepted either that the universe had existed forever in an unchanging state, or that it had been created at a finite time in the past'; p. 8: 'The beginning of the universe, had, of course, been discussed long before this. According to a number of early cosmologies of the Jewish/Christian/Muslim tradition, the universe started at a finite, and not very distant, time in the past. One argument for such a beginning was the feeling that it was necessary to have a 'First Cause' to explain the existence of the universe'; p. 131: 'The possibility that space–time [is] finite but [has] no boundary, which means that it had no beginning, no moment of Creation'.

6. This is not to say that the metaphysician must not seek to form conclusions consistent with modern physics; rather, that the physicist cannot simply enter metaphysics and, with no background in the field, attempt to offer positive conclusions for problems associated exclusively with that field.

a thing signifies the mode of its coming into existence. Often the beginning of a thing's existence coincides with its creation, but the two are not necessarily synonymous. The creation of a thing is the bringing of a thing into existence, whereas the beginning of a thing is the time at which the thing came into existence. One cannot have the latter without the former, but one can indeed have the former without the latter, given that one can conceive of a non-temporal causal dependency, such that some entity, x, is the cause of F in y, without F's ever having had a beginning in y. For instance, imagine that the sun and the moon have existed eternally, and accordingly the light of the sun has eternally illuminated the surface of the moon. Despite the illumination of the moon never having begun to exist, because both sun and moon are assumed to be eternal, the moon nevertheless depends on the sun for its illumination. Thus, a dependence on another for a given characteristic, illumination in this case, does not entail that that characteristic need have begun in the thing. The light of the sun is thus analytically, though not temporally, prior to the illumination of the moon.[7]

If Hawking is correct and a beginningless universe is an uncreated universe, one would think that a Christian philosopher like Aquinas, convinced of the creation of the universe, would surely *not* hold the view that the universe could be without a beginning; after all, in Hawking's account, if such a philosopher were convinced of the creation of the universe, then that philosopher would be committed to the view that the universe had begun to exist. Yet Aquinas holds that the universe could be both created and eternal, that is, without a beginning. So there must be a

---

7. The example is from Richard Taylor, 'The Metaphysics of Causation' in *Causation and Conditionals*, p. 44. It is precisely the intuition at the heart of Taylor's example, that one can have non-temporal causal dependency, that feeds into Aquinas's metaphysics of creation: dependence on God for existence does not necessarily entail a beginning of existence, even though Aquinas knew that the universe began to exist, and this through God's revelation in scripture.

conflicting philosophy of creation at work here (I will outline this in detail in the next section). It is worth pointing out however that one reason Aquinas holds the view that a created universe could be without a beginning is his own dissatisfaction with the arguments offered in support of the beginning of the universe.

The reasons urged for the beginning of the universe that Aquinas considers take a number of different forms, and Aquinas finds all of them to be lacking in some way. The following are some of the reasons pertinent to the theme of this particular chapter.

(1) If the world was made it had a beginning (this is in fact Hawking's assumption). Given a positive proof for God's existence as primary cause, it can be shown that the world was made by God. Hence the world had to have a beginning. However, in response Aquinas distinguishes between (i) an event that is caused successively and (ii) an event that is caused instantaneously, and he argues that in (i) a cause must temporally precede its effect, whereas in (ii) it need not, yet the effect still depends on the cause; in other words, an instantaneous cause is analytically though not temporally prior to its effect. Consequently, the fact of something's having an origin (being made) is not enough to establish that it had a beginning.

(2) If the world was made from nothing, then after it was nothing the world is something. But if the latter is the case, then the world came into being at a particular time. In response Aquinas clarifies the notion of *creatio ex nihilo* and claims that in holding that the world came from nothing, one need not hold that it came *after* nothing, but that it is not made from anything. Consequently, the world can be *ex nihilo* and yet not come into existence *after* nothing.

(3) If the world were eternal, then it would be equal to God; but the latter consequence is impossible, at least for Aquinas and his contemporaries; hence, the world could

not be eternal and must have begun to be. In response Aquinas claims that even if the universe were eternal, it would not be equal to God, since God's eternity is all at once, whereas the universe's eternity would be successive. God is thus a fundamentally different kind of being than created beings, and His mode of being is wholly different from that of created beings.

In Aquinas's more positive view, even if the universe were eternal, that is, without a beginning, it would still require a cause for its existence. This is because, as Aquinas sees things, the universe, whether finite or infinite, is not self-existing, in which case it depends on another for its existence. Therefore something eternal could stand to receive existence from without, and be thereby created. What this implies is that a thing, x, need not have a beginning, and yet could still be dependent on another, y, for its existence, in which case y would be analytically though not temporally prior to x. The foregoing offers us something of the flavour of Aquinas's view, and its metaphysical scaffolding will be explored in the next section.

7.2 AQUINAS ON CREATION

Whilst he denies that the creation of the universe in time could be established, it being an article of faith, Aquinas does believe that reason could penetrate somewhat into the nature of creation and demonstrate the creation of the universe *ex nihilo*.

In the *Sentences* commentary, Aquinas offers us, for the first time in his career, the view that to create something is to produce a thing in existence according to its total substance.[8] This is a view that Aquinas repeats in several of his major works.[9] Taken in itself,

---

8. *In II., Sent*, dist. 1, qu. 1, art. 2: 'Hoc autem creare dicimus, scilicet producere rem in esse secundum totam suam substantiam'.
9. *Summa Contra Gentiles*, Lib. 2, Cap. 17: 'Ubi autem tota substantia rei in esse producitur, non potest esse aliquod idem aliter et aliter se habens: quia illud

this concise formula and its variations does not seem to convey much; indeed, all of the quotations in note 9 were listed somewhat out of context, for they are presented by Aquinas as conclusions, not principles. Aquinas does not begin with the principle that creation is the production of the total substance in being, he arrives at that conclusion. The question is, how does he do so?

In order to juxtapose creation from simple change, Aquinas argues that change or motion requires some underlying subject within which it occurs; creation, on the other hand, does not presuppose such a subject.[10] Thus, given a being that embraces all that is (*esse tantum*), including the most basic subject within which all change occurs, that being's productive activity will be properly called creation; and implicit in this is the view that the act of creation presupposes nothing, but everything presupposes such an act.[11] If everything presupposes such an act, then that act itself brings into existence things whole and complete, in which case the act of creation does not modify some pre-existing subject, in which case creation is the total production of the substance in being.

God is *esse tantum* and as such God embraces all that is and nothing that is not. It follows then that creation, as it is the

esset non productum, sed productioni praesuppositum. Non est ergo creatio mutatio'; *De Potentia Dei*, qu. 3, art. 1: 'Per suam actionem [Deus] producit totum ens subsistens, nullo praesupposito'; *Summa Theologiae*, Ia, qu. 45, art. 1: 'Non solum oportet considerare emanationem alicuius entis particularis ab aliquo particulari agente, sed etiam emanationem totius entis a causa universali, quae est Deus, et hanc quidem emanationem designamus nomine creationis'; *De Substantis Separatis*, Cap. 10, n. 57: 'Nullum agens post primum totam rem in esse producit, quasi producens ens simpliciter per se, et non per accidens, quod est creare'.

10. See the discussions in *De Potentia Dei*, qu. 3, art. 3; *Summa Contra Gentiles*, lib. 2, cap. 17; *De Substantiis Separatis*, cap. 9, n. 49, and cap. 10, n. 56 for why creation is not change or motion, given that change or motion presupposes some subject, but creation presupposes nothing.

11. *Summa Contra Gentiles*, Lib. 2, Cap. 21: 'Creatio autem est prima actio: eo quod nullam aliam praesupponit, omnes autem aliae praesupponunt eam. Est igitur creatio propria Dei solius actio, qui est agens primum'.

production in being of the total substance and presupposes nothing, is solely attributable to God; for everything other than God is composed of essence and *esse*, in which case nothing other than God embraces everything that is. No creature, therefore, can create, because no creature can produce a total substance in being; rather, a creature must presuppose some pre-existing subject on which to work. Effectively, a creature does not cause *esse*, but presupposes it passing it along to other creatures. Thus, a creature's productive activity is really only a form of change in what has already been created, whereas God's productive activity, embracing the total substance and presupposing nothing, is properly called creation.

Aquinas accordingly sees the notion of creation as involving two implicit commitments. First, as noted, creation does not presuppose any component of the thing created, i.e., in creation there is no underlying subject on which to work, and in this respect creation is juxtaposed to change.[12] Secondly, non-being must precede the being of the thing created. Aquinas is quick to qualify the latter remark by stating that the priority of non-being to being in the thing created is not, at the moment, to be taken as any kind of temporal priority. What he has in mind is a priority in nature (or what I have termed 'analytical priority'), whereby the essence of the thing created receives its existence from some superior cause.[13] What Aquinas is here articulating in this second point ties in with what has been shown with regard to essence-*esse* composition and God, to the effect that all such composites depend on God (*esse tantum*) for their *esse*.

---

12. *In II Sent*, dist. 1, qu. 1, art. 2: 'Primum est ut nihil praesupponat in re quae creari dicitur: unde in hoc ab aliis mutationibus differt, quia generatio praesupponit materiam quae non generatur'. Given this point, Plato's Demiurge does not engage in any creative causality.
13. Ibid: 'Secundum est, ut in re quae creari dicitur, prius sit non esse quam esse: non quidem prioritate temporis vel durationis, ut prius non fuerit et postmodum sit; sed prioritate naturae, ita quod res creata si sibi relinquatur, consequatur non esse, cum esse non habeat nisi ex influentia causae superioris'.

According to Aquinas, the two foregoing aspects of creation determine its status as *ex nihilo* in two ways: first, because creation presupposes nothing and so is from nothing presupposed, and second, because the thing created comes to being from non-being, that is, from nothing.[14] Aquinas then claims that if these suffice for the nature (*rationem*) of creation, then creation *ex nihilo* is demonstrable in a philosophical fashion and has indeed been defended by the philosophers, because a commitment to such is a commitment to the theses outlined above.[15] Thus reason can penetrate the doctrine of creation to a certain degree since reason can demonstrate: (i) that God's productive causality presupposes nothing, and (ii) that in the creature, non-being naturally precedes being. It is the task of the metaphysician to establish the foregoing aspects of creation.[16]

14. Ibid.

15. Ibid, note in particular the following: 'Si haec duo sufficiant ad rationem creationis, sic creatio potest demonstrari, et sic philosophi creationem posuerunt'. However, it should be emphasised that even though he believed creation *ex nihilo* to be demonstrable, because the two theses on which it is based are demonstrable, Aquinas did not believe creation *ex nihilo* in time to be demonstrable, for he did not think that any of the reasons offered for accepting that the universe had a beginning in time were compelling.

16. Aquinas adds a third aspect, one that he believes the philosopher cannot establish, and this is to the effect that creation has a beginning in time, see *In II Sent.*, dist. 1, qu. 1, art. 2: 'Si autem accipiamus tertium oportere ad rationem creationis, ut scilicet etiam duratione res creata prius non esse quam esse habeat, ut dicatur esse ex nihilo, quia est tempore post nihil, sic creatio demonstrari non potest, nec a philosophis conceditur; sed per fidem supponitur'. The latter conclusion is one that Aquinas retained his entire career; for some of his characteristic discussions of this issue see Aquinas *In II Sent.*, dist. 1, qu. 1, art. 5, *Summa Contra Gentiles*, Lib. 2, Cap. 32–38, *De Potentia Dei*, qu. 3, art. 17, *Summa Theologiae*, Ia, qu. 46, and *De Aeternitate Mundi*. For commentary see Wippel, 'Aquinas on the Possibility of Eternal Creation', in *Metaphysical Themes in Aquinas Aquinas Vol. 1*, pp. 191–215. Wippel argues that throughout most of his career Aquinas defended the views that: (i) the non-eternity of the world has not been established and (ii) cannot be established, but it was not until very late in his career, with the *De Aeternitate Mundi* (1271), that he defended the view that an eternally created universe is possible. Despite this fact, I am arguing that the possibility of an eternally created universe is

At this point, enough has been said to distinguish creation from natural generation. As noted, (i) God's creative act presupposes no underlying subject and (ii) a creature's non-being naturally precedes its being, such that without the activity of some superior productive cause the creature would be precisely nothing. Natural generation could possibly fulfil the second criterion, to the effect that a naturally generated substance would not exist prior to its current existence, in which case its non-being precedes its being. However, natural generation does not fulfil the first criterion, given that natural generation presupposes some underlying subject within which the generation takes place. And this, as will be recalled, is precisely why Aquinas does not think that creation is a kind of change or motion, because change or motion (or indeed natural generation) presupposes some underlying subject within which the change or motion (or generation) takes place.[17]

As is clear from the commentary on the *Sentences*, Aquinas qualifies the mode by which non-being precedes being in the thing created—at least as this is demonstrable by the philosopher. He states that non-being precedes the being of a creature in the order of nature, that is to say, creatures do not naturally possess being, but derive their being from another (a superior cause) which presumably does possess being naturally. This then ties in the metaphysics of creation with Aquinas's thought on essence-*esse* distinction and composition and God as the cause of *esse*.

In every essence-*esse* composite, there is a potentiality for the *esse* it receives from God. God is not so composed, in which case He does not stand in potency to any such act. Therefore, as has been established, the *esse* that all and anything possesses is derived from God. God then is the unique source and fount of *esse*. Given that God causes the *esse* of things but does not presuppose any *esse* distinct from Himself, God creates out of nothing—that

consistent with Aquinas's overall metaphysical position, even though he only came to articulate this possibility towards the end of his career.

17. See the references in n. 10 above.

is to say, God's creative causality does not presuppose anything on which to work. God originates everything that exists and is thereby master over and superior to all that derives existence from Him.

Given the above considerations, what can be said about the view that in the created thing non-being naturally precedes being? Creatures do not possess *esse* essentially—that is, it is not natural for a creature to exist, it must receive its *esse* from another. If left to themselves, creatures would not exist, because *esse* is not something identical to the nature of any creature, rather, *esse* is identical only with the nature of the creator. Thus in the creator, being naturally precedes non-being. God, as *esse tantum*, is naturally prior to non-being; other than God there is nothing and it is from nothing other than His own *esse* that God brings things into being. Creatures on the other hand do not exist of themselves, instead, they depend on God for their *esse*. Thus, non-being naturally precedes their being; their natures are nothing until brought into being by God. And the latter is what Aquinas means when he states that non-being precedes being in created things.

Given the metaphysics of the matter, there is a philosophical demonstration of the natural priority of non-being to being in created things, and this because they are subject to distinction of essence and *esse*, in which case they do not exist in virtue of what they are, in which case they do not exist unless they receive *esse* from some superior cause: God. Creatures then, as caused by and dependent on God, participate in God's creative activity for their *esse*; and this is nothing more than the participation framework outlined in Chapter 3, to the effect that every creature participates in *esse commune*, which in turn participates in God in order to be. This participation framework is an important one, the consequences of which shall be drawn out in the next section. Suffice to say it entails for Aquinas the view that it is not through two distinct acts that God (i) brings things into being and (ii) sustains them in being; rather, insofar as creatures participate in the *esse* granted to them by God, it is the self-same act by which God gives *esse* to creatures and sustains them in *esse*.[18]

Given that it is a single divine act by means of which things are (i) created and (ii) sustained in being, and given that this divine act is *ex nihilo*, it follows that the sustaining of temporal creatures in being is also *ex nihilo*. So, temporal creatures, for as long as they exist, are caused to exist *ex nihilo* through a divine act embracing all that is. For instance, a creature, x, may begin to exist at t_1 and continue to exist through t_2 to t_n, whereat it ceases to exist. In Aquinas's account, from t_1 to t_n, x participates in a single act of creation from God, and such an act is *ex nihilio*, given that (i) it presupposes no underlying subject on which to work, and (ii) it is located in God and thereby naturally precedes the being of x. Therefore, in a single act of creation *ex nihilo* God causes a being, x, to exist at t_1 through t_2 to t_n, but this does not entail that at t_1 through t_2 to t_n God causes x to exist.

The foregoing serves to highlight that for Aquinas God is not an agent at the beginning of a linear chain of events starting everything off; rather, God is at the head of all created being, and anything that was created, is currently being created, or will be created participates in a single act of creation from God. The temporal reference point is thus to be found in the creature receiving an act of existence, and not in God, who creates and sustains by a single act of creation. If a visual analogy is required, the example of the sun's eternally illuminating the moon can be recalled to serve our purposes.

Imagine once again that the sun is eternal, spreading its rays over anything that comes within its periphery, but imagine this time that the moon is temporally finite, that is, that it began to be

---

18. *Summa Theologiae*, Ia, qu. 8, art. 1: 'Cum autem Deus sit ipsum esse per suam essentiam, oportet quod esse creatum sit proprius effectus eius . . . Hunc autem effectum causat Deus in rebus, non solum quando primo esse incipiunt, sed quandiu in esse conservantur . . . Quandiu igitur res habet esse, tandiu oportet quod Deus adsit ei, secundum modum quo esse habet'.

and that it will cease to be. So, for as long as the moon is illuminated, it is participating in the illumination of the sun, the latter of which is eternally illuminating anything that comes within the scope of its rays; from the moment it came into existence until the moment it ceases to exist, the moon will be illuminated by the sun. Nevertheless, once the moon goes out of existence and ceases to be illuminated, no concomitant change occurs in the sun; the sun still shines eternally and illuminates anything that comes within its scope. Transferring the analogy then to divine creation, by a single act God brings into being and keeps in being all created essences, and for as long as such essences participate in God's single creative act, such essences are sustained in being. Nevertheless, should such created essences undergo change and go out of being, no such concomitant change need occur in God. Thus, Aquinas's metaphysics of creation and the related participation relationship between God and creatures implied therein places Aquinas firmly within the Augustinian-Boethian tradition of understanding God's eternity as a single instant that is present to all events past, present, and future.[19]

As a final point let us return to the difficulty highlighted in Chapter 4 concerning existential causality. Recall that in many causal contexts, the causal property in question often presupposes

19. See Eleonore Stump and Norman Kretzmann, 'Eternity', *The Journal of Philosophy*, 78 (1981), 429–458, for what is now taken to be a classic defence of this notion of divine eternity. Note in particular the discussion of ET-simultaneity in §. II. Within the context of the metaphysics outlined above, one could say that God is ET-simultaneous with creatures insofar as (i) God is eternal and creatures are temporal, (ii) from the eternal reference frame, God is present to creatures as granting them *esse*, (iii) from the temporal reference frame, creatures are present to God as receiving *esse*. As noted by Stump and Kretzmann, p. 439, on this account God is neither earlier than nor later than, neither past nor future, with respect to creatures. Furthermore, God and creatures do not exist at one and the same time when considered within any reference frame, in which case they are not temporally simultaneous. And given that God and creatures are not temporally simultaneous, it follows that a single act of creation *ex nihilo* is capable of (i) bringing things into being and (ii) sustaining things in being.

some pre-existent subject sufficiently potential to be modified in some way. The causality of *esse* cannot presuppose any pre-existing potency to modify, because without *esse* there is nothing, in which case the causality of *esse* brings a thing into existence whole and complete; it does not modify something pre-existing. This, as noted, entails that creation is not any kind of change, but something different and unique to God alone. In Chapter 4 this created a problem for how to conceive of creative causality, and in that chapter the problem was resolved sufficiently to progress by pointing out that existential causality cannot presuppose any sort of passive potency in the subject created, but it can presuppose an active potency in the creator such that the creator is capable of bringing about a creature.

As *esse tantum* God is capable of bringing into existence any possibility of being, that is to say, God's ability to create is limited by being itself; whatever is an impossibility of being is precisely nothing, because possibility is a necessary though not sufficient condition for actuality. As seen in Chapter 3, Aquinas does not consider possibility in terms of possible worlds independent from any sort of actuality, be that God's mind or the actual world. Thus, for Aquinas possibility is rooted in actuality. Now, when it comes to the possibility of creatures, such possibility cannot be rooted in the actuality of creatures, because their possibility must be necessarily prior to them. Consequently, the possibility of creatures must be rooted in God's actuality. But God's actuality is a pure actuality signified by God's being pure *esse*. Thus, the possibility of creatures must be located in God's *esse*.

Now, the possibility of creatures is signified by their essences; a creature is possible precisely because its essence can be. The ontological foundation then of any creature's possibility and thus its essence is rooted in God's *esse*, such that contained in God's *esse* prior to its actual existence is a creature's essence. The creature's essence as contained in God's *esse* is not actually distinct from God's *esse*, for it is only so when it is granted its own distinct act of existence, its own *esse*. Thus, the creature's essence is contained in God's *esse* in a primordial fashion as a possible way in which God's *esse* could be imitated, that is, as something to which God could unite a distinct act of existence.

The essences then of all possible creatures, including those that have been actually created, are contained primordially in God's *esse* signifying possible imitations thereof. When God creates, he unites an essence with a distinct *esse* and thus brings about an actually existing thing distinct from Himself. Whilst this creature is distinct from God, it is dependent on God in order to be, and thus would not be unless it stood in such a relationship to God. The standing in such a relationship of the creature to God entails a passive potency in the creature, a potency which is only the result of the creature's being created and not metaphysically prior to creation. What is prior to creation is God's *esse*, and thus the active potency for God to create; having created, all creatures stand in potency to God, in which case passive potency is a result of creation and not a condition thereof.

Given that God's creative activity is not successive, but rather a single act embracing all that is whether, from our point of view, that is past, present, or future, God does not create by assembling all the components of creatures and then putting them together as one would bake a cake. Rather, God brings into existence the composite entity whole and complete whose metaphysical components are distinct yet united in the thing thereby created. This also entails that God's act of creation is ongoing from our point of view, and that God does not initially create over a temporal period (a number of days) and then leave things to themselves; but rather that there is a single act of creation and what is created has several metaphysical components—layers as it were—that are united to produce the great chain of being that we have.

I will draw this work to a close by recapitulating some of Aquinas's characteristic views on the metaphysics of creation, and from that determine how he can consistently defend the possibility of an eternally created universe.

7.3 GOD AND THE METAPHYSICS OF CREATION

Hawking's view that the beginning of the universe is synonymous with its creation was introduced earlier; this is a view that is commonly accepted by atheist and theist alike. Accordingly, any model of the universe that denies its beginning also denies its being created. And this was precisely Hawking's model: a finite universe with no boundary, in which case he takes the universe to be beginningless and therefore uncreated. However, what this position does not consider is the notion of a creator as a cause of existence. A cause of existence need not begin the universe; such a cause need only grant existence to the universe. The granting of existence to the universe does not exclude the possibility of a beginningless universe; for there is no contradiction in the notion of a universe being without a beginning yet requiring a cause of its existence, in the same way that there is no contradiction in the notion of an eternally existing sun's illuminating an eternally existing moon. An effect, y, depending on a cause, x, for its existence does not entail that y had to have a beginning of its existence. And this is precisely what Aquinas's metaphysics has shown us: that one can consistently adhere to the creation of the universe without adhering to its having had a beginning.

To insist on the need for a creator is not to insist on the need for something outside of the boundary of the universe giving it its first nudge into existence, nor is it to insist, in a quasi-design fashion, on something that sets up the conditions for the possibility of the universe. Rather, to insist on the need for a creator is to insist on the need for a cause of existence. In Hawking's account we can have finite space–time without a boundary. This merely tells us that the universe did not have a beginning; it tells us nothing of the actual existence of the universe. For either the existence of the universe is gratuitous, in which case it receives existence from without, or it exists in virtue of what it is. But it is arguable that the latter is not the case, for existence in no way enters into the understanding of the essence of the universe; different models of the universe can be entertained all of which could exist, thereby indicating that what it is to be a universe is not what it is to be. So, arguably, whatever the universe is, it is not existence itself, even though it is itself existing. Consequently, Hawking's model presupposes the existence of the universe and does not explain it. Thus the question arises: what accounts for the existence of the universe? And it is precisely the latter sort of question that marks the entryway into the metaphysics of creation adopted by Aquinas.[20]

Hawking and his followers are of course free to reject the metaphysics that Aquinas proposes. However, such a rejection would miss the point. If Hawking were to reject Aquinas's metaphysics and deny the need for a creator on the back of a denial of the beginning of the universe, Aquinas or one of his followers could simply reply that Hawking's denial of a need for a creator is really only a denial of a need for something to kickstart the whole universe—but this is what Aquinas and his followers also deny, and yet they are committed to the notion of a creator. So, in order for there to be anything at all threatening in what Hawking has posited, he or his followers must show that the universe does not have any characteristics that require a cause outside of the universe itself. Specifically, it must be shown that the very existence of the universe is either (i) causally irrelevant or (ii) determined by means of natural causes.

Hawking does not approach the issue in this manner, given that he is primarily concerned with the boundary conditions of the universe and with the beginning or seeming beginning thereof. He is not concerned with the sheer existence of the universe, a concern more suited to the metaphysician. But surely the creation of the universe is connected directly with the question of its existence, because the question of the creation or otherwise of the universe is the question of its mode of existence, which is

20. If the foregoing reasoning smacks of the fallacy of composition, the discussion can be conducted along the lines of the existence of things rather than the existence of the universe, and Aquinas's reasoning still follows; for the existence of things, unless they are self-existing, demands a cause of their existence.

in turn a species of the question: why is there something rather than nothing? And this is the question of metaphysics par excellence. Consequently, the question of the creation of the universe is a question of metaphysics, and is somewhat distinct from the question of its beginning. Thus, anyone wishing to deny that the universe is created will have to enter the metaphysical arena and contend with the metaphysics that Aquinas has outlined. Otherwise, one cannot confidently claim that contemporary scientific models which posit that the universe is without a beginning remove the need for a creator.[21]

The universe no doubt exists, and if Hawking is right, it is a self-contained physical system without a beginning, but this does not preclude dependency on a higher cause for its existence. In the context of Aquinas's metaphysics, this dependence on a higher cause is dependence on a creator; and within the same metaphysical framework, a creator, precisely as creator, is not a composite of essence and *esse*, as creatures are, but is pure *esse* itself. Such a being is not simply an entity that has *esse*, but is an entity that encompasses within itself that which it is to be: the fullness and perfection of being. Creatures, on the other hand, limit the fullness of being to their own particular modes. Thus, every creature signifies a certain mode of being, a certain way in which being could be realised. The imperfection of creatures in relation to the creator, then, is cashed out in Thomistic terms precisely insofar as creatures do not and cannot realise the fullness of being, and so depend on that which encompasses in itself the fullness of being. Creatures thus do not depend on just another extremely powerful being of the same ontological kind as they, but on a being of a

---

21. Of course, Hawking can deny the validity of metaphysics in favour of physical science in discussing such issues, and he has very publicly done just this in recent years. I find it difficult to entertain such a rejection of metaphysics, because it is often based upon implicit metaphysical reasoning canvassed in support of the all-embracing validity of contemporary physical science. Such a position no doubt will look down upon most if not all branches of philosophy, but it is hard to see how anyone could be reasonably motivated to adopt this position since it seems *prima facie* to be a philosophical position.

radically different kind, one that can plausibly be construed as a superior being insofar as it is not dependent in the way that creatures are.

Furthermore, insofar as creatures only realise a certain mode of being, and this in juxtaposition from God who encompasses the fullness of being, the creator–creature relationship is best thought of in terms of participation. In the latter account creatures take a part in the causal power of their creator, who, precisely as creator, is a superior being than they and whose creative causality is not simply that of providing the first nudge to the series or winding up the clock. Conceiving of creative causality in terms of participation entails that creatures are in fact dependent on a higher kind of being, and this cause is higher insofar as it is that without which the causal property in question (in this case, *esse*) would be absent from the lower beings if it were not present thereto. This is the typical Platonic view that beings of a lower kind (participants) depend on some being or beings of a higher kind for certain properties that the former do not possess essentially whereas the latter do. And this conception of creative causality serves to exorcise even further the notion that to be created is necessarily to begin to exist, because if God's causality as creator is exercised in terms of the granting of *esse* to creatures who in turn participate in the *esse* so granted, then God's relationship to creatures is not best understood as a temporal causal priority, or even in terms of efficient causality, but in terms of the analytical priority of a being who is pure *esse* to beings who only have *esse*. More Platonically, one could say that God is that which it is to be and creatures participate in this so that they can be said to exist, but not to be identical to the *esse* that they thereby possess, since the latter is proper only to God.

Now, the granting of *esse* to any creature and, conversely, the participating in the act of existence so granted provides an explanatory account of both the origin and the sustaining of creatures in being. Creatures exist insofar as they participate in the *esse* granted to them by God, and creatures continue to exist for as long as they participate in the self-same *esse* granted to them.

Thus it is a single creative act by which creatures are both brought into being and remain in being. In §. 1, I borrowed the analogy of an eternally existing sun's enlightening an eternally existing moon as the means by which to conceive of the possibility of an eternally created universe. This analogy can also go some way to show how the creator–creature relationship is one of participation, since according to the analogy, the moon very clearly participates in the light of the sun in order to be illuminated, and the sun not only causes the moon's illumination, but sustains it, thereby acting as both cause and sustainer in one and the same act. Nevertheless, the analogy is deficient insofar as there is presupposed something on which the sun's causal activity is exercised, and this is the moon which it illuminates. Transferring the case to God's creation, the analogy would suggest that when God creates, He shines light upon some underlying subject, thereby bringing it into existence. But it is precisely the latter that Aquinas sought to deny when he argued that the act of creation presupposes nothing. Thus, whilst it has served us well in elucidating some key points, the analogy of the sun's illumination of the moon is somewhat deficient as an aid to understanding divine creation.

In my opinion the best analogy that we have for the creator–creature relationship can be taken from the arts, namely singing. When a singer sings a song, both the material for the song and the structure that it takes originate in the singer. The song is sustained in being for as long as the singer keeps singing, and the song follows its own logic note by note, but all within the context of the singer's bringing the song about. Thus, in the singer–song relationship the act by which the singer sings the song and the act by which the singer sustains the song are one and the same. I submit that the relationship between song and singer is precisely the relationship that Aquinas envisages between creature and creator.[22]

---

22. The analogy is not my own and is adapted almost *verbatim* from T. A. F. Kelly 'Ex Possibili et Necessario: A Re-examination of Aquinas's Third Way', *The Thomist*, 61 (1997), §. II.C. The analogy to song can also be found in St

If a contemporary theist seeks to search after a creator whilst at the same time honouring the insights of contemporary science, he or she really ought not to go looking for God in the boundary conditions of the universe. Rather, what the theist must do is seek out reasons for why there must be a being of a fundamentally different kind from creatures—one on which creatures depend in order to be. The task for the theist then is to show that creatures are entities of such a kind that they could not be unless there existed a being of a fundamentally different kind; and if the latter can be established, then one would be on the clear path towards affirming the existence of a creator of the universe.

The available options, then, for a successful argument for God's existence, where God is understood as a creator, are significantly reduced. This is because not all of the traditional arguments for a first cause will establish a being from which all existing things flow and in which all existing things participate for their existence. In order to establish the latter one must, in a rather Platonic sense, observe certain characteristics within the universe, the cause of which cannot be found within the universe itself, but which nonetheless point to some cause that in itself possesses such characteristics. This is precisely what Aquinas's proof of God in *De Ente*, Cap. 4 delivers: a being that is pure *esse*, from which all other things derive their *esse* and on which all things depend. Such a being is a single, immaterial, individual, transcendent yet immanent cause of all that is, which, if anything, is what we understand God to be.

Augustine's reflections on creation *ex nihilo* in *Confessions* (Oxford: Oxford University Press, 1991), Bk. 12, n. 29. It should be noted that this analogy concerns solely the relationship between singer and song and abstracts from a consideration of the conditions for the possibility of the singer's existence, such as a suitable environment or the physical laws governing that environment.

BIBLIOGRAPHY

Adams, Robert. 1974. 'Theories of Actuality', *Noûs*, 8: 211–231.

Anscombe, G. E. M. 1975. 'Causality and Determination', in Ernest Sosa (ed.), *Causation and Conditionals* (New York: Oxford University Press), pp. 63–82.

——. 1981. *Collected Philosophical Papers Volume I: From Parmenides to Wittgenstein* (Oxford: Blackwell).

Aquinas, Thomas. 1926. *Summa Theologiae* (Turin: Marietti).

——. 1927a. *Quaestiones Disputatae De Potentia Dei* (Turin: Marietti).

——. 1927b. *Summa Contra Gentiles* (Turin: Marietti).

——. 1927c. *Quaestio Disputata De Anima* (Turin: Marietti).

——. 1927d. *Quaestio Disputata De Spiritualibus Creaturis* (Turin: Marietti).

——. 1927e. *Quaestiones Quodlibetales* (Turin: Marietti).

——. 1929. *Scriptum Super Libros Sententiarum* (Paris: Lethielleux).

——. 1935. *In Metaphysicam Aristotelis Commentaria* (Turin: Marietti).

——. 1950. *In Librum Beati Dionysii De Divinis Nominibus Expositio* (Turin: Marietti).

——. 1954. *In Octo Libros Physicorum Aristotelis Expositio* (Turin: Marietti).

——. 1955. *In Aristotelis Libros Peri Hermeneneias et Posteriorum Analyticorum Expositio* (Turin: Marietti).

——. 1962. *Tractatus De Substantis Separatis* (West Hartford, CT: St Joseph College).

——. 1972. *In Librum de Causis Expositio* (Turin: Marietti).

——. 1976a. *De Ente et Essentia* (Rome: Editori di San Tommaso).

——. 1976b. *De Aeternitate Mundi* (Rome: Editori di San Tommaso).

——. 1992. *Super Boethium De Trinitate et Expositio Libri Boethii de Ebdomadibus* (Rome: Commissio Leonina).

Augustine. 1991. *Confessions* (Oxford: Oxford University Press).

Ayer, A. J. 2001. *Language, Truth, and Logic* (London: Penguin).

Bobik, Joseph. 1965. *Aquinas on Being and Essence: A Translation and Interpretation* (Notre Dame, IN: University of Notre Dame Press).

Braithwaite, R. 1968. *Scientific Explanation: A Study of the Function of Theory, Probability and Law in Science* (Cambridge: Cambridge University Press).

Brown, Raymond Edward, and others (eds.). 1990. *New Jerome Biblical Commentary* (London: Burns & Oates).

Chisholm, Roderick (ed.). 1960. *Realism and the Background of Phenomenology* (Illinois: Free Press).

Clarke, W. N. 1994. *Explorations in Metaphysics: Being—God—Person* (Notre Dame, IN: University of Notre Dame Press).

Copleston, Frederick. 1955. *Aquinas* (Middlesex: Penguin).

Davies, Brian (ed.). 2000. *Philosophy of Religion: A Guide and Anthology* (Oxford: Oxford University Press).

Davies, Brian, and Eleonore Stump (eds.). 2012. *The Oxford Handbook of Aquinas* (Oxford: Oxford University Press).

De Anna, G. 2006. 'Causal Relations: A Thomistic Account', in Craig Paterson and Matthew S. Pugh (eds.), *Analytical Thomism: Traditions in Dialogue* (Aldershot, UK: Ashgate), pp. 79–101.

Dewan, L. 1984. 'St Thomas, Joseph Owens and the Real Distinction between Being and Essence', *The Modern Schoolman*, 61: 145–56.

——. 2001. 'St. Thomas and Infinite Causal Regress', in William Sweet (ed.), *Idealism, Metaphysics, and Community* (Aldershot, UK: Ashgate), pp. 119–31.

Ducasse, C. 1926. 'On the Nature and the Observability of the Causal Relation', *Journal of Philosophy* 23, reprinted in Ernest Sosa (ed.), *Causation and Conditionals* (New York: Oxford University Press), pp. 114–26.

Edwards, P. 2000. 'The Cosmological Argument', in Brian Davies (ed.), *Philosophy of Religion: A Guide and Anthology* (Oxford: Oxford University Press), pp. 202–13.

Fabro, C. 1938. 'Intorno alla Nozione 'Tomista' di Contingenza', *Rivista di Filosofia Neoscolastica*, 30: 132–49.

——. 1950. *La Nozione Metafisica di Partecipazione secondo S. Tommaso D'Aquino* (Turin: Società Editrice Internazionale).

——. 1961. *Participation et causalité selon s. Thomas d'Aquin* (Louvain: Publications Universitaires de Louvain).

Farrell, Walter. 1940. *A Companion to the Summa* (New York: Sheed and Ward).

Feser, Edward. 2009. *Aquinas: A Beginner's Guide* (Oxford: Oneworld).

——. 2011. 'Existential Inertia and the Five Ways', *American Catholic Philosophical Quarterly*, 85: 237–67.

Frege, Gottlob. 1950. *The Foundations of Arithmetic* (Oxford: Blackwell).

——. 1979. *Posthumous Writings* (Oxford: Blackwell).

Garrigou-Lagrange, Réginald. 1934. *God, His Existence and His Nature* (London: Herder).

Geach, P.T., 1969. *God and the Soul* (Indiana: St Augustine's Press).

Geiger, L.-B, 1942. *La Participation dans la philosophie de s. Thomas d'Aquin* (Paris: Librairie Philosophique J. Vrin).

Gilson, Étienne. 1936. *The Spirit of Medieval Philosophy* (Notre Dame: Notre Dame University Press).

Haldane, John (ed.). 2002. *Mind, Metaphysics and Value in the Thomistic and Analytical Traditions* (Notre Dame, IN: University of Notre Dame Press).

Hawking, Stephen. 1998. *A Brief History of Time* (London: Bantam Press).

Hieke, Alexander, and Edgar Morscher (eds.). 2001. *New Essays in Free Logic* (Dordrecht: Kluwer).

Hume, David. 1985. *Dialogues Concerning Natural Religion*, R. Popkin (ed.) (Cambridge: Hackett).

——. 2003. *A Treatise of Human Nature* (London: Everyman).

John Duns Scotus. 1950. *Opera Omnia Volume II* (Civitas Vaticana: Typis Polyglottis Vaticanis).

Kelly, T. 1997. 'Ex Possibili et Necessario: A Re-examination of Aquinas's Third Way', *The Thomist*, 61: 63–84.

Kenny, Anthony. 1969. *The Five Ways: St. Thomas Aquinas' Proofs of God's Existence* (London: Routledge).

——. 1980. *Aquinas: A Collection of Critical Essays* (Oxford: Oxford University Press).

——. 2002. *Aquinas on Being* (Oxford: Oxford University Press).

Kerr, G. 2008. 'The Meaning of *Ens Commune* in the Thought of Thomas Aquinas', *Yearbook of the Irish Philosophical Society*, 32–61.

——. 2012a. 'Aquinas's Argument for the Existence of God in *De Ente et Essentia*, Cap. IV: An Interpretation and Defence', *Journal of Philosophical Research*, 37: 99–133.

——. 2012b. 'A Thomistic Metaphysics of Creation', *Religious Studies*, 48: 337–56.

——. 2012c. 'Essentially Ordered Series Reconsidered', *American Catholic Philosophical Quarterly*, 86: 541–55.

——. 2015. 'Thomist *Esse* and Analytic Philosophy', *International Philosophical Quarterly*, forthcoming.

Kim, J. 1973. 'Causation and Counterfactuals', in Ernest Sosa (ed.), *Causation and Conditionals* (New York: Oxford University Press), pp. 192–95.

Klima, Gyula. 1988. *Ars Artium: Essays in Philosophical Semantics— Medieval and Modern* (Budapest: Institute of Philosophy, Hungarian Academy of Sciences).

——. 1993. 'The Changing Role of "Entia Rationis" in Medieval Semantics and Ontology: A Comparative Study with a Reconstruction', *Synthese*, 96: 25–59.

——. 1996. 'The Semantic Principles underlying St Thomas Aquinas's Metaphysics of Being', *Medieval Philosophy and Theology* 5: 87–141.

——. 1999. 'Ockham's Semantics and Ontology of the Categories', in Paul Vincent Spade (ed.), *The Cambridge Companion to Ockham* (Cambridge: Cambridge University Press), pp. 118–43.

——. 2001. 'Existence and Reference in Medieval Logic', in Alexander Hieke and Edgar Morscher (eds.), *New Essays in Free Logic* (Dordrecht: Kluwer), pp. 197–226.

——. 2002. 'Contemporary vs. Aristotelian Essentialism', in John Haldane (ed.), *Mind, Metaphysics and Value in the Thomistic and Analytical Traditions* (Notre Dame, IN: University of Notre Dame Press), pp. 175–94.

——. 2004. 'On Kenny on Aquinas on Being: A Critical Review of *Aquinas on Being* by Anthony Kenny', *International Philosophical Quarterly*, 44: 567–80.

Knasas, John F. X. 2003. *Being and Some Twentieth-Century Thomists* (New York: Fordham University Press).

Knuuttila, S. 'Medieval Theories of Modality', in Edward N. Zalta (ed.), *Stanford Encyclopedia of Philosophy*, http://plato.stanford.edu/archives/fall2013/entries/modality-medieval/.

Kripke, Saul. 1981. *Naming and Necessity* (Oxford: Blackwell).

Kwasniewski, P.A. (ed.). 2007. *Wisdom's Apprentice: Thomistic Essays in Honour of Lawrence Dewan* (Washington: The Catholic University of America Press).

Lerner, Eric. 1991. *The Big Bang Never Happened: A Startling Refutation of the Dominant Theory of the Universe* (New York: Random House).

Lewis, David. 1970. 'Anselm and Actuality', *Noûs*, 4: 175–88.

——. 1986. *On the Plurality of Worlds* (Oxford: Blackwell).

Lonergan, Bernard. 1992. *Collected Works of Bernard Lonergan Volume 3: Insight—A Study of Human Understanding* (Toronto: University of Toronto Press).

Long, S. 2003. 'On the Natural Knowledge of the Real Distinction of Essence and Existence', *Nova et Vetera*, 1: 75–108.

——. 2005. 'Aquinas on Being and Logicism', *New Blackfriars*, 86: 323–47.

MacDonald, S. 1984. 'The *Esse/Essentia* Argument in Aquinas's *De Ente et Essentia*', *Journal of the History of Philosophy*, 22: 157–72.

Maurer, Armand. 1951. 'Form and Essence in the Philosophy of St Thomas', *Mediaeval Studies*, 13: 165–76.

——.1968. *Thomas Aquinas: On Being and Essence* (Toronto: Pontifical Institute of Medieval Studies).

May, W. 1970. 'Knowledge of Causality in Hume and Aquinas', *The Thomist*, 34: 254–88.

McDowell, John. 1996. *Mind and World* (Cambridge, MA: Harvard University Press).

McGinn, Colin. 2000. *Logical Properties: Identity, Existence, Predication, Necessity, Truth* (Oxford: Oxford University Press).

Meinong, A. 1960. 'The Theory of Objects', in Roderick Chisholm (ed.), *Realism and the Background of Phenomenology* (Glencoe, IL: Free Press), pp. 76–117.

Miller, B. 1975. 'In Defence of the Predicate "Exists"', *Mind*, 84: 338–54.

——. 1986: ' "Exists" and Existence', *Review of Metaphysics*, 40: 237–70.

Nagel, Ernest. 1961: *The Structure of Science: Problems in the Logic of Scientific Explanation* (London: Routledge).

Owens, J. 1955: 'The Causal Proposition—Principle or Conclusion', *The Modern Schoolman*, 32: 159–71.

——. 1965: 'Quiddity and the Real Distinction in St Thomas Aquinas', *Mediaeval Studies*, 27: 1–22.

——. 1981. 'Stages and Distinction in *De Ente*: A Rejoinder', *The Thomist*, 45: 99–123.

——. 1985a. *An Interpretation of Existence* (Texas: Center for Thomistic Studies—University of St Thomas).

——. 1985b. *An Elementary Christian Metaphysics* (Houston: Bruce Publishing Company).

——. 1986. 'Aquinas's Distinction at *De Ente et Essentia* 4.119–123', *Mediaeval Studies*, 48: 264–87.

Paterson, Craig, and Matthew Pugh (eds.). 2006. *Analytical Thomism: Traditions in Dialogue* (Aldershot, UK: Ashgate).

Plantinga, Alvin. 1974. *The Nature of Necessity* (Oxford: Clarendon Press).

Pruss, Alexander. 2006. *The Principle of Sufficient Reason: A Reassessment* (Cambridge: Cambridge University Press).

Putnam, H. 1975. *Mind, Language and Reality: Philosophical Papers Volume 2* (Cambridge: Cambridge University Press).

Quine, W. V. O. 1961. *From a Logical Point of View* (New York: Harper and Row).

——. 1969. *Ontological Relativity and Other Essays* (New York: Columbia University Press).

Ratzinger, J. 1969. *An Introduction to Christianity* (San Francisco: Ignatius Press).

Roland-Gosselin, M.-D. 1948. *Le 'De Ente et Essentia' de s. Thomas d'Aquin* (Paris: Librairie Philosophique J. Vrin).

Russell, Bertrand. 1956. *Logic and Knowledge: Essays, 1901–1950*, Robert Marsh (ed.) (London: Allen and Unwin).

Salmon, N. 1987. 'Existence', *Philosophical Perspectives: Volume 1—Metaphysics*, 49–108.

Sosa, Ernest (ed.). 1975. *Causation and Conditionals* (Oxford: Oxford University Press).

Spade, Paul Vincent (ed.). 1999. *The Cambridge Companion to Ockham* (Cambridge: Cambridge University Press).

Stalnaker, R. 2003. *Ways a World Might Be: Metaphysical and Anti-Metaphysical Essays* (Oxford: Oxford University Press).

Stroud, Barry. 1977. *Hume* (London: Routledge).

——. 2011: *Engagement and Metaphysical Dissatsifaction: Modality and Value* (Oxford: Oxford University Press).

Stump, Eleonore, and N. Kretzmann. 1981. 'Eternity', *The Journal of Philosophy*, 78: 429–58.

Sweeney, L. 1963. 'Essence/Existence in Thomas Aquinas's Early Writings', *Proceedings of the American Catholic Philosophical Association*, 37: 97–131.

Sweet, W. (ed.). 2001. *Idealism, Metaphysics, and Community* (Aldershot, UK: Ashgate).

Te Velde, Rudi. 1995. *Participation and Substantiality in Thomas Aquinas* (Leiden: E. J. Brill).

Twetten, David. 2006: 'Really Distinguishing Essence from *Esse*', *Proceedings of the Society for Medieval Logic and Metaphysics*, 6: 57–95.

Van Steenberghen, F. 1980. *Le problème de l'existence de Dieu dans les écrits de s. Thomas d'Aquin* (Louvain-la-Neuve: Éditions de l'Institut Supérieur de Philosophie).

Vallicella, W. 1983. 'A Critique of the Quantificational View of Existence', *The Thomist* 47: 242–67.

——. 2002. *A Paradigm Theory of Existence: Onto-Theology Vindicated* (Dordrecht: Kluwer).

Von Wright, G. H. 1975. 'On the Logic and Epistemology of the Causal Relation', in Ernest Sosa (ed.), *Causation and Conditionals* (New York: Oxford University Press), pp. 95–114.

William of Ockham. 1970. *Opera Theologica Volume II* (New York: St Bonaventure).

Williams, D. 1962. 'Dispensing with Existence', *The Journal of Philosophy*, 59: 748–63.

Wippel, John. 1979. 'Aquinas's Route to the Real Distinction', *The Thomist*, 43: 279–95.

——. 1981. *The Metaphysical Thought of Godfrey of Fontaines: A Study in Late Thirteenth-Century Philosophy* (Washington, DC: Catholic University of America Press).

——. 1984. *Metaphysical Themes in Thomas Aquinas Vol. I* (Washington, DC: Catholic University of America Press).

——. 2000. *The Metaphysical Thought of Thomas Aquinas: From Finite Being to Uncreated Being* (Washington, DC: Catholic University of America Press).

Wittgenstein, Ludwig. 2001. *Philosophical Investigations* (Oxford: Blackwell).